BDSM Relationships

Books 1, 2, and 3

# BDSM Relationships

# Books 1, 2, and 3

Peter Masters

Copyright © 2012, Peter Masters

All rights reserved. No part of this book may be reproduced or transmitted in any form or by any means, electronic or mechanical, including photocopying, recording, or by any informational storage or retrieval system, except with permission in writing from the author.

Books in the present series:

*Understanding BDSM Relationships*

*BDSM Relationships - How They Work*

*BDSM Relationships - Pitfalls and Obstacles*

Also by Peter Masters:

*The Control Book*

*Look Into My Eyes - How To Use Hypnosis To Bring Out The Best In Your Sex Life*

*This Curious Human Phenomenon - An exploration of some uncommonly explored aspects of BDSM*

Cover art by Peter Masters

http://www.peter-masters.com/

ISBN 978-1-4774-6778-7

# Contents

**Understanding BDSM Relationships**     1

1   Introduction     3

2   The three pillars of BDSM relationships     13

3   BDSM and sex     31

4   Uncomfortable thoughts     37

5   What a BDSM relationship provides     45

6   Foundations of a BDSM relationship     55

7   Compatibility     81

8   Life aspects     87

9   People     93

10   Artists and tinkerers     127

11   Assembling the pieces     137

# BDSM Relationships - How They Work    141

| | | |
|---|---|---|
| 12 | Introduction | 143 |
| 13 | Trust, honesty, openness, communication, and all that stuff | 147 |
| 14 | Meeting people | 153 |
| 15 | Build your own partner | 161 |
| 16 | Criteria | 165 |
| 17 | Motivations | 171 |
| 18 | Dominance and submission | 225 |
| 19 | The lists | 259 |
| 20 | Maintaining balance | 307 |
| 21 | Online BDSM | 311 |
| 22 | Here's the thing | 315 |

# BDSM Relationships - Pitfalls and Obstacles    319

| | | |
|---|---|---|
| 23 | Introduction | 321 |
| 24 | The False Self | 325 |
| 25 | Trust | 331 |
| 26 | Communication | 339 |

| | | |
|---|---|---|
| 27 | Surrender versus submission | 347 |
| 28 | Dominance and submission | 351 |
| 29 | Wrong reasons why people do BDSM | 361 |
| 30 | Recognising pitfalls and obstacles | 387 |
| 31 | Pushing the kinky sex line | 443 |
| 32 | Incomplete needs meeting | 447 |
| 33 | False righteousness | 453 |
| 34 | Conclusion | 459 |

# Bibliography 463

# Glossary 465

# About the author 471

# Book One

# Understanding BDSM Relationships

# Chapter 1

# Introduction

For the uninitiated I'd like begin with a few words about BDSM. "BDSM" is a cunningly compact acronym which stands for the terms: Bondage and Discipline, Dominance and Submission, and Sadism and Masochism.

BDSM is about relationships and interactions between people. It's about power, control, dominance, surrender, humiliation, pain, and discomfort. Sometimes, but not always, it's about sex. It is often intense and can involve extreme sexualization or objectification.

People practise BDSM in a variety of places: in their bedroom, around the house or garden, or in specially set up rooms which are often called dungeons due to their connection with pain and torture. They may go to social events where they have the company of like-minded enthusiasts and where they get to indulge their desires either with their own regular partner or with

## UNDERSTANDING BDSM RELATIONSHIPS

BDSM is huge and before making my next point I'd like to mention a few more activities to go with the quite small number of examples I've given so far:

- Inflicting pain on your partner or, contrariwise, being tortured by your partner,
- Cutting designs into your partner's skin with a scalpel,
- Being whipped by your partner until your back is raw or bleeding,
- Flogging your partner's back and buttocks with a heavy leather flogger until they're red, raw, and possibly bleeding,
- Caning your partner's buttocks or thighs until they are bright red or bleeding,
- Locking your partner in a cage,
- Teasing your partner,
- Torturing your partner,
- Being humiliated or embarrassed by your partner,
- Dressing or behaving as an animal, such as a pony, dog, or cat,
- Pinching your partner's nipples until they are in agony,
- Using hypodermic needle tips to pierce your partner's skin multiple times—including their genitals and nipples—often creating decorative patterns of needles,

- Ordering your partner around, or being ordered around by your partner,
- Depersonalisation or objectification—such as being used or treated as if you were a chair, a table, or a foot mat.

But there's something decidedly odd about the activities listed above. If we step back and look at them objectively, none of them really look like fun. You certainly don't find any of them on the list of attractions at the average theme park. Nor, objectively, do any of them really look that appealing, satisfying, or rewarding. But for those readers who have seen the light, the activities and examples I've discussed could be exactly the menu for your next exciting evening or weekend with your partner and you might already be salivating at the thought.

Another odd thing is that while all of this is definitely BDSM, what do they have in common? Except for boobs, what does being dangled by your nipples have in common with wearing a rope bra? And what does pulling a cart while dressed as a pony have to do with being locked in a cage? And how can you compare whipping your partner's back till it's raw and bleeding to trampling on them in your high heels?

Also, BDSM is frequently a hit-and-miss affair for many people. Why does it work for some and not for others? Why are all these activities so powerful for some and so blah or downright off-putting for others?

Why is it that being embarrassed at work in front of your colleagues by your boss is something bad, while being compelled to lick the boots of your partner at home can be the best thing since sliced bread?

Why is being beaten with a stick in a dark alley by someone who makes off with your money something to get totally pissed off about, but being accurately and deftly caned on the buttocks by your partner so hard and for so long that you can't sit down for days without wincing can be an experience to enthusiastically share with your friends over coffee?

Why would you never think of pulling a knife on someone on the street when you actually have a wide range of knives at home which you quite happily "pull" on your beloved partner, readily drawing blood from them as you carve designs into their flesh?

What is it that makes all these otherwise unpleasant or downright excruciating activities so pleasurable and satisfying?

And, importantly, what is it about the person with whom we do these BDSM activities that lets this astounding transformation of suffering or pain into pleasure happen? Is it the person? Is it the relationship we have with them? Is it both?

And, perhaps sadly, why does this magic sometimes stop working?

Being without answers to these questions puts us in a position where we don't actually have any control of our BDSM. This is very weird, even paradoxical, because a lot of BDSM is precisely about taking and using control. But the truth is that when a hoped-for relationship fails, or when an existing relationship falters, many BDSM practitioners don't know what to do to fix it. Often, their only solution is to move on to a new partner and hope that the next relationship works.

I've noted in other writings[1] that there's an air of magic to BDSM. While BDSM is not rocket science, many BDSM folk have no idea what makes it tick. For them, it is simply magic.

---

[1] [MASTERS2008, pp. 4 - 5]

## UNDERSTANDING BDSM RELATIONSHIPS

Indeed, using a flogger the right way on the right person can be a powerful or even magical experience. But if you find that waving your magic flogger no longer leads to sub-space or orgasms, or that the magic knots which used to bring so much joy have become merely blah, where do you go and what do you do to fix it? Google? Facebook? Phone a friend? Trial and error?

Understanding BDSM and BDSM relationships means that we can get ourselves out of the situation where we just have to suck-it-and-see and into the situation where we know why some things are effective and some not, why some things stop being exciting or satisfying and how to get them back on the rails again, and how to take control and set about making our BDSM work.

I have a number of goals for this book and its two siblings[23]:

1. To explore and explain the nature of BDSM,

2. To examine what people look for in their relationships with their BDSM partner,

3. To point out the reasons why we do the most common BDSM activities,

4. To look at some of the reasons why BDSM relationships fail and at the ways in which they fail, and

5. To look at ways these failures can be prevented.

Unfortunately, some relationships are doomed from day one. Some, in fact, should have prominent red labels attached saying,

---
[2] *BDSM Relationships - How They Work*
[3] *BDSM Relationships - Pitfalls and Obstacles*

Do Not Resuscitate. But others have a chance, and I am hopeful that what I say in these books can assist in making that chance into reality.

No two people do BDSM for the same exact reasons. As I make my meandering journey through the whys and wherefores of BDSM, keep in mind that while some of what you read here may not apply to you today, it may apply to your partner. As you grow and explore, it may even apply to you sometime in the future.

# Questions

At this point, I'd like to ask you to stop and reflect on your connection to BDSM. As I mentioned earlier, the subject of BDSM is huge and I'd like you to start thinking about where in this huge space you see yourself.

- How do you see BDSM? What does it mean to you?
- Why do you do BDSM, or why are you interested in it?
- Do you know what can excite you in a scene?
- Is this satisfying in a long-term sense? Do you need anything else from a BDSM relationship?
- If yes, what do you need long-term? How does this differ from what's exciting during scenes?
- If you have a partner, do you know what they desire to get out of their relationship with you?
- Do you know what they need from the relationship?

- What part do you play in getting their needs met?
- If you don't currently have a partner, what will any future partner be getting from you?

And:

- Why are you reading this book?
- What do you hope to get out of it?

be. It could be that this couple is a master and his slave having lunch together and that what looked like a request for her to get the salt and pepper was actually an order. In fact, during their lunch together she could be following a strict protocol imposed by him dictating what she can eat, how she can eat, when and how she should speak, and so on.

This brings up an interesting point: even if we do see two people in a dungeon busily doing things with some rope and a handful of floggers, this may not be all there is. Just as something quite powerful can be going on between a master and his slave in circumstances which seem quite innocuous such as a cafe, there might well be something quite intense going on in the dungeon which we can't see. The obvious stuff with the floggers, etc., may not actually be the main event. Underneath the physical displays of prowess with knots and stamina against the heaviest flogging, something else more psychological, emotional, or even spiritual could be going on.

Even if we're sure that there's BDSM going on, how can we tell if what we're seeing is a relationship with a sound, deep, and effective BDSM basis or whether we're just seeing some kinky fun? These questions are important because if we're trying to develop a relationship with a current or potential BDSM partner then we need some idea of the nature of the beast we're dealing with. It's no use, for example, trying to explore the depths of delightful BDSM depravity when all we or our partner are interested in is an occasional kinky sex session with pink, fluffy handcuffs. On the other hand, if we are in a developing relationship which has the potential to be very profound and intense for us BDSM-wise and we approach it with a lack of respect and treat it as light, kinky fun, then we may quickly find ourselves looking for a new partner.

In this chapter I'd like to suggest that there are two things we can use to recognise effective BDSM, and an additional third which we can use to recognise that two people have a significant BDSM relationship rather than just being two folk doing BDSM together. I call these three things the pillars of BDSM relationships. They provide the solid supports on which any BDSM relationship rests. They are:

- Disparity of power,
- Penetration, and
- Engagement.

## 2.1 The first pillar: disparity of power

Those of us into BDSM sometimes refer to *vanilla* people or *vanilla* folk or *vanilla* activities. When we talk about vanilla what we're generally talking about is the egalitarian world outside of BDSM where everyone supposedly has equal rights and equal power to direct their destiny.

This is not the world of BDSM.

In BDSM, we often don't talk about husbands, wives, girlfriends, or boyfriends because these don't hint at or suggest anything more than a completely power-balanced relationship. In BDSM, we instead talk about tops, bottoms, masters, slaves, dominants, and submissives. These names or roles have built in to them a distinct idea of who is in charge, who directs or decides, and who follows or submits.

This difference in power usually appears in the form of one person leading or setting the direction for what goes on between the two, and the second person following or being directed. Many people would like to think that this first person is the top, the dominant, or the master, and that this second person is the bottom, the submissive, or the slave. This is not always the case.

There are many ways in which power can be different between two people, and to a large extent the fact that there are a great many ways this power difference can exist or be created is why BDSM is so varied.

A power difference can be innate, or it can be learned, or we can simply choose for it to be so. When power is innate it can be something like physical strength, or a susceptibility to fetish, or a desire or need to control.

When it's physical strength it means that this power can be expressed through manhandling, or by grabbing your partner by the hair and hauling them physically to where you want them, or by physically wrestling them and overpowering them. This can be very primal.

When you have a susceptibility to fetish, instead of having a power to use over someone else, this is a power which can be used over you. If your particular fetish is feet, for example, then your partner has two excellent tools at the ends of his or her legs which they can use to control, inflame, or extinguish your sexual feelings.

And when your own desires or hungers lead you either to take control of your partner or to be controlled by them, then you're moving into dominance and submission where actions can be less important than the intent behind them. Instead of focussing on particular or stereotypical BDSM activities involving rope, whips, or canes, the important thing is that you are decisive and authoritative and use this to direct and control your partner, be it in a dungeon, on the street, or even in a cafe.

## Understanding BDSM Relationships

Power can also be learned. In this case, we often call it skill or ability. An ability to tie amazing networks of knots is something that's learned, and it's a skill which you can then use on someone else. Flogging, whipping, piercing, cutting, and a range of other forms of BDSM play are also skills which take practice to learn, after which an endless stream of submissives will beat a path to your door. These skills and abilities are tools which give us power to affect our partner and to which our partner will surrender.

We can even choose when and how power should appear for us to use. If you and your submissive go out to a relatively isolated bit of forest and she is naked then you have created a situation where you, as her dominant, have an exploitable advantage over her. You can humiliate her or make her feel vulnerable and defenceless. You can play psychological games with her such as by saying, "I think I hear someone coming!" It's simply a matter of picking some place or circumstance where one of you has an advantage or the other has a disadvantage. Another example: giving your submissive subtle orders when you're both together with her vanilla friends. This challenges her to obey, but she also feels the need to try not to be embarrassed or exposed by how she must behave towards you. A final example: having your submissive wear a rope harness under their clothes while you're both out in public or while visiting family.

Differences in power can often be subtle. A volunteer at a BDSM demonstration or workshop can be a good example here. An obvious difference in power lies with the demonstrator. He or she has skill, expertise, and confidence which makes them powerful in regards to performing the particular activity he or she is demonstrating. But, less obvious is that the volunteer also wishes the activity done to them. This readiness creates an opportunity for the demonstrator to exert his or her skill or

*The three pillars of BDSM relationships*

ability on the volunteer. Without this readiness to experience the power of the demonstrator there would be no BDSM at all. The disparity in power isn't just that there is this difference, but also that there's an opportunity to exert it.

Another, perhaps unexpected, choice which can cause a disparity of power is when we create a goal. For example, as a dominant I might decide that I want my submissive to learn how to kneel gracefully. If I am determined about this goal then this determination is a strength or power which I can use. It gives me a drive and a focus which I can direct towards my submissive. Having a goal and choosing to use or involve my submissive in attaining it is something which I can assert and is something to which she can surrender. It is a force within me which I can bring to bear on my submissive, such as in the present example by exercising her repeatedly until her movements are smooth, fluid, and look effortless.

## 2.2 The second pillar: penetration

Penetration is my second pillar of BDSM. Although it's tempting to think the word refers to sexual penetration, it actually refers to the ability to make your partner feel you. In particular, it's about exploiting or using the difference in power which I discussed above. The fact that there is a difference or inequality in power is not sufficient. You need to use it or experience it. It must be felt. Until you use the power it is only potential BDSM. Going to an isolated area of forest, for example, and undressing your submissive is not going to be powerful or effective unless you do something with this situation to affect both you and your partner.

## Understanding BDSM Relationships

When a top has a bottom strapped to some diabolical apparatus and is busy flogging them mercilessly, or is dropping molten wax on some sensitive part of their anatomy then, ideally, both of them are getting something positive out of it.

While it's clear that the bottom is getting some serious stimulation via the flogger or the wax, it's not so clear what the top is getting out of it. Indeed, if the bottom is doing an impression of a dead fish and is simply standing or lying there without moving or saying anything, then the top is probably not getting anything at all out of the scene except practice. In fact, life might be simpler for him if he simply sets up a pillow and hammers that instead or blows out the candle and goes to watch some TV.

On the other hand, if the bottom is moving, writhing, moaning, or begging in response to the flogger strokes or the drops, then the top is getting feedback and the bottom is directly stimulating the feelings and responses of the top. The writhing, moaning, etc. cause the top to react and be aroused.

If one or both people involved are not actually feeling something as a result of the actions of their partner, then there is little or no BDSM there for them.

It's easy, for example, for a top at a BDSM party to demonstrate their skills at flogging or caning and for the recipient to have a jolly good time. It might well be though, that the top is not being particularly involved and is instead merely going through the motions for the purpose of the demonstration. Thus there might be BDSM activities going on, but the penetration is only one way. Only the person being flogged or caned is being penetrated. This can happen with an established couple as well, with one person doing the appropriate deeds because their partner wants or needs them without the first partner being involved or excited

*The three pillars of BDSM relationships*

by it at all. In fact, here we find one of the first ways in which a BDSM relationship can fail, namely lack of involvement when penetration only occurs in one direction.

Penetration can also take other forms. I was at a BDSM party once where a number of the dominants were sitting in a circle talking while their submissives sat at their feet. During the conversation, one of the female dominants decided to make a point by ordering her female submissive to perform oral sex on one of the male submissives. This was notable because of the different forms of penetration involved:

- Firstly, and obviously, the female submissive was orally penetrated and felt the penis of her cohort in her mouth.

- The female submissive was also penetrated by the authority of her dominant who ordered her to perform such a public exercise. In other words, the submissive felt the exercise of her dominant's authority over her.

- The female submissive was penetrated by those of us watching. Certainly the experience would have been less intense for her, and possibly less challenging, had there been no audience. As it was, a number of the dominants made comments thus adding to the penetration and experience of the female submissive.

- The female dominant herself was penetrated by experiencing her submissive responding to her authority, and by seeing how everyone else present responded to what her submissive was doing under her orders.

- Those of us watching were penetrated or effected by the performance.

It is this multiple penetration aspect of BDSM which can make sex hotter. Beyond the feeling of cock-in-cunt (or cunt-enclosing-cock) which gives a purely physical penetration, BDSM allows for authority to be exercised, another form of penetration, and for the use of pain or physical manipulation such as through impact play or bondage, which is an additional form of penetration. This allows BDSM to effectively triple (or more) the different types of penetration occurring during sex thus giving much more intensity.

Using an unequalness in power to penetrate our partner is largely what defines BDSM. Disparity of power alone, or penetration alone don't do it. But using power to create penetration does. This can be a complex and subtle dance. As I mentioned above, a bottom or submissive can and does penetrate their top or dominant. In an impact play scene, for example, they do it with their moans and writhing as they are struck by the cane or whip. In effect, this is a power which the bottom or submissive has over their top and it highlights that even though in a scene it might seem that the top or dominant is nominally in charge, power to affect the other lies with both people involved.

This begs the question: if both people in a scene have power over the other, then doesn't this render the idea of one being a master and the other a slave, or of one being a dominant and the other being submissive, meaningless? This isn't the case. The idea of a top, dominant, or master is that they are the one who leads or who takes charge. It may not necessarily be that they are the ones with all the power, but it is frequently the case that they are the ones who determine when and how the power is directed, be it by them over their partner, or by them creating or allowing situations where their partner can use power over them.

## 2.3 The third pillar: engagement

BDSM is not done solo. Even the aficionados of self-bondage can have an Other present with them when they are practising bondage alone. In their case, where they employ a strategy to prevent themselves from being able to escape—such as by using a combination lock at night thus forcing them to wait until the daylight to escape, or by encasing the key to the final padlock in a block of ice thus requiring them to wait until the ice has melted— this Other is Time. Time compels them to remain restrained, regardless of any protestations they may make, until it is ready to allow their release[1].

However, just because there's another person taking part in a BDSM scene with you doesn't necessarily mean that you have any sort of meaningful BDSM relationship with them. It is important to recognise this difference between simply doing BDSM and being part of a BDSM relationship. Doing BDSM may merely be allowing someone to tie you up and enjoying the embrace of the rope, or can be flogging someone and watching them writhe and see their back turn red. Both of these and other activities may be enjoyable, but don't necessarily mean that you're part of any sort of BDSM relationship.

We could say that a BDSM relationship requires an intimate and personal involvement rather than just a technical involvement. Indeed, the idea of engagement means that what we are doing is interacting with our partners in some form or other and that they are interacting with us. Merely hitting them and seeing them jump is not necessarily such an interaction. You could go around

---

[1][MASTERS2008, pp. 53 - 54]

hitting all sorts of people and watching them jump but it doesn't mean that you are having a relationship with them.

Engagement is my third pillar of a BDSM relationship. Going to a BDSM party, meeting some cutie, tying her up, flogging her, and being turned on by it is not engagement. She is not engaging us and we aren't engaging her. In fact, we really don't know her from a bar of soap although she may have better breasts. Instead, we are actually engaging ourselves by imagining that she is feeling or thinking in some particular way. We respond to what we imagine she is feeling, not to what she is actually feeling. In other words, while we are performing the physical aspects of our BDSM on her we are actually engaging something conjured up in our own imagination. This something we have in our imagination could perhaps be called the Average Bottom or the Average Submissive. If we do want to play with someone new then we do what we know the Average Bottom likes or what the Average Submissive likes.

The same thing applies to submissives and bottoms who want to play with or impress a top or dominant they fancy. Not knowing this person they do what the Average Top or the Average Dominant likes and hope for the best.

This is an important idea because until we know someone well, until we know what triggers they have, how they feel and respond, and what their own intimate wants and needs are, then we are limited to engaging what we think they want or need and what we think they are feeling, not what they actually want, need, or feel. It may well be that with a lot of experience we can get pretty good at guessing what makes someone else tick, but until we do actually know the real them then we're still only going to be engaging what we think they are, not what they really are.

## UNDERSTANDING BDSM RELATIONSHIPS

Once we have made the transition from imagining or guessing our partner's BDSM experiences to actually engaging our partner on the basis of their real feelings, needs, and responses then we can have a BDSM relationship with them. Before this point we can't. We might think we can, but the key is knowing them, not thinking that we know them, and not filling in the gaps of what we know with what we'd like to imagine them to be.

When we intimately engage someone else we use our personal knowledge and awareness of their strengths, weaknesses, triggers, emotions, desires, and needs to cause a real, rather than imagined, reaction in them. This is what happens when a top or bottom actively engages his bottom or submissive during play. But this engagement works in both directions. Bottoms and submissives who know their partner well can moan, wriggle, yell, scream, lubricate, get an erection, smile, and wink in ways which intimately impact their top or dominant.

Understanding this is important to the shape of any BDSM relationship you may have.

Consider this: if someone can get their rocks off by flogging anything with breasts and a vagina, then they're not engaging you. Likewise, someone who's deliriously happy to be tied up by anyone who can do knots isn't being engaged by you. They're being engaged by their relationship with the rope. You just happen to be holding it.

*The three pillars of BDSM relationships*

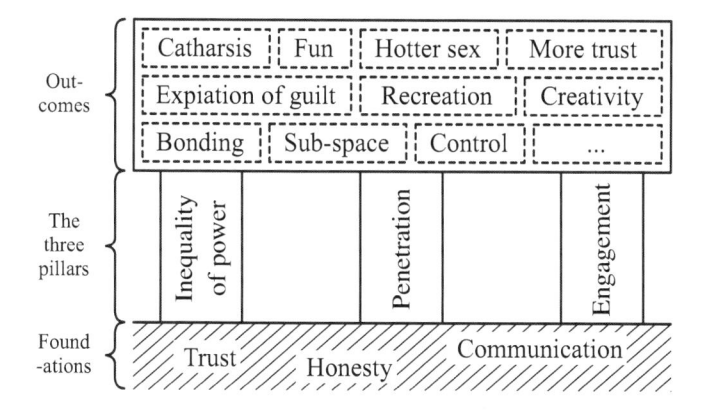

Figure 2.1: The levels of BDSM

## 2.4 The place of the three pillars

When we step back from BDSM and try to see it in its entirety, we may be able to see it as three levels, each one building upon the other. I've represented these levels in figure 2.1. They are:

1. Foundations

2. Three pillars

3. Outcomes

The foundations will always be trust, communication, and honesty because these provide the solid base which holds up everything else. Without honesty the foundations can become like shifting sands, moving about as circumstances change, and on which nothing substantial can be constructed. Without communication there won't be any relationship because relating is explicitly about communicating. And without trust there will always be barriers and distance which limit or prevent engagement.

On top of the foundations are the three pillars, and resting on top of the three pillars are the outcomes. The outcomes are what we get out of our BDSM. We don't do BDSM because we just want inequality of power, or because we just want penetration, or because we just want engagement. We want what these things give us, where they take us. Take pain, for example. No one does BDSM for the pain. They do it for where the pain takes them, for the state of mind they can achieve through the pain, for the release they get from experiencing intense pain. If someone went into a BDSM scene, experienced a lot of pain, and then finished the scene feeling exactly the way they did when they started, then they wouldn't do it at all. The pain needs to do something, change something, release something. Pain alone, while it might be intensely penetrating, needs to do something useful.

The same applies to rope and bondage. A dominant doesn't tie someone up just for sake of tying. They need to feel some outcome. Maybe their partner ends up feeling super horny and after the scene is ravenously sexual, or maybe the dominant finds that focusing on the fine detail of decorative bondage is relaxing, or maybe they get their own rush from experiencing power over their partner. Whatever the reason, there needs to be an effective outcome from the use of the inequality of power, the penetration, and the engagement, otherwise we don't use them.

There are many things which we look for in our BDSM relationships, many more than the super horniness or relaxation

I've just mentioned. We could include fun or recreation as an outcome, or greater bonding with our partner, increased trust, and increased intimacy. These are all valid and quite common outcomes, and often they are important parts of building a strong relationship with our partner. There are many more outcomes and in book two of this series I'll be looking at these a lot more closely.

I hope that at this point you can begin to see the structure and the pillars that I've been talking about, particularly in relation to your own BDSM and to the people you share it with.

One of the important things which I've noted elsewhere about BDSM when compared to vanilla relationships, is that in BDSM we do things to our partners or they do things to us. In vanilla-land, we instead do things with partners, not to them. This difference of "with" versus "to" is one of the key things which lets us actually see or define a difference. This goes hand in hand with the first two pillars I mentioned, unequalness of power and penetration, because we use these to do *to* our partners. We don't necessarily need to actually be more powerful in a physical sense, though we can be. More, it is the desire or need to actually use our skills, abilities, strength, desires, or determination to create situations in which we can penetrate our partners and have them feel us doing things to them, and to create situations in which their responses can affect or penetrate us.

These two pillars let us recognise BDSM, but this book and the others in this series are about BDSM relationships and to have a BDSM relationship we need to actually engage the person with whom we do our BDSM. This is the third pillar.

There are lots of things we can consider here. For example, if we have a long-standing friendship with someone and as part of that we satisfy our BDSM needs by, say, tying them up or being tied by them, are we having a BDSM relationship along with the friendship? Or are we merely friends who do BDSM? Can we be friends on one level and have a BDSM relationship on another?

I'd like you to keep in mind that sex isn't necessary to BDSM. In fact, you don't even need to get horny at all and still do BDSM. Is it possible therefore, to have a perfectly satisfying sexual relationship with someone and to separately have a platonic BDSM relationship with that same person?

Considering BDSM in terms of the three pillars I have listed also lets us see a difference between the, er, "classical" idea of a master or slave—such as in the old American South, or in the ancient world—and our present BDSM incarnation of these roles. A classical master used a slave for the service that they received, for the benefit from the slave. It wasn't the act or fact of mastering which was important. It was the service or the utility the slave provided. That was the sole value.

In BDSM terms however, a master doesn't just order a slave around to get service or some utility benefit. They use their slave precisely for the experience they get from doing so, for the penetration they themselves experience. The service can actually be secondary.

Likewise, a BDSM slave or submissive doesn't serve solely to be beneficial to their master. They serve to feel penetrated.

By talking about three pillars, what I'm trying to do is allow us to recognise a <u>BDSM</u> relationship as distinct from some other type of relationship. A relationship doesn't need all three pillars, but without them it isn't BDSM. With them, it is. For example, there doesn't need to be inequality of power for there to be penetration. Someone can be penetrated or strongly affected by the looks, sense of humour, attitudes, or caring nature of their

## Understanding BDSM Relationships

partner. This doesn't mean that there's an unequalness of power being exercised though.

Penetration can be absent in a relationship and this means it isn't BDSM, but it can still be a successful vanilla relationship. As we've seen, BDSM is about doing to rather than with. Two people who enjoy bungee jumping and get an intense rush out of it might spend a lot of time together, know each other's desires intimately, and put a lot of time into planning their bungee adventures, but when it comes down to it, it is the bungee jumping which is doing the penetrating, not the partner.

Even engagement can be missing and two people can still have an entirely satisfactory relationship which they both find rewarding. It just isn't a *BDSM* relationship. For example, two people who backpack the world together may feel comfortable in each other's company, and may share the burden of organising hotels, trains or flights, but they may not actually know much about each other or, indeed, care. The scope of their relationship may merely be as travelling companions and it might be a highly successful one, with them both ending their adventures saying what a fantastic time they had, but it wasn't really with each other even though they both happened to be there at the time.

By understanding the nature of these three pillars we can gain the ability to distinguish a BDSM relationship from other types of relationship. In particular, when we're trying to understand or troubleshoot a BDSM relationship it is often the nature of these three pillars which tells us how that relationship works, what its strengths are, and its vulnerabilities.

## Chapter 3

# BDSM and sex

There seems to be a great deal of confusion about the nature of BDSM. A lot of people, and I mean A LOT, seem to think it's just about sex. If it were just about sex then this would make many things very easy. Unzip your fly or take off your panties and the BDSM can begin. Zip up your fly or put your panties back on and the BDSM is over. There'd be no need to wonder whether you're crazy or not because you like being tied up or because you like whipping your partner so that they howl and bleed. If BDSM were only about sex you could say that the pain and the rope are just a part of a big sex game and that what you do in your dungeon or your bedroom is not a reflection of who you really are.

It's true that there are many people who use BDSM activities, such as light bondage or flogging, as a sex aid. This includes the countless thousands or millions who use a hint of BDSM for titillation in the bedroom. They may use silk scarves or cheap, fluffy, plastic handcuffs from the local sex-aid shop for bondage, or they may use light, soft floggers for sensual teasing. This is often simply symbolic. The scarves and plastic handcuffs are not robust and can't withstand any real struggling, and the light floggers do little more than suggest pain, but the idea of being tied or flogged can be powerful and may lead to mighty erections and voluminous lubrication. For some people, the fact that it is only symbolic can be very reassuring because the real thing can be, for any of a number of reasons, quite frightening.

It is a very important and very significant step to be able to divorce your BDSM interests from sex. By saying that the pain, the rope, the service, or any of the other aspects of BDSM are important and significant to you just on their own and without sex, you are stepping away from a safe intellectual harbour. You can no longer justify to yourself or to others that what you do is just "kinky sex." But taking this step can be very empowering. It can actually allow you to fully embrace BDSM because you no longer need to maintain a veneer of plausible deniability either for others or for yourself. Trying to believe that your BDSM practices are just about sex can actually hold you back from exploring other areas of BDSM which may be even more rewarding and satisfying for you.

While BDSM isn't necessarily about sex, sex can be a very effective tool to use in BDSM play. As I've already noted, BDSM is about power, control, domination, and surrender. To control, to dominate, or to surrender there must be something powerful involved. Sex can be that powerful thing. I stress that it can be. It need not be sex. Pain is also powerful. Ropes and restraints can be powerful. Even fear can be powerful. All these things are excellent BDSM tools. For the moment however, we're talking about sex.

## UNDERSTANDING BDSM RELATIONSHIPS

Making a guy feel horny and then preventing him from having an orgasm can be a very effective use of sex. You might put his cock in a cage with spikes on the inside to torture him so that when his cock becomes erect the spikes stick in. Or you might take a woman, tie her down with her legs apart, and then apply a very powerful vibrator to her clitoris. We could debate the relative merits of no orgasms versus too many orgasms, but suffice it to say that they are both very effective in their own way. They are both tools to create feelings of helplessness or surrender for the submissive, and for the dominant they create feelings of power or of being in control.

Your own BDSM play may involve a lot of sex. There's nothing wrong with that and I'd never suggest that there was. But in this chapter I'm trying to stress that BDSM is not sex, nor is sex BDSM. While there are those folk out there for whom BDSM is merely sexual foreplay, there are also many hard-core BDSM folk for whom their BDSM activities are the goal rather than being merely a warm-up for some hot-'n-horny nude gymnastics. In case your own particular BDSM circumstances make this distinction difficult to see, I'd like to give a few more examples to make my point.

A couple into cutting, where one cuts designs into the other's flesh with a scalpel without the aid of an anaesthetic, don't generally engage in a long session of carving designs into flesh and then suddenly whip off their clothes and get at it. It's often the pain and the artistry which are important for them, and despite what some people might like you to think, it is actually agony and it doesn't necessarily make you horny[1].

---

[1] It is appropriate to note that cutting also can be done so that it involves minimal or no pain. This is the case when the knife is used very lightly to cut

*BDSM and sex*

In a similar way, a couple into heavy impact play, such as whipping, caning, or spanking, are not going to have a long session where the top puts in every bit of energy he has to hammer his partner with every whip and flogger at his disposal and then, sweat dripping off him and barely able to stand any more, leap vigorously onto his partner (who is feeling similarly exhausted) and have energetic sex. No. More likely they will both curl up somewhere and either rest or fall asleep.

Finally, a guy into suspension bondage with his partner is not going to construct some amazing rope bondage, winch his partner high into the air, then whip off his clothes and start leaping into the air with an erection hoping to fortuitously (and briefly) enter his partner in some satisfying fashion before falling back to the ground.

## 3.1 BDSM and fetish

There's another bit of sexual mystery which also gets mixed in with BDSM sometimes. It's called fetish. A fetish is an object, thing, or a non-sexual part of the body which atypically stimulates someone sexually. Rubber and latex are common fetish materials; corsets and stockings are common fetish clothes; and feet and elbows are common fetish parts of the body. They become a fetish when these typically non-sexual objects make someone feel sexually aroused.

---

through only the top one or two layers of skin. Oftentimes this form of cutting also doesn't draw any blood.

## Understanding BDSM Relationships

There's a very important element to this definition of fetish. This is that fetish doesn't need to involve a second person[2]. Remember that with BDSM we always have a second person involved, such as the person tying the knots, the person giving the orders, the person cutting the flesh, or the person wielding the cane.

BDSM differs from fetish in two important ways:

1. BDSM always involves a second person while fetish never does,

2. BDSM doesn't always involve sex while fetish always does.

BDSM can go hand-in-hand with fetish, but it isn't fetish. But because fetish is about causing sexual excitement and because—as we've seen—sexual excitement can be a powerful BDSM tool, it means that fetish can be a powerful tool in BDSM play. If your partner is intensely aroused by latex, then when you wear latex you have something which you can use to control or manipulate your partner. You can arouse them with a caress from your latex-clad hand or stroke between their thighs with your latex-clad foot. Or you can deny them your latex by tying them up and standing just a bit too far away for them to touch or smell you.

Using your partner's fetish means you have sexual power over them. And power is the name of the BDSM game.

---

[2] Or, at least, not a whole person in the case of feet or elbows.

# Chapter 4
# Uncomfortable thoughts

There are many uncomfortable thoughts and ideas associated with BDSM. I say uncomfortable because they may not sit easily with the things we'd sometimes like to believe, particularly about ourselves. For example, many people can have trouble accepting the idea that:

- They enjoy striking or hurting their partner,
- That their partner enjoys being struck or hurt,
- That they enjoy being struck or hurt by their partner, or
- That their partner enjoys striking or hurting them.

I suspect that this discomfort is the source of many people's view that "BDSM is about sex" because the idea of two people having sex is socially acceptable. Even in the most conservative of families or societies the need for sex is understood. The need to strike, bruise, cut, or pierce your partner with needles is not. But, if you can dress up this striking, bruising, cutting, and so on as "kinky sex", regardless of how bad the fit, then suddenly it enters the realm of the acceptable. You can say, even to yourself, "Oh, yes! I do BDSM, but it's just another way of doing sex."

However, sometimes the heavier or more intense forms of BDSM play simply can't involve sex. We need to ask what happens when a couple who enter the world of BDSM via fluffy handcuffs start looking for more or heavier BDSM. While at the fluffy handcuff stage, it's easy to call what they do merely "kinky sex". But, once things start to get heavier, and maybe bruising and bleeding start to happen on a regular basis, or when perhaps they start exploring humiliation or a master/slave relationship, then trying to maintain the illusion that it's still just a kinky form of sex becomes much, much harder. At this point one or both of them may experience enough of an internal conflict that the BDSM must stop. Perhaps they simply cannot reconcile what they do to their partner, or what their partner does to them, with what they think a relationship should be. What happens then to their partner if for this partner there is no such conflict?

BDSM in many of its more intense forms can be a challenging idea to accept. Taking the step beyond justifying your BDSM in terms of kinky sex, light fun, simple role play, or merely as "adding variety", can be hard to make. It means accepting that pain, service, controlling your partner, being controlled by them, and other BDSM-type activities are right for you. You actually need to embrace and fully accept these ideas.

This creates a very concrete dichotomy, a division between BDSM being only about sex (and therefore a safe idea), and BDSM being about something else as well as sex (and therefore an uncomfortable idea). There is no grey area between these two positions. It's also a one-way trip to move from the first position to the second. It can require a lot of revisiting of what you thought you knew about yourself as you come to accept the new role which pain, humiliation, and other BDSM experiences have in your life.

Ideally, both people in a relationship either make this step from sex-only BDSM to a wider view of BDSM together, or have already made the step before they get together.

But when one partner has made this step and the other has not, the path ahead can be gloomy. It's likely that there'll be frustration on both sides—one pushing for more, the other pushing for less. There is not necessarily any right or wrong in this. It just simply may be the way it is.

Can this difference be resolved? Perhaps. But like all such issues the answer, if one is to be found, lies in communication and openness. If one partner cannot or does not make that step to embracing BDSM and its intensity, it might easily be that they don't need it as much as their mate. If other aspects of the relationship are satisfactory and rewarding then maybe something can be worked out.

## 4.1 Tough to swallow

Although maybe still uncomfortable, some of the more well-known BDSM activities, such as flogging or rope bondage, are easier to swallow in this regard than others simply because

*Uncomfortable thoughts*

they are portrayed in TV shows and movies, or because they sometimes bear a passing resemblance to childhood games such as cowboys and indians.

Sometimes though, what our partners are looking for can be intense, even disturbingly so.

I was at a BDSM workshop recently in which cutting was being demonstrated. Although I've mentioned it before, I haven't actually explained what it is. Cutting is a BDSM activity involving using a sharp knife or scalpel to make cuts into the skin of a submissive or bottom. Some people do this to create designs in the form of scars, some do it for the psychological effect—for the fear or apprehension, and some do it for the raw pain.

At this particular workshop, the submissive being cut as part of the demonstration remarked that it was good that she was there at the workshop because otherwise she'd be cutting herself at home. This leads us to one of the rarely spoken, and sometimes uncomfortable truths about BDSM, and that is a connection for some people between BDSM and self-harm.

Self-harm may develop as a coping mechanism depending on a person's external circumstances, or it may become desirable or needed by someone for no obvious reason. Self-harm can sometimes be a symptom of borderline personality disorder (BPD), or of other psychological disorders. Self-harm appears to be more prevalent in younger people, though it can be found in all age groups and both genders. Self-harm doesn't imply suicidal tendencies. The person who does it might only feel the need every few months and otherwise be entirely fine the rest of the time.

## UNDERSTANDING BDSM RELATIONSHIPS

There is a clear attraction for those who self harm and BDSM because BDSM often deliberately involves pain. Those seeking pain can find it in BDSM... on a platter, so to speak.

More important for us than why some people seek pain or seek to harm themselves is the simple fact that they do. For them, it is a need. It can involve a lot of embarrassment for them. It is not seen as socially acceptable. It isn't discussed, and the people who do feel the need to cut often do so alone without letting anyone know about it.

When the need is strong, the people who cut tend to cut deeply looking for strong pain. There's a big risk in this, particularly the risk of bleeding out and dying from loss of blood.

We may debate about this, or argue that self-harm is a symptom of some sort of illness, or that it's a poor coping strategy, but whether it is or isn't is not my place to judge. However, I will say that if someone is going to cut or hurt themselves anyway, it's far better for them either to do so when they're with someone, or for them to be hurt by someone who is able to make sure that it doesn't go too far and who is there to render assistance.

This is a good place for BDSM to come into the picture. A BDSM relationship can provide a safe and supportive environment for someone who needs pain. They can get that experience without needing to do it alone. When they are not alone, or when their partner cuts or hurts them, they can get the pain they need with far less risk, and get it with someone to hold them and support them before, during, and afterwards.

A danger here has to do with the difference between enabling and supporting. A friend of mine recently announced that she was going to run a workshop on the spiritual side of cutting and scarification. She had to turn many people away because it was

*Uncomfortable thoughts*

clear that they were simply looking for somewhere to go and cut themselves. They were looking for somewhere where they'd be allowed to, or be given permission to, or even encouraged to cut themselves. They were wanting someone else to take the responsibility.

BDSM isn't about giving up responsibility. Someone who gives up responsibility is a doormat and probably doesn't have a place in any sort of relationship, BDSM or otherwise.

It can be difficult to draw a line between enabling and co-dependency on one side, and being supportive on the other. When we care about someone we might stray too much towards actually creating situations which encourage them to self-harm when better or healthier options exist. Instead of supporting them, we can make things worse. There is a big difference between supporting someone who has a need for pain, surrender, or humiliation on one hand, and cheering them on on the other.

## 4.2 Positioning ourselves

When we engage in BDSM, a lot of the time the needs, hungers, and desires which surface are not necessarily the sorts of things you can talk about in church or during a game of bowling with the lads. But with our partners—our submissives, our dominants, our slaves, and our masters—what does arise presents us with opportunities to support and encourage our partners, and for them to support and encourage us. It is perhaps a measure of our commitment to ourselves, to our partners, and to our BDSM, how far we go with this.

This brings us to one of the three pillars of BDSM which I mentioned earlier: engagement. If there are ideas, thoughts, or attitudes which come our way in our BDSM explorations with our partner and we refuse to engage those ideas just because they are uncomfortable, then we necessarily limit where we can go and what we can do.

## Chapter 5

# What a BDSM relationship provides

For two people exploring BDSM, being part of a relationship creates opportunities to satisfy their BDSM wants and needs in a number of different ways.

Firstly, the relationship can create a context in which they can do more things, or experience things more intensely than they could with a casual play partner. By having an ongoing relationship with a partner who has complementary interests to yours—such as when you like being flogged and they like flogging—it means that you have more opportunities to explore and try out new things. You can afford to experiment because if some new technique turns out to be a disappointment one day, your partner will still be around the next day so you can do something different. In casual play, because it might be the only time you play with this person, you have to get it right first time. You don't take chances or try new things. You stick with what you know works, and you don't try to expand your horizons.

Secondly, because of the trust which comes with a longer-term relationship, you can go to more intimate places in your play than you can with a casual partner. You can even take chances with more intense play, knowing that your partner will be around the next morning or the next day so that you can take care of them or so that they can take care of you.

Thirdly, when you're part of a relationship with your BDSM partner, you don't have the need to make each and every scene a complete episode in itself as you do with a casual play partner. With a casual partner you can't be sure they will be around to continue where you left off next time, or if there will even be a next time. Having a regular partner allows you to adopt the view that what you start today doesn't need to end today, but can be open-ended and continue to play out over the next days, weeks, or even months.

Fourthly, the relationship that you have with each other allows you time to develop an awareness of each other's wants and needs, to establish ways of communicating, to develop trust in each other's intentions and abilities, and to develop your own routines and preferences for when you play together. This can be very comforting, but watch out for complacency!

Another thing which an ongoing relationship provides is an opportunity to more deeply explore BDSM. Profound surrender, submission, dominance, and mastery all become possible when you know that your partner is going to be there for you and with you every day. In a scene with a casual partner you can, at best, only superficially explore control and authority. This is because at the end of the scene you both need to walk away with the same control and authority with which you entered the scene. When you have a regular partner, particularly a live-in partner, this is not the case. When you know that you'll be seeing and interacting with your partner multiple times per day, any handing over of control or exercising of authority can quite realistically last for days, weeks, months, or the length of the whole relationship. For example, in such a relationship a submissive can effectively, productively, and completely hand over control of her sexuality and how she expresses herself sexually to her partner. He will be there to use, administer, and exercise that control in the long-term. On the other hand, the best that can happen in a casual scene in this regard is perhaps some orgasm denial for a couple of hours. And keep in mind that when we're talking about sexual control, a period of only a couple of hours is extremely short when we consider that sexual arousal and sexual tension can be held and built for days with some people.

You can see here that I'm talking about both penetration and engagement, the second and third pillars of BDSM relationships which I discussed in chapter 2. Having trust in your partner and knowing that your activities aren't confined to a simple evening's entertainment together means that you can develop and explore more intense and profound forms of BDSM, and this means more penetration. In casual play, you simply can't go too deep. Casual play might involve intensity, but not depth.

In addition, having a longer-term knowledge of, and experience with your partner builds engagement. Instead of being limited to doing what works for most people—and hence, what will probably work with your partner-of-the-moment—you can learn your actual partner's actual buttons and triggers. You can learn what they respond to and what they need, and then you can engage the Real Them and not an Average Partner.

*What a BDSM relationship provides*

## 5.1 Particular explorations

I'd like to spend a few words here talking about some particular BDSM activities and how they are affected by whether they are performed in the context of a relationship or whether they are just done casually at a play party or just with someone who is only an occasional play partner.

### Bondage

Bondage is very much a scene-based activity. This means that bondage lends itself well to being rolled out for quick and casual scenes either at parties or when you're with BDSM acquaintances. These can be rewarding in themselves because for some bottoms and submissives the effect of the embrace of the rope, even if just for 15 or 20 minutes, can be quite intense. Likewise, some tops enjoy the challenge and concentration involved in creating the initial tie and are then happy to move on.

For two people in a longer-term relationship however, more profound and intimate explorations can occur. For example, the top can put his partner into a rope harness over which she wears her normal street clothes for the day.

In addition, studies have shown[1] that bondage can have strong, positive, physiological effects—such as deep relaxation, feelings of floating, and emotional release—which are more easily experienced in a safe and secure environment with someone you trust.

---

[1] [MASTERS2008, pp. 103 - 105]

Bondage also has its intimate side, and being tied up—particularly while naked—can create intense feelings of exposure and vulnerability. Indeed, you can be extremely exposed, vulnerable, and helpless in bondage, and the security of being in a relationship with your trusted partner can allow you to fully surrender yourself into this experience. In a casual scene at a play party or with someone who is merely a BDSM acquaintance, you might leave your clothes on for the bondage for security reasons and thereby lose out on the experience of sexual vulnerability or exposure.

## Catharsis

Catharsis is a release of built-up emotional energy in response to something intense, dramatic, or powerful. The events or emotions which cause the initial build up of energy may have no relationship with whatever triggers their eventual release. For example, the built-up energy could come from something that happens at work—something positive, such as a promotion, or something negative, such as irritation with a colleague—which you can't fully let out of your system while you're in a staid working environment and while you're wearing a suit. The energy build up could also come from something that happens with family or with friends, or from something that happens while you're out and about.

When you don't have the opportunity to let those feelings out at the time, you need to find some other opportunity later. This is called catharsis. A trigger for the release of this pent-up energy can be found in some BDSM play such as heavy flogging, cutting, whipping, and humiliation, all of which can be—even just to those watching—quite dramatic and intense.

While floggings are sometimes handed out at BDSM events and parties with the same readiness as canapes, cheese, and biscuits, the more profound and satisfying experiences leading to catharsis come when two people who know each other take the time to develop such a scene in full awareness of each other's needs.

For example, the common attitude that BDSM equals sex often means that a flogging from Master Gregory The Brutal at a BDSM party will include some gratuitous fondling and heavy breathing. This can seriously detract from a submissive's emotional release when he is actually looking for some regular and heavy thudding into which he can allow himself to sink for ten or fifteen minutes.

This is not to say that a good flogging can't lead to some serious and satisfying nookie, but this works best when the two people concerned do so in the context of a longer-term relationship. Intimacy and long experience with a play partner means that limits are familiar and that the buttons which can be pushed are well known. This means greater intensity and less need for caution. Importantly, it also means that when you do play with your partner you can afford to say, "This scene is for catharsis, and later tonight we'll go for the nookie." Many people engage in BDSM scenes for the cathartic or cleansing effect which intense BDSM can have. This is far easier to achieve with a familiar partner in a familiar context than on a casual basis with a casual partner because you have the time and the opportunity to focus on one set of wants or needs in one scene, knowing that your partner will be around for a different scene later on when you'll be exploring other wants and needs.

# Guilt

Not all BDSM is about having a good time. Some BDSM is about making a bad time less bad. Guilt fits into this "less bad" category. For reasons beyond the scope of this book, some people carry a burden of guilt around with them. This is not to say that they've just robbed a bank or stolen candy from a baby. Instead, what I'm talking about is the guilt which for some people stems from childhood, from their upbringing, from their family, or even from their religion. It's either there all the time, or it builds up depending on what's going on in their lives. The archetypal way of dealing with this in a BDSM context is through a spanking—especially in a schoolroom scenario—but any sort of discipline-type activity can serve the same goal. This includes caning, being locked up, being spoken to sternly, and so on.

People don't generally go around telling anyone who'll listen that they feel guilty, need a good spanking, and then ask would this person help them out. Punishment and discipline work best when there is a foundation of trust and a longer-term relationship, and where the "guilty party" can be open and honest about how they feel, and about the sort of discipline, pain, or punishment which they need, for how long, and how intensely. This has some similarity with the point I made above in regards to catharsis. Sometimes, perhaps often, a scene will have a functional purpose beyond mere pleasure and it needs to be recognised as such. If BDSM play is sometimes used to mitigate guilt or to trigger catharsis, this is more easily done in the context of a relationship where you can devote whole scenes to this openly, knowing that there will be scenes at other times for other wants and needs, and that it won't always be about catharsis or guilt.

*What a BDSM relationship provides*

## Cutting

Some activities are, by their very nature, quite intimate. Cutting is one of these and it necessarily involves close personal contact. This can be contrasted with, say, flogging which inherently involves far more physical distance between the top and the bottom. Because of the closeness required for cutting, and because it is often performed on parts of the body which are usually private, some form of trust and respect between the cutter and cuttee is needed. This is easier to come by when there is a relationship underpinning the whole deal.

This doesn't mean that cutting can't be done on a casual basis, but it does mean that the cutter and cuttee are likely to be able to immerse themselves in the intimacy and profundity of the scene far more when they know each other well, than when they are ships passing in the night.

## Play involving power

Established relationships also lend themselves to unplanned and spontaneous power play. Even when there's no actual long-term exercising of control or authority going on, such as that which I discussed at the beginning of this chapter, a dominant and a submissive who have a long-term relationship can enter into role either for some playful fun or for something more serious whenever the mood takes them. A good foundation of intimacy, honesty, and trust means that any overture by one—such as the submissive kneeling at her partner's feet, or the dominant grabbing his partner by the scruff of the neck—can be either accepted by the other and lead into something more intense, or can be politely and safely deferred until a later time.

## Endorphins

The human body reacts in different ways to prolonged and intense pain. In some cases, it tries to deal with it by releasing neurochemicals which allow us to continue to function in spite of the pain. Some of these chemicals create a "high". This can be a feeling of detachment, for example, or withdrawal. It can also be a feeling of intoxication.

Whatever it is though, it leaves us vulnerable, and while we're in this vulnerable, intoxicated, neurochemically-impaired state, we need a partner who'll watch over us and take care of us until the chemicals have faded away and we're back to what passes for normal. And, again, this is going to be safest, and we're going to be able to surrender ourselves most to such an experience, when we have a trusted, long-term partner with us.

## Continuity of context

Continuity of context means that any situation, state of mind, or role which is entered into can continue through to a safe completion. BDSM between casual partners often has less of a guarantee of continuity than BDSM in a longer-term relationship. This is because there is a lack of certainty that attitudes, roles, thoughts, or situations will be picked up from where they left off with a casual partner. Because of this, it often happens that casual BDSM play leaves one or both of the people involved feeling like there has been a lack of closure, that something was missed out on. It can also leave them feeling quite alone.

Combined with the development of intimacy and trust, this idea of continuity is one of the main things which distinguishes

BDSM in a relationship from casual BDSM play. It allows roles to be established, built up, explored and exercised over extended periods and to greater levels of satisfaction than is possible in casual BDSM. Something unfinished in one scene can be picked up in the next and there's no need for fear or concern that this opportunity won't occur.

# Chapter 6

# Foundations of a BDSM relationship

BDSM is many different things to many different people. For some people it is about pain, for some it is about sex, for some it is about bondage or confinement, for some it is about surrender or profound submission, and for others it is about fear, embarrassment, or humiliation. Some people see it as the focus of their lives, some see it as a sort of hobby, and some see it merely as a kinky adjunct to their sex lives. Because of the large difference in levels of interest in BDSM, and because of the wide range of possible BDSM activities, it follows that the sorts of relationships in which we get involved are also many and quite varied.

This can make it difficult to work out exactly what we are looking for from BDSM. In part this is due to a natural tendency to look at what people are doing around us, compare ourselves to them, and simply imagine what it'd be like if we were doing what they're doing. But, when we examine the sorts of relationships other people are having, what we see might be entirely different from what is going to work for us. These other people might be having entirely reasonable and profoundly satisfying BDSM experiences; they are just going about it in a completely different way from what we might need. This can lead us to doubt ourselves or question whether we're on the right path.

There are however, many right paths and we might just need to find our own.

A challenge to finding our own personal flavour of BDSM is that what we might call mainstream BDSM tends to embrace only a small portion of what BDSM has to offer. When we look at what other people are doing or what is going on around us, we necessarily only see a very, very small subset of all of BDSM. If we look at the folk around us for inspiration they may indeed be practising a variety of interesting styles of BDSM, but the one which would work best for us might not be among them.

This can be a big problem because without having seen, heard, or read about particular approaches to BDSM, it can be hard or even impossible to think them up yourself. The one which is perfect for you might be out there just waiting for you to notice it and start doing it.

In this chapter, I want to present to you a variety of different ways of thinking about BDSM relationships. If you haven't yet worked out what's right for you, these may give you a clue, and if you already have something which works, the ideas here may help you make it better.

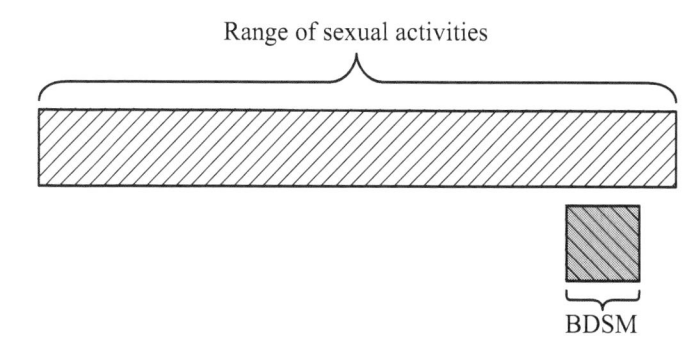

Figure 6.1: BDSM as a small subset of sex

## 6.1 The quantity of kink

Some people see BDSM primarily as an extension of their sex lives. They view it as kinky sex, or sometimes just "kink". For them it might be that BDSM is strictly a clothes-off activity which always starts or ends with sexual intercourse. This doesn't mean that BDSM equals sex. It means that BDSM is a type or flavour of sex. Figure 6.1 represents this view of BDSM. For such a kinky person, their range of sexual activities includes everything they do with BDSM. It means that they don't see, and sometimes can't even imagine, BDSM without sex.

I've drawn the box representing BDSM activities quite small. For some people it could be smaller, for some people it could be that the BDSM proportion is much larger. When we start considering the sorts of relationships in which BDSM is such a subset of sex, one of the things we can look at is what this proportion is. In effect, this means that we try to determine how much of the sex is vanilla and how much is kinky.

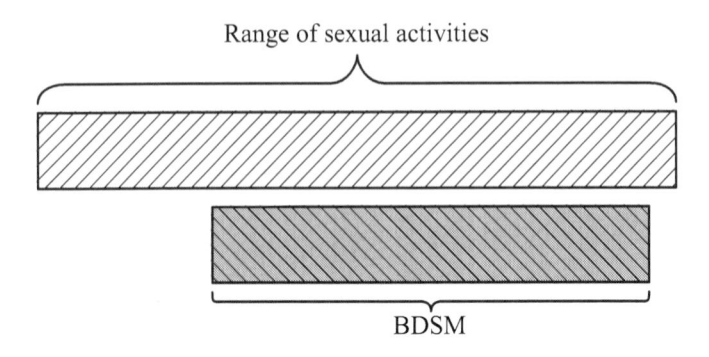

Figure 6.2: BDSM as a large subset of sex

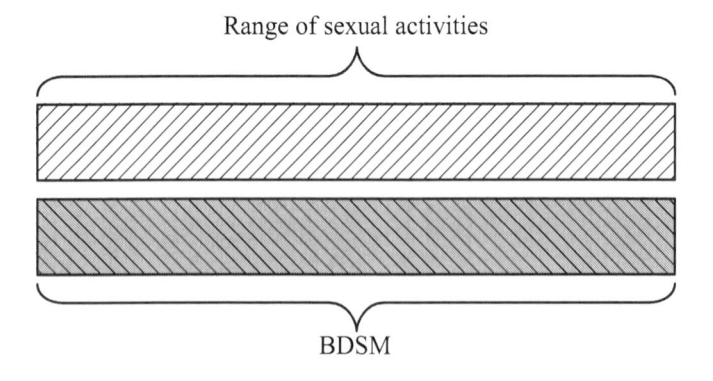

Figure 6.3: BDSM is sex and sex is BDSM

## Understanding BDSM Relationships

When we look at the sorts of relationships this can involve, one simple way of categorising them is the degree to which kink is involved such as:

- Vanilla with a touch of kink (the BDSM proportion is very small - figure 6.1),
- Mostly kink with a touch of vanilla (the BDSM proportion is very large - figure 6.2), or
- Kink exclusively (sex is BDSM - figure 6.3).

Importantly, these categories will significantly determine which wants and needs can be satisfied for the people involved in them.

For example, someone who is looking to regularly experience intense pain or profound submission during sex is probably going to want to be in a mostly kink relationship. If they're with someone who is looking for a mostly vanilla relationship with just a bit of kink every now and then, then this want or need for pain or submission is probably not going to get met to the extent they need.

Conversely, someone who is only into the occasional use of fluffy handcuffs is going to be best suited for a relationship which is mostly vanilla. They would probably be overwhelmed with a partner who is looking for 100% kink.

Let's look a little closer at these categories and see how the relationships might shape up.

## Vanilla with a touch of kink

When a kinky relationship is mostly vanilla, the BDSM elements will only appear now and then. BDSM may just be used to

*Foundations of a BDSM relationship*

make sex more exciting or adventurous. Perhaps sex with BDSM will simply become part of the couple's sexual repertoire along with sex in a glass-walled elevator, sex in a forest, sex while swimming in the ocean, sex while riding an elephant, and sex while skydiving. It's just another situation or context in which to have sex.

When a relationship is mostly vanilla, the people involved refer to themselves in mostly vanilla terms—such as husband, wife, boyfriend, girlfriend, lover, etc. They don't see themselves in BDSM terms.

Because the BDSM side of their relationship is a subset of the sexual side, and because most people don't fuck 24 hours a day, 7 days a week, this means that the BDSM aspect can be separate from and still coexist with other aspects of the relationship between these two kinky folk.

They could be friends (or "friends with benefits") who have a friend-type relationship including sex and occasionally some BDSM. They may engage in BDSM casually, or sometimes at play parties, or in the privacy of one or the other's apartment or home.

It could be that one or both have mild BDSM and sexual needs and they recognise this. It might be that these needs aren't strong enough to support a long-term live-in relationship and they just get together nookie-wise as needed.

Alternatively, they could actually be lovers. They could live together or just date. Sex is common or frequent, and sometimes it involves BDSM.

They could be married, and with this level of commitment to each other, they might have decided to invest in equipping a dungeon in their basement with all the paraphernalia they typically use in their BDSM sessions.

One of the important features of this type of relationship is that it's scene-based. The BDSM shenanigans, like most sexual activities, have a clearly defined start and end, and once they've ended the couple go back to being vanilla.

## Mostly kink with a touch of vanilla

Some couples like a lot of kink, and they like it to add flavour to much of their lives. In other words, it leaks out of their bedrooms and they allow both it, and references to it, to colour their lives in general. Because the BDSM aspect is often a focus, they may think of their partner in BDSM terms—such as being their dominant, submissive, master, mistress, slave, etc. This may be some or most of the time.

In contrast to those people for whom BDSM plays a minor part in sex, these kinky folk will often see their sexuality in terms of BDSM. But, like their less kinky counterparts described above, they won't be doing it 24 hours per day, seven days per week.

They might be two kinky people who get together almost solely to get their kinky needs met. Again, this could be because that their kinky needs aren't enough to support a long-term committed relationship. They could be a top/bottom or dominant/submissive couple who don't live together, but who get together from time to time to play and fuck, and who maybe also do non-sexual things together occasionally, such as have coffee or go to the movies. They might have other people in their lives who they also fuck vanilla-wise, but when the two of them are together it is almost always BDSM.

Or they could live together in a partnership or marriage. They would be a top/bottom or dominant/submissive couple who share a life together, who live together and who play regularly. Their sex is almost always with a BDSM flavour.

## Kink exclusively

When two people have a relationship where sex and BDSM can't be separated at all then it really only matters whether they have anything else together.

If all they ever do together is have sex/BDSM then that pretty much defines the relationship. In this case, you couldn't say that they even have a friendship. Although they may completely trust and respect each other, they may not have any common activities or interests except for their sexual and BDSM adventures.

On the other hand, they could be "friends with benefits", in which case the benefits are always sex with BDSM.

Also, they could be married or they could be life partners. In this case, their sex is always about BDSM.

## Compartmentalising

It's important to keep in mind that we're talking about sex here. When you always see BDSM in terms of sex then it makes compartmentalising it easy. Some people like this. It lets you define a simple boundary between BDSM and the rest of your life. If there's no sex then there's implicitly no BDSM.

It also makes managing BDSM simple. If the BDSM side of things breaks down then it isn't your whole life which is affected.

If you're one of those folk who strongly links sex and BDSM then a breakdown in your BDSM activities may affect a large chunk of your sex life, but the rest of your life will continue on. And if BDSM is only a kinky adjunct to an already-varied sex life, then the BDSM, if and when it stops working, can be put aside—temporarily or permanently—with no major loss.

It's worth pointing out that actual sexual intercourse, exactly like many BDSM activities, is scene-based. It has a start and an end, and this makes it really, really easy to combine with scene-based BDSM.

## The vanilla folk

When we consider vanilla relationships, factors which contribute to their success typically include:

- Shared and common interests,
- Similar tastes in music, entertainment, food, or sport,
- Complementary sexual needs and desires,
- Aligned political and religious attitudes,
- Shared interest in raising a family, and
- Same taste in friends.

All of these are things which you can find in advertisements by vanilla singles who are looking for long-term partners. Success in such a relationship may be considered to be a measure of peaceful longevity, of how long the people involved remain together and continue to find the sharing of their lives to be rewarding.

## A closer look

I don't want to dwell too much on the vanilla side of relationships because it's both beyond the scope of this book and because there are already numerous books and TV shows which deal with them in more than sufficient and sometimes prurient detail.

Instead, I'd like to look now at what do we get if we only consider relationships when viewed from the BDSM perspective?

# 6.2 When BDSM doesn't mean sex

While some people view BDSM in terms of sex and consider what they do to be merely kinky variations on sex, there are also people who explore BDSM separate to sex. They still may bonk each other senseless after some BDSM scenes, but at other times they explore the BDSM for the sake of BDSM and not for sex.

Having this awareness that for them BDSM and sex may overlap (figure 6.4 on the facing page) but aren't the same changes their perception and experience of any relationships they have in which BDSM plays a part.

Separating out sex from BDSM (figure 6.5) both increases the range of possible activities and relationships they can have, and at the same time tends to increase their complexity and richness.

In particular, once detached from sex and its private, one-on-one, scene-based nature, the BDSM aspect of a relationship can be extended beyond the time constraints of a scene, out of the privacy of the bedroom, and into many other aspects of life.

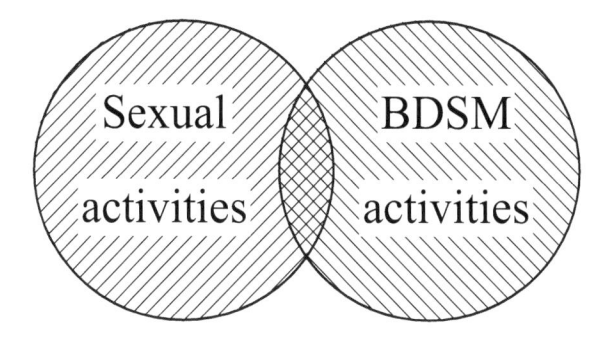

Figure 6.4: BDSM and sex overlap

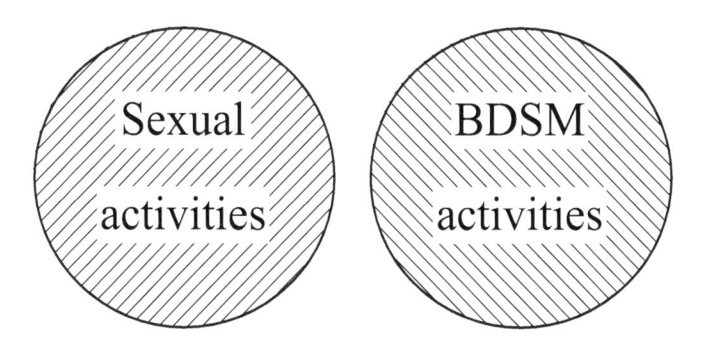

Figure 6.5: BDSM and sex with no overlap

## Full-time relationship, full-time BDSM (24/7)

"24/7" BDSM refers to a BDSM relationship which maintains its BDSM flavour 24 hours per day, 7 days per week, 365 days per year.

Some people claim such relationships can't exist. I can understand this point of view because for someone who is into the straight, physical side of BDSM—such as flogging or bondage—it's pretty clear that the flogging must stop from time to time if only due to exhaustion or because bruises and abrasions need time to heal. In fact, any sort of BDSM based solely on specific physical activities—cutting, piercing, humiliation, erotic denial, etc.—has to stop from time to time and so can't be 24/7.

Having said that, it becomes clear that 24/7 BDSM—if it can't be based on particular activities—must be based on something else. That something else is attitude. For example, even a mere inclination towards staying full-time in a submissive or dominant attitude with your partner can become a powerful and ever-present component in a relationship when it is recognized and embraced by both people involved.

BDSM doesn't need to be only about activities or scenes which have a clearly defined start and a clearly defined end. For some BDSM couples, the exercise of power, authority, and control is their thing and it plays out in a D&s[1] or M/s[2] relationship between them. This is much less a set of activities and more a set of attitudes and behaviours. When one person—the slave

---

[1] Dominant and submissive
[2] Master/slave

or submissive—has given up authority over themselves to their partner, this context of deliberately imbalanced power can be a 24/7 constant awareness and experience.

Even when they're not with their partner, a slave or submissive can feel the bonds their partner or their relationship has placed on them in terms of tasks or duties to perform, acceptable behaviour, priorities, and allowable choices. These can include how to dress, how to behave towards others, when to be home, what to eat, what to buy, and so on. The slave or submissive knows that they have a partner above them, and they are constantly aware of the position of service they hold. They know that their partner may, at any time, get in contact and give them directions which they must follow.

The master or dominant is just as much a part of this "24/7-ness" as they plan for and take advantage of the behaviour of their submissive or slave partner. In the same way that their submissive/slave partner is aware of the bonds in place on them, their dominant/master is aware both of the bonds they have placed and of the service their partner is performing even when the two of them are apart.

Perhaps we can consider this in terms of actual rope bondage. A submissive who is tied is going to feel the restraint when she moves or struggles. This is the power her dominant partner asserts over her. But even when she is lying there and the embrace of the rope is merely holding her in place, she has the awareness that she is bound. Likewise, a dominant who has delightfully tied his partner isn't going to suddenly cool once the last knot is in place. His pleasure from the bondage continues while his partner is restrained, even just from knowing that his handiwork is having its effect on her.

*Foundations of a BDSM relationship*

Full-time, 24/7 BDSM tends to best exist when the people concerned are living together or are frequently in each other's company. This is no different to a vanilla full-time relationship where constant presence—such as waking up in the same house in the morning and going to bed in the same house in the evening—is the norm. This provides the time needed for the two people involved to stay on the same track together. Too much time apart allows for one to drift onto a different path to the other.

## Full-time relationship, scene-based BDSM

Not everyone is looking for the intensity or immersion that 24/7 dominance and submission or mastery and slavery requires. BDSM folk can be married or live together and not have the same 24/7-type relationship as discussed above.

Many people, in fact, are happy to have a relatively vanilla relationship with just a hint of BDSM, perhaps combined with occasional BDSM scenes which may be quite intense. These people might have BDSM-type decorations scattered around their house or apartment, socialise with other BDSM folk and share war stories about the sub that got away, but their actual BDSM engagements only take place at set times, possibly in a custom-built dungeon in a spare room, or in the main bedroom on the nights when a private box of toys is opened and the chains, ropes, and floggers come out.

The sort of BDSM we're talking about here is scene- or activity-based and it will typically happen when both people involved feel a need. There's a clearly defined start and end to the activities, and when it's all over the toys get put away and the people involved return to "normal" until the next scene.

The advantage of this type of relationship is that any BDSM-related wants or needs can be met when and as required because the two people concerned are available to each other all the time.

This contrasts with a 24/7-type of BDSM relationship where BDSM would colour or infiltrate every aspect of their lives. For those without such a strong need, having a full-time partner to share in the vanilla side of life—such as work, family, movies, theatre, zoo, and holidays—means that each person can do their own thing when they want, do vanilla things together when they want, and tie and flog each other when they want.

## Part-time relationship, some BDSM ("friends with benefits")

An interesting term has arisen in modern social life, and that is "friends with benefits". This is a friendship which includes sex and it is something I mentioned a few pages back. It is about two people who care about each other as friends, and who trust each other enough to go to bed together knowing that it's not going to lead to awkwardness such as unwanted talk of marriage or having to meet the parents.

BDSM has the same phenomenon. In this case, it is two people who are friends or good companions and who enjoy a healthy BDSM scene together from time to time. Importantly, they know that their friend/partner isn't going to start clinging to them and isn't going to want to set up a dungeon-for-two.

On the negative side (at least in terms of BDSM), there is the risk that one of the people involved might set up house with someone else and the "benefits" consequently cease for their previous partner.

*Foundations of a BDSM relationship*

Another problem is that even if they are both unattached, they are likely living separate lives and the opportunities for them to scratch each other's itches might not be so easy to arrange as in 24/7 or living-together relationships.

## Part-time relationship, only scene-based BDSM

Then there are the people who get on well in a scene-based BDSM context but who tend not to have any shared interests or desires to see each other when floggers or rope aren't in play.

While it might sound like these folk have very limited opportunities, this can actually include the same sort of thing we see with people who belong to car clubs or who go to science-fiction conventions. This can be social, or intimate, or both, and may involve meeting for lunch or dinner with other like-minded BDSM folk.

These encounters can provide opportunities to let the BDSM side of your personality out for some fresh air with others who happily talk about and share the same BDSM interests. When the socialising is done, BDSM scenes can follow.

This socialising can occur in public cafes or restaurants, in someone's private home (often with BDSM toys or dungeon available), or on specially-planned weekends away with like-minded enthusiasts.

A narrower aspect of this type of relationship includes the people who get together just to scene for their own mutual satisfaction. They may have met at a BDSM party or social event, decided they had similar BDSM interests, and arranged to meet again afterwards for some extra activities.

A variant on this latter type of relationship can be what you get with professional BDSM services where visits are paid for and the goal is strictly a BDSM encounter.

## Party-only or scene-only BDSM

While some folk in a relationship might attend and scene at BDSM parties as a couple, some people go to BDSM parties strictly for no-strings BDSM play. They might make themselves available as a demonstration bunny for a workshop on bondage, or as a human torch during a fire play show-and-tell. Or, alternatively, they may take a bag of rope and offer to tie up all comers.

The point is that they can stretch their BDSM "muscles" a bit at the party, and then walk away at the end with their want or need met and with no strings left attached.

## One-way BDSM and professional BDSM

The BDSM part of some relationships is strictly one-way. The situation where a person visits a professional BDSM dominant, dominatrix, or submissive, pays their money, and gets what they need, is a good example of one-way BDSM. This is not to say that the professional isn't also getting something out of the engagement, but the obligation is on the professional to satisfy their customer's needs. It's not mutual as it is in other relationships.

Some non-professional relationships can also be one-way in BDSM terms. A case in point can be where someone has BDSM wants or needs which aren't as frequent or as strong as their

*Foundations of a BDSM relationship*

partner's. This may involve BDSM play when you aren't in the mood. There's nothing wrong with this. Taking care of your partner can be a natural part of a caring and supportive relationship. As long as this is balanced overall and there's no resentment then it's fine.

The previous paragraph refers to BDSM which is one-way only some of the time. This has more of a chance of succeeding than BDSM which is one-way all the time. This can happen when one person loses interest in BDSM (for whatever reason) or where one person never has had any BDSM interest but the two of them are together for other reasons—such as other common interests, children, etc.

## 6.3 The needs or wants which get met in a relationship

When two people have a relationship involving BDSM, there are two ways that their BDSM wants or needs get met:

1. The relationship itself satisfies the wants or needs. This happens where the relationship involves dominance and submission, or mastery and slavery, and the actual exercising of the relationship—such as the use and experience of power, authority, and control—provide the satisfaction to the people involved.

2. The relationship provides a context in which wants or needs are explored and satisfied. For example, a couple who use flogging as a sort of cathartic release on weekends, or as a lead-in to kinky sex, have a relationship

which creates a safe context in which to engage in flogging.

There can be significant overlap between the above two ways in which needs are met. For example, a couple who have a significant D&s element in their relationship might also use flogging, bondage, cutting, piercing, etc., to satisfy other needs while still staying within the dominant/submissive context.

## The relationship itself satisfies want or needs

Sometimes there won't need to be ropes, floggers, leather outfits, dungeons, chains on the wall, or any other obvious signs of BDSM-in-progress for a couple to have an entirely satisfying BDSM relationship. Sometimes it can be the nature of the relationship itself, rather than what goes on inside it, which is satisfying.

This will mostly happen when an important aspect of the couple's relationship has to do with the experience of power; i.e., one person experiencing or exercising power over their partner while their partner experiences power being asserted over them. This can happen in a number of ways. Some of these are obvious, and some not so obvious.

It's obvious when one partner takes the role of dominant or master and then explicitly takes control of, and gives orders and directions to their submissive or slave partner. This can be made extremely evident by the clothes that each wears—or doesn't wear, in the case of a slave or submissive who is kept naked by their partner. In addition, the way each talks to the other—such as the use of "Sir"—makes concrete the sort of relationship they are involved in. The control-taking in this sort of relationship is overt and may even be aggressive.

It's less obvious when the control-taking is more subtle and less imperative. A situation where a dominant provides firm guidance and direction for their naturally-yielding, submissive partner can be perfectly rewarding for some BDSM folk and there may not be any outward sign that BDSM is involved. Such a situation might be where they're both in the car and the submissive is driving. Along the way, the dominant might always choose the route. Or they might go out to dinner together and the dominant always chooses the restaurant. He might even choose and order the meal she eats. There may not be any special clothes or ways of addressing each other in their relationship, but the power and control can be just as pervasive and satisfying for them both.

Power can also be less obviously experienced through teasing, tickling, taunting, or tantalising. That this is BDSM becomes apparent when it's not done out of malice or meanness, when it's almost always one particular partner on the receiving end, and when both see it is a positive aspect of their relationship. This can be a rewarding form of attention which the dominant is happy to give and to which the submissive is happy to surrender. This sort of play reinforces the role or rank which each has in the relationship, and these acts of reinforcement—such as tickling or teasing—are a subtle, but often quite effective, exercise of power.

Service-based relationships can also be powerful BDSM experiences, even without any orders or commands being given by the dominant. While service can be based on a slave or submissive obeying the explicit orders of their partner, in many cases a submissive or slave can fully submit to the desires or wants of their partner without them. All it needs is that their dominant clearly expresses his or her preferences, values, and priorities. This automatically creates a framework for the submissive in which they can direct themselves while still being under the control of their partner.

As an example, a master may have strong ideas about how he wants things done around his house. Once his submissive partner knows these, she can fully surrender to them and provide useful service to him even though he might not have once given her an actual order. The sorts of things he might say are, "I like my bed sheets changed weekly, the house dusted from top to bottom twice a month, and dinner on the table by 6:30pm." He won't be saying to his submissive, "Scum-of-the-earth, prepare my dinner!" or "Slave! Change the bed sheets!" Instead, she has a framework or structure in which she is able to conform to his wishes and desires without the need for explicit orders.

This can work very well for couples where the submissive or slave partner has a background where actually being submissive was frowned upon—such as if they were brought up by a women's liberation mother or in a feminist household. She can submit to her master's wishes and desires while still not being told what to do!

What I have been talking about here effectively creates a 24/7 relationship.

## The relationship provides a context

I'd like to spend a few words now talking about topping and bottoming, and about how they change depending on the nature of the relationship between the two people involved.

Topping and bottoming usually refer to scene-based BDSM activities, i.e., to activities which have a clearly defined start and end such as a bondage scene, a flogging scene, or a cutting scene.

At first glance, we might think that what's important about these very physical activities is how well they are executed technically, about the aim of the person wielding the flogger, about the firmness of the knots and the layout of the rope by the person doing the bondage, or about the steadiness of the hand of the person doing the cutting. It's true that these are important, but what is often neglected is the people factor.

We can see this people factor when we compare the differences between doing one of these scenes at a BDSM play party with someone we might know only casually, and doing the same scene at home with someone who we know well.

At a play party with a casual acquaintance, the scene needs to be strictly self-contained. There can't be any overrun because this person we're with is not going to be around for much time after the scene ends. We, and the scene, are limited by their availability. Not just by their physical presence or not, but also limited by their ability or willingness to be supportive. With a casual topping or bottoming partner we need to be self-contained ourselves. We often can't lean emotionally on the person we're with or expose our inner selves too much. A casual scene with a casual partner is typically just a straight technical or mechanical affair, and that's that.

There's nothing wrong with this sort of arrangement. For the sorts of BDSM wants or needs which can be met in a strictly scene-based context—such as a straight need for pain, or for some physiological release through bondage—well-defined and limited scenes can be fine.

What happens between two people who have a long-standing relationship is very different to this.

Firstly, they are prepared to invest in each other. In a long-term relationship of any sort, there is an understanding that not every day or every encounter is going to be perfectly wonderful for both people. Sometimes things aren't going to work due to distractions, medical issues, and other transient problems which affect us all at some time or another. Any scene these people do together doesn't need to be balanced in the sense that each gets their needs met then and there. Instead, they look more at the long term, and if a scene doesn't work out today, maybe it'll work out tomorrow. This is not the case in play with a strictly casual partner where there is only one chance to get it right and where the pressure to perform can be much higher.

Secondly, with people who know each other, there's not so much need to tightly contain the scene or to tightly contain yourself. The scene can afford to run over time. Its effects—such as when you enjoy being tied up so much that you want to stay tied up all night and through until the morning—can even afford to leak into the next day because any time and availability problems can often be flexibly managed. There isn't the same need to pack up and be Joe or Jane Normal straight afterwards as there can be in casual encounters.

And with someone you know you can afford to open up, knowing that your partner is not going to feel burdened by your tears, and that they're not going to be judgemental if you show weaknesses.

Even when your partner isn't a live-in lover, husband, or wife, knowing that they aren't going to disappear from your life means that you don't have to be so independent. You don't have to make sure that a scene and all its psychological and emotional ramifications end when the ropes come off, when the knife is

*Foundations of a BDSM relationship*

cleaned and put away, or when the floggers are put back in the toy bag. This creates a very different, more open, trusting context in which scenes can play out.

This doesn't mean that there's anything more than topping and bottoming going on between you and your partner, nor does it suggest that there's any 24/7, D&s, or power/control aspect to what you do together.

The important thing is that having a long-standing and ongoing relationship with your play partner does dramatically change the context of your play, as well as create opportunities for play which scratches different sorts of itches than strictly casual play with a casual partner.

## Overlap

Being part of a relationship where the relationship itself provides satisfaction (such as M/s or D&s) doesn't prevent you from engaging in more "traditional" BDSM pursuits—such as wax play, bondage, or caning. Indeed, the overarching power/authority relationship can provide a powerful context itself for these other activities.

For example, being compelled by your master to engage in BDSM scenes at his pleasure can be an effective context in which to explore and exercise power. The feeling of having no choice but to obey and submit to the pain or torture he wishes to inflict can be a very intense experience for both you and your master.

## 6.4 Discussion

An extremely quick way of considering what you're looking for in a BDSM relationship can be summarised as:

- What are you looking for?
- How often do you want it?
- How intense does it need to be?

This takes a lot of the fine detail away from the topic, but these three questions can nevertheless provide a good starting point for determining what's going to work for you.

We can supplement these questions with a further three to give an idea about how a potential partner is going to fit in:

- What are you prepared to give back to your partner?
- How often?
- How much of an effort are you prepared to make?

Consider these carefully. If you're actually just looking for occasional intense BDSM scenes, then a partner who is looking for something more regular or even live-in might be disappointed.

# Chapter 7

# Compatibility

For a BDSM relationship to work between two people, there has to be some measure of compatibility. We can think of it as being:

- Some or all of the wants and needs you have being satisfied by your partner, by the relationship, or by both, and
- Some or all of the wants and needs your partner has being satisfied by you, by the relationship, or by both.

There are many different wants and needs which might be involved in a BDSM relationship. For example:

- You might want someone to share your interest in shiny nipple clamps,

- You might be looking for a relationship in which to explore long-term, profound submission,
- You might want someone as an occasional bondage-and-sex partner,
- You might be trying to find a partner simply to accompany you to BDSM parties,
- You might be needing someone to tie you up regularly,
- You might be wanting to find a submissive partner with whom to satisfy your need to control or overwhelm,
- You might be looking for a house-mate who shares your passion for wax play, or
- You might be simply looking for cuddles and affection with an occasional hint of BDSM.

Regardless of what your reasons are, you need to make sure that any partner you select has a reasonable chance of satisfying your wants or needs. Sometimes it can be too easy to be distracted by the wrapping—the clothes, the leather, the way of talking, the skills with a flogger, or the knack with a knife. When this sort of distraction occurs, the result can be briefly exciting, but it can also quickly fade. If all you're looking for is a quick bit of excitement—the BDSM equivalent of a one-night stand—then this could be entirely fine. If you're looking for something which will last, you have to pay attention to the real criteria which need to be met for the relationship to work for you in any long-term sense.

At the same time that you're picking a partner for yourself, you need to be sure that you will be able to contribute towards satisfying your potential partner's own wants and needs. This is very important because it's sometimes easy to skip over the fact that your potential BDSM partner also has wants and needs which their relationship with you must satisfy. In the heat of the moment, you might think that you have found Master Magnificent or Subbie Superb and proceed at full speed to attain them without considering or realising that you might not be right for him or her. This can be a difficult thing to accept or admit, but the price you may have to pay for not doing so—namely, ending up in a badly-functioning relationship, or being rejected down the track—is far higher than accepting the inevitable now and devoting your time and energy towards finding a better match.

When you're looking for a BDSM partner, the responsibility for making the relationship work is shared by you both. To make the right—or, at least, the best—choices you need to talk, be honest about your goals, discuss your wants and needs as much as you know about them, and listen to your potential partner as they do the same. Regardless of on which end of the flogger you normally find yourself, you need to learn what works for your potential partner and how to help them get it. While power, control, and authority might lie in the hands of the dominant, that doesn't ever absolve the submissive from making an effort.

Sometimes in the BDSM world you can find the strange ideas that firstly, dominants are the ones who both make relationships work and who have all the responsibility, and secondly, that the submissives are the ones who merely follow. This isn't the case. Each person involved, be they dominant, submissive, top, bottom, master, mistress, or slave, has just as much responsibility as their partner for the success or failure of the relationship. Some submissives think that because they are capable of achieving a deep sub-space, or because they can have multiple orgasms at the drop of a flogger, this must clearly be

*Compatibility*

sufficient for a line of dominants to form at their door with each dominant being desperate to bring the submissive unbridled bliss. This is not so.

## 7.1 It's doing to, rather than doing with

One of the important differences between a BDSM relationship and a vanilla relationship is that in BDSM you do things *to* your partner while in vanilla relationships you do things *with* your partner. In vanilla relationships or in vanilla sex, it is sufficient merely to do things with someone else. In BDSM it is not.

This difference between doing to and doing with involves the idea of penetration. In a vanilla relationship you might go to a movie together, to dinner together, or out para-sailing together. But, even if the experiences are intense, it isn't your partner causing them. It is the movie, the dinner, or the para-sailing. With BDSM however, we cut our partner with a knife, we tie them up, or we crawl at their feet and beg. In BDSM, we do things directly to our partner. We make them feel. We create the experience. We don't just keep them company while exciting things happen.

This is a big difference in terms of relationships. It means that the BDSM relationships themselves create the opportunities for satisfaction, pleasure, and excitement. We don't merely accompany our partner; we engage them. If I want to see an action movie or have a great dinner then it's easy to find a cinema or a restaurant to satisfy this desire with or without a partner. If I want an intense bondage scene however, I need a strong relationship with someone who is going to be part of that scene with me.

Seeing this difference helps us to understand one of the ways in which a BDSM relationship can fail—namely when the doing to stops happening and all that is left is the doing with. This is the vanilla-fication of a BDSM relationship. Instead of it being about BDSM any more, it somehow fades and you suddenly discover one day that you are living a vanilla relationship.

## 7.2 Changing needs and personal growth

Sometimes people's BDSM wants and needs change over time. While some needs may vary depending on life's circumstances—such as stressful days possibly leading to a stronger desire for heavy floggings, or that being on holidays may allow time for longer and more relaxed scenes—as people grow and learn about themselves this might change their BDSM wants or needs in longer-term or more profound ways.

Someone who discovers that an aversion for some particular BDSM activity is due to something from their past may work on it and then find that they really enjoy the activity. Someone else may use BDSM as a way of dealing with other issues in their lives, and when they resolve those issues they find that they're no longer interested in BDSM. And some people who never had any interest in BDSM for the first decades of their lives may find themselves drawn to it as they learn more about what makes them tick and as hungers are discovered or recognised.

This is important to understand for a relationship because as time goes by, the wants and needs of the people involved may genuinely change. This change may draw the partners closer together, or it may push them apart. Personal growth doesn't always happen in the direction that is going to strengthen a relationship. It may simply do the opposite.

On the other hand, change itself doesn't mean the end of the relationship. Even if activities you previously enjoyed no longer inspire you, that doesn't mean there aren't other things which can take their place. As your passions for different things wax and wane, talk about the changes with your partner. Don't cover things up and don't pretend to be interested in activities which no longer rock your boat. Keep your partner informed and treat the changes as opportunities to engage in new activities or to see your relationship in new ways.

# Chapter 8

# Life aspects

A useful way of understanding the place BDSM has in our own relationships is to consider which aspects of our lives we want it to effect or to be involved in.

As I noted earlier, some people make a particular effort to compartmentalise BDSM by confining it to only one or two aspects of their lives. One of the most common ways is by limiting BDSM activities to the bedroom and to sex. Such compartmentalising can be a good way of managing BDSM in the face of conflicting demands on our time and attentions.

For example, when we're talking about a couple with children, limiting BDSM to the bedroom can be a very effective way of keeping BDSM out of the sight of the children. The couple is going to be having sex anyway (probably) and will be making any necessary arrangements to ensure that they can do it in privacy. By satisfying their BDSM wants and needs at the same time, they can kill two birds with one stone.

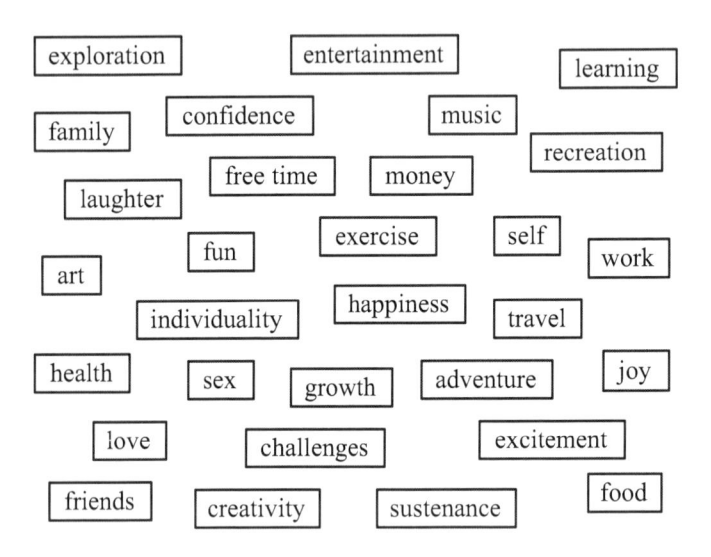

exploration  entertainment  learning
family  confidence  music
  free time  money  recreation
  laughter
   fun  exercise  self
art       work
  individuality  happiness  travel
health  sex  growth  adventure  joy
  love  challenges  excitement
friends  creativity  sustenance  food

Figure 8.1: Life aspects

## Understanding BDSM Relationships

While sex is a common companion to BDSM, there are many other aspects of life which can be involved either directly or tangentially with BDSM. I've listed some of these in figure 8.1 on the preceding page to give you a few ideas. It's worth thinking about these and whether they have a place or not in your BDSM now, or whether they could have a place in your BDSM in the future.

Throughout the course of the day there may be opportunities to interact BDSM-wise with others who aren't our primary partners. **Friends** who are either into BDSM themselves, or who are aware of our inclinations, provide chances for us to express our interest in BDSM, to talk about it, or just to try a few things, even when it's not to the extent which we might explore with a primary partner or in a fully-fledged BDSM scene.

Is this something which might actually add to your friendships? Can you meet people through your BDSM social life or at BDSM parties who can become friends away from a party or outside of a dungeon?

**Exploration** and discovery are aspects of our natural human curiosity. We like to find out new things. In fact, it can be immensely satisfying to speculatively try something and find out that it's the best thing since sliced bread. In BDSM, this can involve new techniques for existing things we do, new sensations, new thoughts, and new feelings. When we are open with our partners, new things become easier to try because we don't feel so awkward about asking, and we don't feel so afraid or worried that something we'd like to explore may turn out to be a dud. Exploring lets us discover new things which we can add to our BDSM repertoire. This adds variety, and gives us more tools to try in different situations. It's worthwhile to take time to try new things and treat the attempts as little voyages of discovery into uncharted and potentially exciting realms of BDSM.

**Entertainment** and **fun** are things we might not directly think about as goals for our BDSM. As a top, I might make an extra effort to tie knots with a flourish, or take some time before a flogging to discuss my collection of whips, canes, and floggers with my partner before I get started. It might be that this doesn't add directly to the BDSM component of the activities, or affect my stamina or where I hit, but it changes what we do from a simple flogging scene to something more encompassing and rewarding.

**Learning** is something for which BDSM provides ample opportunities. The obvious things, such as mechanical technique for impact play, cutting, or bondage, are there for us to learn, but BDSM also gives us a rare chance to see and experience our partners and others we play with at their most vulnerable and helpless. There are many situations and reactions which we get to see that are beyond what we might see in vanilla-land.

**Food** is not normally mentioned in BDSM handbooks, except possibly when talking about molten chocolate and formal meals served by your slave. But food is an aspect of life which can be touched by BDSM in all sorts of ways. Just as some people can seamlessly combine sex and BDSM, the scene-like nature of eating also lends itself to BDSM-ification. There's no reason, for example, why you can't deny your submissive food for the better part of the day and then tie and torture her with nipple clamps, fruit, floggers, cake, and rope.

**Family** can be brothers, sisters, mother, father, etc., but for many people into BDSM, particularly those into longer-term D&s or M/s relationships, it can be important to have supportive fellow masters and slaves to lean on and to share with. These can become a sort of family, providing a similar hierarchy with the head of the household and other family members all contributing to the family as a whole.

When you think about **money** and BDSM, maybe what comes to mind is that there's a door charge to your favourite party, or that an upcoming equipment safari for your new dungeon is going to cost big bucks.

Something else you can think about is: can BDSM become part of how you earn your living? Do you have skills or talents which you can put to work? Are you good at handicrafts? Have you thought of making and selling floggers, for example? Well-balanced and well-constructed floggers are keenly sought after because the ones you find in many kinky sex shops are not really intended for serious use by someone who knows what they're doing. Being able to make them, especially if you can make them to order, could be a good side business. Or, if you are good at carpentry you might be able to make and sell St. Andrews crosses, spanking benches, equipment racks, and all sorts of other things. If you're into the social side of things and have the space, have you thought about organising or running play parties for local enthusiasts? Or maybe you could set up a little business supplying some of the more difficult-to-find items which many BDSMers like, such as bondage tape which doesn't stick to the skin, or low-temperature wax-play candles. And, of course, if you like being spanked, you can hire out your backside by the hour, or if you're good with a flogger or with rope, you can tie people up and flog them and get paid for it.

*Life aspects*

## Understanding BDSM Relationships

The potential for creativity and art to enter into our BDSM and our BDSM relationships is huge and I have devoted a whole later chapter to it[1].

BDSM often provides opportunities to learn about ourselves. It can be challenging because many of the ideas involved in BDSM can be confronting, but as part of getting involved in BDSM we learn to deal with these things and through this we can gain more self-confidence and a better understanding of who we are.

While all the above have to do with more-or-less direct involvement of BDSM, sometimes the things we learn from BDSM can be useful in other areas of our lives. Learning to take control and be authoritative in a D&s or an M/s context, for example, is a skill which you can transfer and use at the office or with non-BDSM friends. This doesn't mean that you need to be rude, arrogant, or rough, but recognising when it's useful to take charge can be effective and productive and can help keep things moving when people get stuck with making a decision or are in conflict. It can help you be seen as a leader.

Likewise, experience with D&s and M/s can let you recognise when someone you spend time with, such as a colleague or a friend, is inclined to either be dominant or to be submissive. When you see this, and when it works for you, you can allow yourself to respond a little. You don't necessarily need to do a full-scale BDSM conversion on them, but merely let that side of them come out in little ways for your mutual benefit.

If they seem naturally deferential or service-oriented, you can create opportunities for them to express it. Ask them, in a polite way, to get you a coffee, and you may well make their day.

---

[1] Chapter 10 on page 127, *Artists and tinkerers*.

# Chapter 9

# People

There's one thing which we can be sure about in regards to BDSM, and that is that the physical side of BDSM—the flogging, the bondage, the torture, and the pain—is not it. By *it* I mean the endpoint, the goal, the destination that we BDSM practitioners are trying to attain when we do *what it is that we do*[1].

This may seem like a radical idea when you look at the wide range of popular BDSM books out there which tell us how to focus on and excel at precisely these things. But, the real point of BDSM is not about how many floggers you own or how many ways you can wield them, or how many different types of rope you have in your toy bag and how many different types of knot you can tie, or about the wildly varying selection of candles

---

[1] Sometimes abbreviated as WIITWD.

which you have on hand to create trails of cooling hot wax on flesh. If it were only about the knots, the red marks, and the pain, then I have a clove hitch, a red felt marker, and a house brick which will really make your day.

The actual doing is not why we are into BDSM. It is where the doing takes us psychologically, emotionally, and even spiritually. Indeed, it is actually about people. It is about us. It is not about floggers, ropes, or wax.

BDSM is a complex beast which many people fail to appreciate fully. Many people choose to see BDSM as merely being about kinky sex, which it may well be in part for some, either because that's honestly all that they see or need from it, or because that's all they are prepared to admit they want from it. Frequently it is not quite so easily categorised.

> *This reality, the sadomasochistic reality, kept me going. It was where I explored everything fascinating about human nature, conflict and resolution, passion and control, anger and conditional love. I ignored the nagging voice in me, which I still occasionally call The Chastiser, which continually wondered why the fuck I was doing this, what I was seeking - [ANTONIOU1995].*

## 9.1 The focus seems to have drifted away from people

It seems that the focus of mainstream BDSM has drifted away from people and is instead moving towards things and the mechanics of things. It can be that dealing with the mechanical side of BDSM—such as how to use a flogger safely, how to tie a person so they can be released quickly in case of blood circulation problems or fainting, how to perform needle play, how to disinfect implements, and so on—is easier than learning what it is that makes you or your partner tick. This mechanical side of BDSM is also much easier to consider than confronting the difficult challenges of navigating a relationship.

Have a look at figure 9.1 on the next page. This is a typical ad for a BDSM workshop. Note that there's no mention of learning how to make it satisfying and rewarding for you and your partner. By the end of the workshop, you may be able to flog in a technically proficient manner. Maybe afterwards you'll be able to throng with the flogging literati, sip fine wine, and discuss the merits of the latest hand-made floggers from the dedicated, if perverted, monks toiling away in quiet solitude in the El Floggo monastery of northern Spain. But will you know how to tell if a flogging is really working for you and your partner and, if not, how to fix it? Will you learn how to recognise what your partner is feeling? Will you know what to say and how to treat your partner? Sorry. These things are not covered.

This is disappointing. How many BDSM folk do you know who have broken up with their partners due to an inadequacy in flogging technique, or through not owning a large enough variety of rope, or due to not being able to discuss corsets or chain *ad infinitum*? Perhaps there are the occasional people for whom a Herculean flogging arm is a requirement for their partner, or who absolutely need their partner to go into the deepest sub-space at the drop of a flogger. Perhaps... though I haven't met any of them yet.

The point I'm trying to make here is that a BDSM-based relationship doesn't collapse because someone has the wrong

*People*

> **Flogging 101 by Master FloggingDude**
>
> Due to popular demand we'll be running our Flogging 101 workshop again on the 15th of May. Flogging is one of the most popular BDSM scenes and this workshop will teach you how to get the most out of it.
>
> We'll be looking at:
>
> - The different types of whips and floggers,
> - How to choose a flogger that's right for you,
> - How to prepare a flogging scene, and
> - What to do and what not to do.
>
> Bring a partner if you can because this is a hands-on workshop. If you can't bring a partner we should be able to find someone to work with you. There'll be a number of experienced instructors on-hand and there'll be plenty of time for questions.
>
> What to bring:
>
> - You,
> - A partner, if you have one, and
> - Your own floggers or you can use ours.
>
> 2pm start.

Figure 9.1: Typical BDSM workshop ad

floggers on hand or because their knots are all saggy[2]. People move on because the BDSM itself is not working, not because of knots.

In a sense, I think that BDSM has become a reflection of the take-total-responsibility-for-yourself, fake-empowerment attitude that pervades our western society. You are required to be responsible for your own world and your own experiences. I may flog you or tie you up, but it's entirely up to you to have a good time. If you don't have a good time... well, that's not my fault. It must be you because I did everything right! The workshop mentioned in the ad above is an ideal example of this. The focus isn't on getting a satisfying or powerful experience. It's about the technical execution of floggings, just add submissive!

Perhaps this drift towards the mechanical is also due to a wider trend towards political correctness.

> *Now it's three-hundred-page manuals on how to make sure nothing bad will ever happen to you and twelve-page party rules that state that the utmost care must be taken to make sure that no one is frightened or offended, that no bodily fluids are spilled, and no cries shock the neighbors - [ANTONIOU1995].*

Being politically correct seems to mean that you don't impact on the lives of other people and that you keep your distance. Good and effective BDSM is contrary to this. It's about engaging and penetrating your partner. It's about having an effect on them. It's about doing *to* them.

---

[2]Like mine.

*People*

## Understanding BDSM Relationships

If you do decide to start treading in the areas where you actually have a real impact on your partner's psychological, emotional, or spiritual experience, then you are taking on a whole lot more responsibility and power than if you're just saying, "Here! Let me flog you." Indeed, perhaps it is fear of this power and responsibility which causes so many people to focus on the "safe" mechanical side of BDSM.

BDSM is fundamentally about people, not about things, implements, or dungeons. When a BDSM relationship fails it's not because the floggers weren't right or because the dungeon was under-equipped. It's because of a people failure. BDSM is about how people feel. It's about their wants and needs. And mostly it's about their relationships with other people. Sometimes—perhaps too often—we forget this.

When a BDSM relationship succeeds, when it flowers, when it meets the deepest needs of the two people involved, it doesn't do so because of dungeon furniture, because of coils of rope, or because of shiny nipple clamps. It succeeds because of the people. It's easy for this people aspect of BDSM to slip our minds. Shiny new nipple clamps, the smell of leather from our floggers, a bright array of multi-coloured candles, the sting of the whip, and the texture of the rope can all distract us.

When things get difficult it can be oh-so-tempting to focus on the mechanical side of it all: on how to flog, on how to disinfect, on how to tie knots, on how to clean our kit when we're done, on how to quickly slip a hypodermic needle tip through a fold of skin, and so on.

While being able to tie knots might be an excellent talent to have, unless there are people skills behind the knots then they will merely be knots and not the path to ecstasy, self enlightenment, or even a good fuck. Without the ability to interact, to explore, to understand, to share, and to experience BDSM with your partner, the BDSM itself can and will be hollow.

What I'm talking about here are two of the themes of this book: penetration and engagement. The mechanical aspects of BDSM—the knots, the floggers, the dungeons, and so on—are tools which we use to engage and penetrate our partners. They aren't the endpoint by any means. We don't go to workshops about bondage or electroplay just so we're technically proficient. Technical proficiency might be nice, but we go to these workshops to learns skills which we can use to engage and penetrate our partners.

In short, we could say that the goal of all this engagement and penetration is to create or to increase *happiness*. We don't just stick hypodermic needles into our partners because we want to increase their metal content or because we want to make them magnetic, and we don't encourage our partners to tie us up because we think they only like to see us immobile, and we don't stand at one end or the other of a whip because pain is the end station. There has to be some positive outcome beyond the activity itself for what we do. That's why we do it. It might be something simple like a quick case of the jollies, a bit of a laugh, maybe an orgasm; or it could be something more profound, such as deep surrender, an opportunity to learn something about ourselves or our partners, or an intimate bonding experience.

Something we don't always notice is that a BDSM relationship can provide an opportunity to be more of ourselves than other circumstances allow. Having a trusted and receptive partner allows you to show more parts of yourself and to say and do more things than you might be able to with someone else. We aren't simply intellectual creatures who show ourselves through carefully chosen words and the occasional gesture. We are

*People*

animals who can and do need to communicate through actions, aggression, sex, dominance, and submission. Being able to use rope to "speak", or to use a heavy flogger to send a very primal message, or to kneel and make ourselves helpless and vulnerable to our partner, are all ways to communicate with our partner at a level other than words. Being able to do this can be a very deep form of penetration and can effect us profoundly. It can be giving life and voice to parts of ourselves which we must normally keep quiet, and can let those parts of ourselves be active and fulfil themselves. This self expression is a form of release. We can look at it as BDSM providing a way of letting ourselves be or become.

In the rest of this chapter I'd like to expand on a few of the things I've just been talking about, and I'd like to look at a few of the other things which BDSM can mean for us and our partners.

## 9.2 Activities

The focus of this book is people—people mainly in the form of our partners, but also in the form of anyone with whom we establish any sort of relationship for the purpose of exploring or meeting wants and needs through BDSM. The penetration part of this occurs through what we do with these people, through what we do with our partners.

When we talk about BDSM activities, we often see them in terms of what is done to submissives. Outwardly, submissives seem to be the ones who are being penetrated by flogging, bondage, mummification, piercing, and so on. The poor little dominants toiling away in the background might hardly get a mention. However, being on the other end of the flogger, rope, cling wrap, or needle can be just as exciting and satisfying. That is why dominants do it. To use a sexual analogy: being the one with the dick doesn't make sex any less exciting or pleasurable for a man because he is the one doing the penetrating rather than being the one who is penetrated. My point is that we BDSM folk tend to define what we do in relation to what happens to the submissives, even though the outcome for a dominant can be just as satisfying or profound—such as catharsis, surrender, sexual arousal, or even service.

Generally speaking, if we aren't there with them, or we have no contact with them, then we can't penetrate our partners. It is through the activities we actually do with our partners, or through the consequences of these activities, that we penetrate them and they penetrate us. Or, put another way, we make manifest penetration and engagement through the activities we explore with our partners. Without activities there is no penetration and, consequently, there is no engagement.

In what follows, I want to talk about a number of the activities we do in BDSM with a focus on the relationship side of them. How can and do they effect a relationship? How do they help us penetrate or be penetrated by our partners? How can we engage our partners more when we do them?

## Terminology

Labels such as bottom, submissive, or slave get used a lot in BDSM. Often, these terms aren't terribly useful because: a) there are only seven terms[3] and they're hardly enough to describe

---

[3] Master, mistress, dominant, submissive, top, bottom, and switch.

the very large variety of attitudes, practices, wants, needs, and desires which we find in BDSM, and b) there's no common agreement on what these terms mean. Even if we could nail down what our regular BDSM companions intend by these terms, we can easily come across other people who use these terms very differently.

The same labelling problem which occurs for bottoms, submissives, and slaves occurs for tops, dominants, mistresses, and masters. The terms are blurred by inconsistent use. The terms "master" and "mistress" are particularly abused and there's a common convention of calling anyone on the handle-end of a flogger or anyone who ties knots, regardless of how well or not, "master" or "mistress" even though by some definitions they might more accurately be described as simply a top.

This is compounded by the fact that there are actually folk around who we can correctly call "masters" because they are master artisans. They are genuine experts at their craft—be it at wielding a cane, making bondage furniture, tying knots, crafting a perfectly-balanced flogger, or whatever.

For some people too, there's a sort of implicit expectation that a master or mistress is someone who masters slaves, who commands authority and obedience, and whose personal aura overwhelms all of those who come before them. Not all masters and mistresses do this. Some masters and mistresses simply top, often dedicating themselves to it and doing it very well.

Until there's some central BDSM labelling authority, linguistic purists such as myself are just going to have to put up with this uncomfortable blurring of terms. For the rest of this chapter I am however going to make my writing life, and your reading life, easier. I am simply going to group tops, dominants, mistresses and masters together and refer to them as "dominants", and I'm going to group bottoms, slaves, and submissives together and refer to them as "submissives".

## Pain

Many submissives look for pain. Sometimes people talk about this as a type of masochism, but in reality submissives want or need pain which they can use to get somewhere emotionally or psychologically. The pain itself is not pleasurable or rewarding, but where it takes the submissive is.

The physical pain a submissive looks for tends to be quite localised, usually limited to a small part of the body such as the buttocks, the shoulders, nipples, etc. More wide ranging pain, such as along the length of both legs, is generally simply painful and isn't useful.

Most commonly in the BDSM world, pain comes from impact play—being hit by a cane, a flogger, a whip, or by being spanked. There are a couple of reasons why this sort of pain is the most common. One of the main ones is that it's easily controllable. The submissive's partner can vary how hard they hit and the rate at which they hit to create just the right level of pain. There are also a wide variety of implements which can be used and these allow the pain to be *tuned* to exactly what the submissive needs.

A second reason why impact play is a common source of pain is that it involves the submissive's partner. Indeed, impact play done on oneself is very rarely satisfying. By having a partner do the striking it means that both partners are intimately involved in this powerful experience. The submissive can also surrender themselves more and immerse themselves more in the experience because their partner takes care of the mechanical aspects.

*People*

There are other sources of pain and although they're quite common, they aren't generally as popular as impact play.

Using clamps or alligator clips on sensitive body parts—particularly nipples, labia, lips, and testicles—is easy, relatively safe for short periods, and the intensity of the pain can be varied by adjusting the tightness of the clamps.

Cutting, the use of a sterile knife to cut through outer layers of skin, is another source of frequently intense pain.

There can be many effects of pain. A submissive might see pain as something to resist or overcome. It might be a test of strength, not against their partner, but against the pain itself. Or they may see it as something which drives everything else out of their mind and leaves them feeling empty and cleansed. It can also be a release. If the pain isn't sharp, such as the thudding from some types of flogger, it might take them into a unique and intensely focused state of mind (sub-space). Where the pain is targeted between their legs, they may find it an intense amplification of sexual penetration. And finally, pain might be a tool which leads the submissive into a state of complete surrender, and this can be a deep and spiritual experience.

When the pain is a tool the submissive uses to reach some psychological, emotional, or spiritual destination it's important to appreciate that too little pain, too much pain, or the wrong sort of pain can make it hard or even impossible for the submissive to get where they want to go. This is where their dominant plays an important role. It is rarely the case that a submissive just needs one sort of pain. Usually, they need a progression of different types of pain, or of different ways the pain is applied, or of different rhythms of pain as they move through different states of mind. Explaining this to their dominant as it happens would be distracting and so the ability of their dominant to determine on their own what pain is required, when to change the pace, when to pause, etc., can be vital for a submissive.

Previous experience with other submissives might help a dominant get this right, but when the dominant knows their submissive intimately, knows what they need, and knows how to read the signals their submissive sends throughout the scene—such as muscle contractions, how the submissive changes position, and so on—then the dominant is going to know what to do and when to do it. Of course, I'm talking about one of my themes in this book: engagement. The road paved with pain which the submissive travels is going to be smoother and with less detours when their dominant engages them personally, rather than engages only An Average Submissive.

When the pain isn't quite right, or is merely adequate, a submissive has to work harder to adapt what they're getting from their dominant to achieve what they need, and this can make the experience or scene less immersive.

# Bondage

Bondage is another common BDSM activity. Although it doesn't hurt, it has many things in common with the sorts of pain we see elsewhere in BDSM. Firstly, it's controllable—a skilled bondage artist can tie or untie someone very quickly and the degree of restraint can vary from simple rope handcuffs to full mummification. Secondly, although there are a few people who practice self-bondage, bondage is most effective when done by a partner. Bondage can create powerful feelings of helplessness and of being controlled. It's also a tool for objectification in a couple of ways.

Firstly, the general physiological definition for a human includes: one head, two arms, two legs, and a torso. Bondage and mummification reduce this. The arms might still be there, but when they're tied a submissive is rendered arm-less, becoming less than before. The same thing can happen when their legs are tied, or when a mask is put on, or when a gag is inserted in their mouth. As well as compelling the submissive to a state of surrender or submission, all of these things reduce the submissive to being less of a person. They take away part of their humanity. They begin to objectify them.

Secondly, depending on how they're tied, a submissive becomes useful to a dominant in ways which they are not when they're not tied. If the submissive is hog-tied, or if they're tied to a piece of furniture, they may simply become a hole to fuck. Not a person to fuck, or a submissive to fuck, but a hole that's ready to be used at the dominant's convenience.

And if we're talking about decorative bondage, the submissive becomes simply a canvas on which the knots, rope, and colours are aesthetically arranged.

With the large variety of ways bondage can be applied—and we haven't even talked about cages, chains, bondage furniture, suspension bondage, or outdoor bondage—it's obvious that there are lots of opportunities for engagement. Basic ties, such as rope handcuffs or hog-ties, tend to be effective for most submissives, but we're trying to talk about actual submissives rather than Average Submissives in this book and when you have a regular partner you can explore things which are particular for you both. For example, outdoor bondage, particularly while naked, is very effective for some, but not all, submissives. Suspension bondage can be exciting and a real challenge for both the dominant and the submissive, but it's not everyone's cup of tea. The important thing is that with such a variety of options, when bondage is something that works for you and your partner it provides a large field for you both to intimately explore and may contain some hidden treasures.

Finally, the tight embrace of rope can create a physiological response in some people, simply giving them satisfying or pleasant feelings of floating, detachment, or release[4].

## Foreplay for sex

Pain play, impact play, and bondage are common precursors to sex. For some people they can act as a sort of foreplay, even while being satisfying for other wants and needs at the same time. They can leave a submissive feeling powerfully penetrated, and can leave a dominant feeling that he has powerfully penetrated his partner. As a result of the play, the dominant and the submissive can become highly aroused and ready for some sexual action.

On the other hand, some forms of BDSM play can be draining and not leave any energy for sex. An intense cutting scene, where designs are cut into the submissive's flesh by their dominant partner, might not leave the submissive feeling horny at all. A heavy interrogation scene, or some humiliation play, might leave the submissive feeling cleansed and refreshed, but not necessarily ready for some between-the-sheets action. Instead, they might just want some quiet time to recover.

---

[4][GRANDIN1992] and [KRAUSS1987].

When a submissive or dominant is looking to use BDSM as foreplay for sex, there are a few activities which can be very effective:

- Sensation play - using touch, heat, cold, feathers, sandpaper, and so on, to create various sensations, often when the submissive is bound or blindfolded,
- Wax or candle play - the dripping of hot, molten wax onto the submissive—such as on their breasts or back—and letting it cool and set on their skin,
- Sensual flogging - using soft floggers to gently strike the skin of a submissive, perhaps near or on their genitals and breasts, or
- Light bondage - using ropes, silk scarves, or handcuffs to render a submissive helpless to the sexual advances of their dominant partner.

Notable about all of these is that they're not intense or draining, and they involve a lot of physical contact which is potentially quite arousing.

## Humiliation

Humiliation play actually has something in common with bondage. Where bondage subtracts from someone physically by taking away their power to move parts of their body, humiliation attempts to remove parts of their identity, their self, their pride, or their self-respect. By criticising someone or by mocking them when they cannot defend themselves, humiliation diminishes them. Like bondage, this diminution is under the dominant's control. The dominant chooses what to say or what to compel the submissive to do, and the dominant acquires the control and power to re-value the submissive, to make them either feel less of a person or more of a person as the dominant chooses.

This is powerful stuff because it reaches beyond the physical, which most of us are comfortable with, and into the self, which most of us are less comfortable with. We're less comfortable because we often have less skills for dealing with these sorts of deliberate attempts to limit us and thus feel humiliation more strongly than, say, rope bondage.

Other forms of humiliation include being compelled to be naked in front of others, being required to use kitty litter in the corner of the room where we can be watched rather than use a toilet in privacy, and needing to perform something we're not very good at where others can see us.

Engagement has its place here too because not every submissive is going to find the same things humiliating. Just undressing someone, pointing at their private parts and laughing is not going to work for everyone. In fact, humiliation is a risky business. Untying someone and packing the ropes away is easy, but putting someone's self back together, or your relationship, after you've said the wrong thing is not. Knowing your partner intimately and having a history of experience together teaches you what works and what doesn't.

## Surrender

One of the most powerful BDSM experiences is surrender, and it is an unspoken, yet very important part of most BDSM activities. Creating pain, restraint, humiliation, or anything else in BDSM is most effective when we can let our defences down and allow these feelings in. In other words, we get most bang for our buck when we can allow ourselves be fully penetrated.

For a submissive to be able to surrender so that this can happen, they need to feel safe, they need to trust that their partner is going to be capable and skilled, and they need to not have any worries or concerns which prevent them from losing themselves in whatever it is that they're doing. Any of these things can get in the way of the process which allows pain or bondage to become pleasure.

Importantly, surrender is just as much a vital part of the experience for submissives as it is for tops, dominants, and masters. A submissive may respond to and be penetrated by what their dominant does to them and by their own reactions to this, while a dominant is penetrated by what they themselves do and by how their submissive partner responds. Surrender is a necessary part of this penetration, and if a dominant doesn't let their own barriers down to allow the experience and their partner to enter them, then no penetration will happen and the dominant will find the experience quite empty.

## Punishment or discipline

Another thing which some submissives look for is punishment or discipline. Being put in a position where they endure a clinical, even detached, caning, whipping, or spanking can be emotionally cleansing. It can be a way of releasing pent-up feelings, frustration, or even guilt.

Instead of wanting the experience to be sensual, such as when BDSM is used as sexual foreplay, or instead of wanting it to be a form of pain which they can use to take them into sub-space, these submissives typically look for sharp and genuinely painful pain.

A common scenario which helps to set the psychological scene for discipline can be a schoolgirl or schoolboy being disciplined by a teacher. This is a form of role play which creates the right mood. A school uniform helps, as does the submissive being required to drop their pants or panties and bend over a desk.

Additionally, striking implements more typical of a disciplinary environment, such as a wooden ruler or a short cane, often work best for this. Over-the-knee spankings can also be effective.

Engagement has an important role in punishment. While there are many BDSM activities which are typically associated with the idea of punishment—such as caning, being compelled to stand in the corner (humiliation), or spanking—it's often a very personal thing. Caning involving a custom-made, leather-padded bench in the dungeon might be the stuff of serious red marks and not being able to sit down without wincing for a week, but caning while leaning over an old school desk might be psychologically more profound. Over-the-knee spanking can be pleasurable and give you a radiant butt for hours afterwards, but for some the better effect might involve dropping your pants, leaning over an old-style school desk and receiving six of the best.

## Service

Service is attending to the wants and needs of your dominant partner. Well, usually that's what it looks like. In reality, a lot of the time what we're talking about is penetration. The acts of

*People*

service need to penetrate the submissive. They need to feel that they are serving or being useful. The dominant also needs to be penetrated. He needs to feel the service of his submissive. If you happened to be a dominant and you happened to have a slave who professed that they'd do anything you asked, you could send them to a coal mine to dig coal for you. In BDSM-land this is probably not going to be satisfying for either of you, though you might get some lumps of coal out of it. It's not going to be satisfying relationship-wise because although having coal dug for you might be your greatest wish, you don't get it as part of your relationship with your enthusiastic, and now grubby, submissive. The service is distant from you. It is detached. Your submissive also doesn't experience any penetration by you because your reaction is something she simply doesn't see in the glow of her headlamp down in the mine.

Because we're talking about BDSM here, and because we're particularly talking about BDSM relationships, penetration and engagement need to be present. Service, at least in BDSM, provides a context in which penetration can occur. However, service can become hollow if service is all there is. It might be fine for a real-life butler (or miner), but they get paid for it. Submissives and dominants need penetration as their reward and, again, I'm not necessarily talking about sexual penetration.

For submissives, it might be that they genuinely need to feel that they are taking care of their partner. This is sometimes the case, particularly for female submissives. When so, the service needs to be personal, such as preparing and serving food, helping their partner dress, or personally delivering lumps of coal and putting them in the fireplace. The submissive can see and feel the benefit, and can feel their own need being met as they serve. It often requires the dominant to show that they are pleased and, notably, it is a case where the submissive does the action and the dominant responds, although it is the dominant whose needs are the ultimate driver for the service.

How satisfying, rewarding, or penetrating it is for a submissive to perform service is going to vary greatly. Some submissives might serve to experience the long-term surrender of themselves to the authority of their dominant and it might not actually have anything to do with personal service for them *per se*.

Because service is a case of horses for courses, when you're considering it you don't need to just think about the general idea of service, but you need to consider the type of service. Here are some to consider:

- Being a chauffer,
- Running errands, doing shopping,
- Household duties - such as cleaning, ironing, or cooking,
- Personal service - being a valet,
- Sexual service - being sexually on-call,
- Personal assistant - organising your dominant's appointments, paying bills,
- Being the home handyman - doing repairs around the house or apartment, painting,
- Technical work - maintaining your dominant's web site, and
- Mining coal.

## Physical handling

Physical handling is where the dominant uses main force or physical strength to manipulate and control their submissive. For a submissive this can be quite a powerful experience. Being controlled is a common BDSM and sexual drive[5], and actual physical manhandling is a very primal expression of this.

Sometimes physical handling can be quite subtle, such as when a submissive is being tied up by their dominant. During ties, the dominant is often in physical contact with their submissive with incidental touches—such as when they brush against their submissive's skin as they position the rope or knots, or more directly as they place their submissive's arms, legs, head, and body in particular positions as they tie the rope.

More direct physical handling can be in the form of the dominant pushing their submissive to their knees, grabbing them by the hair and dragging them around, or even roughly undressing them and fucking them.

Clearly, there's an element of objectification to this because physical handling moves us away from the hands-off, civilised culture we normally live in and instead moves us towards the animalistic, making us handlers of meat, or making us the meat itself.

## To be commanded

Being commanded by a dominant or master can be very powerful and very symbolic for a submissive. I'm not talking about the

---

[5][HILL1996], [MESTON2007].

casual, drive-by commands a dominant might give while they're actually busy with something else. Some submissives' boats are rocked in this regard when commands are given in a serious, or even sanctified context. No jeans and T-shirts here for the dominant. Instead, he or she dresses in their finest and blackest leathers, grasps their submissive firmly by the chin, angles their submissive's head up, fixes the submissive in the eye, adopts a stern, deeper-than-usual, and compelling voice, and then lays down the law.

There may be some fantasy to this, but the goal is for the submissive to feel themselves commanded, to feel the intensity of their partner, and to have their partner's wishes to focus on.

We need to distinguish between being commanded on one hand, and obeying commands on the other because there's not always a one-to-one connection. Many submissives find the experience of interacting with their dominant or master to be the exciting part of their relationship. Being commanded is a very serious and immediate interaction. It is potentially very profound. Actually obeying the commands is not necessarily such a high point though. There are some submissives who revel in being directed or commanded by their partner, but whose interest and obedience rapidly diminishes once the interaction ends... such as when they need to go away and do as they've been told.

This can be a confusing thing for a dominant or master when it first happens, but the key thing to keep in mind is that some submissives require that component of interaction. That is the form of penetration to which they mainly respond. They need to have an immediate sense of the presence of their dominant and to be aware of and feel what their dominant is doing, preferably to them, at all times. Otherwise, their focus wanders to other things which may seem more interesting and penetrating.

*People*

Perhaps this type of submissive is going to be more suited to BDSM activities and scenes which closely involve their partner—such as dungeon scenes—rather than D&s. Again, we're talking about engagement here. We're talking about knowing your partner and knowing what they respond to.

A submissive may well claim to be intensely service-oriented, but the nature of the service, and the context in which they perform well, can vary dramatically. Only by both talking with and exploring a submissive can you find out the details.

## Micromanagement

Rather than simply give a submissive or slave an order or instruction and leave them to work out the details themselves, micromanagement is where a dominant takes a close and active interest in the execution of the order, oversees every particular, and directs or commands his submissive in fine detail as they carry out the order.

When used in the wider or vanilla community, micromanagement has a negative connotation in that it suggests that the person doing the micromanagement is neglecting bigger issues and is making choices and decisions which their minion is perfectly capable of doing on their own. In the BDSM world however, micromanagement can be an exercise of detailed interaction, domination, and surrender. The submissive might be completely capable of cleaning the kitchen or dressing herself on her own, but micromanagement requires that she give up this autonomy and make herself available, almost puppet-like, to her partner as he directs her through these activities.

Like some other activities in BDSM, there can be an element of objectification in micromanagement. Through having her ability to choose how to perform ordinary tasks taken away, her status as a person is reduced and she becomes more and more a puppet whose strings are controlled by her dominant.

In the wider community, micromanagement is often a sign of lack of trust, but in BDSM it can be an effective exercise in control and penetration, requiring close interaction and supervision on the part of the dominant, and this close interaction itself can be the payoff.

This payoff isn't just for the submissive. If we continue with the puppet analogy for a moment, the dominant also gets to feel his submissive partner in the same way a puppeteer feels the weight and resistance of his puppet as he pulls the strings. If there's some unexpected resistance he can pull harder or change the direction he pulls. With his submissive, the dominant can adapt his commands depending on her skills and ability to execute them, and depending on any resistance she displays.

## Penetration of a dominant

Following on from what I said earlier, a lot of literature, and even a fair chunk of my own, focuses on the reactions, feelings, needs, and wants of submissives. Often this is the case because a submissive is, in some ways, more *visible* than a dominant. What a submissive suffers and experiences is usually more apparent and more easily viewed than the experiences of a dominant. Submissives are often also louder. However, a dominant also explores BDSM and engages in BDSM activities because they want something out of it, i.e., because they have wants or needs they wish to satisfy through individual BDSM activities or through their BDSM relationships. And, in fact, the same three pillars of BDSM which I mentioned early in this book have the same place in satisfying a dominant as they do in satisfying a submissive.

For example, it must be the case that a dominant experiences penetration. If they aren't affected by their partner or by what they do with their partner then the experience is simply hollow and unfulfilling. And to actually have a BDSM relationship they need to be engaged by their partner. Their partner needs to know them and treat them as the individual they are, rather than just as Another Dominant.

In many cases, the penetration a dominant experiences comes from two sources:

- The first source of penetration is the dominant's own actions. For some dominant's the presence of their submissive can be a chance to let the dominant part of themselves out, to express that part of themselves which they might otherwise need to keep bottled up. For example, a dominant who has a primal need to manhandle or to physically express control or power is going to have that chance to unleash this side of themselves when they're with their willing and receptive partner. Just on its own, this can be a powerful experience, one which the dominant feels deeply inside themselves.

  This self expression doesn't need to be a deep primal urge though. Some dominants might have a creative or artistic side[6] and this part of themselves is something which they can release with their partner. While this sort of activity might not seem as intense as giving a partner a heavy

---

[6] See chapter 10, *Artists and tinkerers*.

beating, it can be just as important and significant to the dominant.

- The second source of penetration is the response of the dominant's partner. Seeing your partner being turned on by what you do, seeing reactions being triggered, or seeing needs being manifested and met, can also have a very strong effect on a dominant. Mother Nature is partly responsible for this by making sure that when we become aroused—and not just sexually—we transmit signals to our partners which trigger them into doing more and becoming more aroused themselves. This happens even when we're not aware that we're sending these signals.

When the little BDSM centre in my brain turns on and I feel like tying someone up or torturing them, this initial stirring may be what actually starts me doing BDSM stuff or what starts me having BDSM thoughts, but the pleasure and satisfaction doesn't just come from actually carrying out these desires. It comes from the reactions of my partner. As they respond and are aroused by what I do, their actions and reactions penetrate and trigger me. As I respond to them and the dynamic we create together, I become more aroused and what I do intensifies, which triggers them to greater heights, which triggers me, and so on. It is an ever-increasing spiral as we penetrate, feed off, and engage each other.

## Surrender of a dominant

Surrender is a term we might normally associate with a slave or submissive, but as I noted above, surrender is vital for a dominant as well. In his case, the surrender is of himself to the experience. The dominant must be open to the effect of his own actions, and to the effect on him of the actions and reactions of his partner.

It can be tempting for a dominant to try to be in control all the time and perhaps there is a bit of a misconception about this. Trying to be in control all the time can actually be counterproductive. For example, if you have a skilled and talented service-oriented submissive you can be fully in charge but *delegate* to him or her the tasks you want them to do. You might say to this talented possession of yours, "Make me a fine meal of lasagna with a rich, minced beef filling and a tasty cheese sauce[7]." They can go off on their own and devote themselves to satisfying this desire, and later serve this culinary delight to you. You then surrender to this experience they have prepared for you and soak up any associated wine or dessert. Through all of this—from the initial order to the final burp—you are in charge, but you're not micromanaging. You're delegating and reaping the rewards of the exercise of your authority.

The same upwards spiral of penetration I mentioned above is at play in this situation as well. You don't send your submissive out of the room when you eat. Instead, you might have them dress for the occasion and then keep you company. They are going to see and experience the pleasure they have brought you. And perhaps this will bring out more of the submissive in them as they serve the meal, pour the wine, etc., which might trigger more of Little Dom inside you, and so on.

If you have trouble delegating then it's much harder for your submissive to both contribute to your experience and to create

---

[7] Any female submissives or slaves who want to know how to show me a good time, take note [PM].

situations which penetrate you. Indeed, when you don't let them take their own initiative, they probably can't do much for you at all. Continuing with the lasagne example, if you keep a supervisory eye on every single step of its production then effectively you are cooking it yourself and are just using your submissive as a replacement set of hands for your own. There's no surrender in this for you. If instead you give your partner the initial instruction to make lasagne and then leave them to it, the result is surrender on your part, as well as seeing the results of their determination to serve you well—both of which can be quite penetrating. Micromanaging is a good tool at times, but it can also create a barrier between you and your submissive. And one way to get past that barrier is to surrender yourself to your submissive.

## Training

A common activity in a BDSM relationship is training. Exactly what this means can vary from partnership to partnership. For some people it is closely associated with heavy physical play, such as whipping or flogging, and involves habituating the submissive so that he or she is able to endure heavier and longer sessions. The benefit for the dominant is that they don't just finish their own warm-up and find their partner has already reached their pain or tolerance limit. Part of the training in this case might be simply developing endurance, but can also be teaching the submissive ways that their endurance can be prolonged—such as by controlling or pacing their breathing, changing position or flexing their muscles, by performing relaxation exercises, etc.

For other folk, training can be the process by which a dominant teaches a submissive the behaviours and attitudes he wishes them to exhibit as part of their involvement with him. These might be rituals and structured rules[8] which give the submissive an overarching way of behaving outside of direct interactions with their dominant. In addition there will be training in how the dominant wants his submissive to behave in direct interactions, such as when she is giving personal service, when she is receiving orders, when she is speaking, and so on.

In all cases though, the result of training is that the dominant can see and experience the changes he is causing in his partner's behaviour (which is, of course, penetrating her as well).

## Empowering

> *Two are better than one; because they have a good reward for their labour. For if they fall, the one will lift up his fellow: but woe to him that is alone when he falleth; for he hath not another to help him up -   Ecclesiastes 4:9-10*
>
> *Two heads are better than one - Proverb*

My point with the above two quotations is that when you are a dominant working with your submissive then the two of you together are potentially better than you just working on your own. And because you're the dominant, you are the one in the driver's seat and you get to decide the projects which you both work towards. Instead of it just being you, your submissive can become an extension of you, an extra set of arms, or an extra brain, working towards the goal you set. This can be very

---

[8] See also [MASTERS2009, pp. 143 - 156].

empowering. It can be an intense feeling of being able to do more, of being stronger, of being more potent.

Not only is your submissive partner a fully-functional human being, they are there to be pressed to your will, to enable you to achieve what you want with twice the capability of just you on your own.

Beyond this is something I mentioned earlier, which is allowing you to be yourself, allowing you to express the feelings, desires, lusts, and needs which you can't express with anyone else. Your partner is your target for manhandling and rough treatment. Metaphorically, she is the one you overpower with a club and drag off to your cave. She can also be the one who suffers under your rigorous training regime, or she is the one you role play with, or she is the one you tie with your diabolical array of knots. Your submissive empowers you to be you. And, at the same time, you empower her to be her.

## Meditation

For both the dominant and the submissive, many BDSM activities allow them to enter into a reflective mental state somewhat like meditation. This can be a state of intense inwards focus. It's often associated with physical relaxation and sometimes with feelings of floating.

Primitive and not-so-primitive folk sometimes use heavy, regular drumming to get into such a state. Others might use some experience which requires or demands quiet and close attention to some activity. We can easily find such situations in BDSM through things like heavy flogging in the first instance, or through piercing in the second.

There can be a strong element of surrender in these sorts of meditative states, and it can often be the case that both the dominant and the submissive react the same way to what's going on.

For example, in a heavy and regular flogging, both dominant and submissive share the same regular thudding, even though they are at opposite ends of the flogger. Similarly, a submissive being pierced with hypodermic needle tips is going to be just as intensely focussed on the placing of each needle as their dominant is in ensuring the needle goes in just right.

This same close attention to what's going on to the exclusion of what's happening around you can occur with some forms of detailed bondage, stylised impact play such as florentine flogging, wax play, and many others.

## Catharsis

Catharsis, which I mentioned earlier, is associated with intense or dramatic experiences. It is an outlet for strong, built-up emotions and feelings which can't find an easy release any other way. BDSM has the possibility of this intensity through activities like pain play, heavy flogging or whipping, role play, and others. In contrast to meditation, which is a surrender to what's happening, catharsis can often involve reacting to or against what's happening. For example, a submissive who is tied to an A-frame, who is being heavily flogged, and who is strongly writhing and straining against her bonds, can get a very powerful release through her own physical actions and reactions. This is very different to a quiet meditative state. Similarly, intense role play, such as an interrogation scene, provides many opportunities for drama and emotional release.

In terms of relationships, catharsis has more of a chance of occurring when there is no distraction from the experiences and when limits are well known. When both the dominant and the submissive know themselves and each other well, each can work towards their own catharsis without having to wonder or question what they need to do for their partner because they already know.

Flogging is one BDSM activity which very strongly involves the dominant in the drama. While the outward purpose of a flogging might be to give the submissive a severe hammering, by carefully choosing their floggers and the way they apply them, the dominant can control how much of themselves and their raw effort they put in. Choosing a flogger which requires little effort to wield can distance the dominant from what's happening, while a perhaps shorter or softer flogger can mean that the dominant needs to put more of themselves into getting the same result from their submissive. This extra effort involves the dominant more and gives them potentially more cathartic release.

## 9.3 Conclusion

When we look at BDSM—both at the activities we do and then at the relationships we have with our BDSM partners—we can find that although the activities themselves can be rewarding and satisfying in themselves, the relationship we have with our partner changes the nature of our activities and the effect they have on us.

Trust is a big part of this, and it is a major contributor to how much we can surrender. This directly impacts how profound our experiences are.

*People*

## Understanding BDSM Relationships

In addition, when we explore BDSM in the context of a longer-term relationship we have the option of allowing our activities to become less scene-based and to embed aspects of our activities in what we do outside of the dungeon. For example, if we talk about a couple who like rope, the dominant can tie his partner into a rope harness at the beginning of the day and let her go to work wearing it under her clothes. This can create a low-level penetration for both of them for a whole day. Or, when we talk about D&s, a dominant can decide in the morning what his submissive will be eating and drinking during lunch or during any breaks she has while working.

Longer-term relationships also create the opportunity to learn our partner's particular interests, preferences, and triggers so that what we do engages them and is targeted at them and their needs. This increases the satisfaction we both get. A possible analogy is off-the-shelf clothing versus tailored clothing. It can take a long time to go through a rack of clothing looking for something which is the right fit, and there's no guarantee that you'll actually find what you need anyway. Tailor-made clothing, clothing made exactly for you, will be the right fit every time. When we as dominants or submissives know our partner's BDSM "measurements", then what we do can be a perfect fit for them most, if not all, the time.

What we do in BDSM creates opportunities to engage our partners, not just to do technical proficient BDSM scenes. This engagement, finding and recognising our partner as an individual instead of just as A Submissive or A Dominant, is what makes a BDSM relationship.

# Chapter 10
# Artists and tinkerers

BDSM frequently provides opportunities to be creative. Sometimes these opportunities can be quite obvious. Shibari, a style of bondage focussing on the visual appearance of the bound figure and on the pattern of the ropes and knots, is a good example.

There are many other ways for creativity to appear in a BDSM context. Recognising that this is happening is important in terms of a relationship because it may be that a creative or artistic outlet is very significant either to you, or to your partner, or to you both. When it is, it needs to be supported and encouraged just as any other want or need. If it isn't recognised and supported, it's like you spending a week or more painting a fine erotic mural on your bedroom walls and then finding that your partner complains that it doesn't match the pillow cases. You end up feeling that the effort which you've put in to enrich your life and theirs with art has suddenly been treated as valueless.

In the context of actual BDSM activities, creativity can show up in a number of ways. Beyond Shibari (and erotic wall murals) there are also:

- Patterns of lines created on someone's butt from caning,
- Patterns of needles placed during piercing, often in the forms of circles, lines, flowers, or other designs. In addition to the needles themselves, some people weave coloured ribbons or laces between the needles,
- Designs created during cutting, and
- Patterns created from wax as it runs and cools over someone's body, and the intermix of colours from the different waxes as they run together or run over each other.

Because of this artistic component, most of the activities I've mentioned above can have a strong effect on a submissive beyond the activities themselves. This happens through the submissive experiencing being used as a canvas for their partner's artistic expression. This can be a powerful form of objectification where the submissive becomes merely a tool for their dominant or master to use while creating art.

Submissives can also be creative. This creativity can appear in bondage in the form of escapologist bottoms who take delight in finding new and inventive ways of escaping the bonds placed on them by their top.

Predicament bondage is an opportunity for inventiveness from both the submissive and their top. For the top, it is by means of constant refinement of the bondage through devising new knots, new angles, and new positions. The cleverness of the situation, rather than the appearance, is important. For the submissive, cleverness and lateral thinking can defeat, even if only temporarily, the postural predicaments their top creates.

In D&s and M/s, masters and dominants can be creative in designing training regimes and exploring their partner. Instead of simply working or using their partner, they may look for new, challenging, unusual, and demanding exercises for their partner.

## 10.1 The tinkerer

When talking about art we mustn't forget the tinkerer. Just as you see in the old teen movies from the 60s where young males souped up their new cars so they could go cruising for girls, or where home handymen spent hours in their workshops building who-knows-what, or now where modern day geeks fine-tune their computer desktops or add the latest-and-greatest software to their computers, BDSM also has its tinkerers.

These are the people who use BDSM as an excuse or as a context in which to tinker or muck around with stuff. It used to be that tinkerers would fiddle around under the bonnet of their cars way back when, and then moved on to fiddling under the bonnet of their computer when cars became too complex for mortal man. Our tinkerers fiddle with different types of rope, experiment with different types of knots, devise new pinching and clamping devices out of discarded stuff, or build bondage or torture furniture in their garage.

Many forms of tinkering aren't directly connected with play. They are often done in the days or hours before or after play. Here are a few examples:

- Cleaning or conditioning ropes,

- Building nuclear-powered nipple clamps out of things found in kitchen drawers,

- Shopping for new BDSM toys,

- Constructing bondage furniture out of bent coat-hangers and duct tape,

- Kitting out a dungeon,

- Making and oiling canes,

- Reconditioning a second-hand dentist's chair,

- Designing and making corsets,

- Designing weird spanking implements from bargains bought at the local charity shop,

- Making floggers with intricate patterns of braids on the handle, and

- Seeking out and acquiring obscure BDSM tools and equipment, such as hunting down antique violet wands on eBay® and restoring them.

## 10.2 Collector hobbyist

A variation on the tinkerer is the collector hobbyist. These are people who collect things. Some collectors look for particular types of BDSM tools, equipment, or gadgets. They might be fascinated by flogging and look out for floggers with tails made out of unusual material, or floggers of unusual designs, or specially-designed, one-off, custom-made floggers. My aunt used to collect salt and pepper shakers from around the world, but this probably isn't relevant.

Some collector hobbyists collect activities. They try to discover, or invent, as many different activities as possible so they can try them all, such as tree-top wax play or Push-The-Peanut.

## 10.3 Collecting tools, equipment and gadgets

Whenever I think about people who collect BDSM paraphernalia I think of my above-mentioned aunt or of another person I know who collects things shaped like owls. Anyway... for whatever reason, some BDSM people like to collect things based on a theme. Sometimes the collections are useful, sometimes not. Some of the things they collect include:

- Floggers, particularly handcrafted floggers or floggers made from unusual materials (human hair, fishing line, octopus nostril hair, the web of the South American hip-hop spider, etc.),

- Candles from different countries and cultures, or candles made of different types of wax, or with different types of dyes,

- Knives of different shapes and sizes, with and without serrated blades, for cutting and for mind fucks,

- Hypodermic needle tips of various lengths, bores, and different colours for piercing and creating patterns,

*Artists and tinkerers*

- Handcuffs, though having more than one pair of handcuffs begs the question: how many hands does your submissive have?
- Rope of different thicknesses, different materials (hemp, nylon, cotton, plastic, natural fibre, etc.), different textures, different colours, different stiffnesses,
- Pegs, clamps, pincers, and tweezers,
- Attachments for a violet wand.

Collecting often goes hand-in-hand with large amounts of time spent sorting, polishing, and discussing the collections with other people.

## 10.4 Collecting activities

In book two of this series, *BDSM Relationships - How They Work*, I have a chapter containing lists of all sorts of BDSM activities. My lists are intended to be used to enrich your BDSM relationship by helping you discover new activities to share with your partner. Some people however, take such lists as challenges and want to be able to say they've tried every single activity. These people are activity collectors. Their hobby is to find and try everything they can. It's usually not that they need to do so, or that they have some hidden and unsatisfied urge which drives them to try ever more challenging or difficult activities. No. It's often just the same as collecting charms on a charm bracelet or collecting stamps[1] is for other people. It adds a little extra

---

[1] I wonder if foot fetishists collect stamps? [pun intended]

interest to what they do and gives them something to display at show-and-tell or to talk about at parties.

## 10.5 Show and tell

This is one important—but often unspoken—aspect of tinkering. Taking your latest-and-greatest flogger, fucking machine, or amazing hand-woven rope acquisition from the Upper Kalahari to the next play party or BDSM social event and showing it around can be just as important in some ways as using it on your partner. Many creative aspects of BDSM stand up well both as ways of demonstrating your passion and enthusiasm to others, and as chances to get your ego fluffed up a little by the oohs and ahs of those who admire either your handiwork or your diligence at seeking out obscure treasures.

## 10.6 Incompatibility

While tinkering and art can happen in a BDSM context, it can be boring, annoying, or distracting if you're trying to have a scene with your partner and instead of helping you to immerse yourself in the experience they're trying to get a difficult knot just right or they're trying to get the molten wax to pool in a certain way.

They may have a need to be creative sometimes, and you do need to ensure that they have these opportunities. But equally, you will have your own needs which perhaps aren't met while they're being creative. While there might be an element of incompatibility in this, there's no reason why you can't both take

*Artists and tinkerers*

turns at being, on one hand, creative or being the canvas and, on the other, enjoying full-on BDSM.

If you find their tinkering to be getting in the way sometimes, say so. Don't be brutal about it, but try to discuss it. Maybe suggest a compromise where you dedicate some agreed sessions to art and some to needs-meeting.

And if you're a tinkerer, or if you like to use your BDSM play sessions as times to be artistic, make sure you let your partner know and make sure you both agree on the times when art will be the focus or when, instead, savage bloodletting will.

## 10.7 Artistry

Before finishing off this topic I'd like to just briefly list a few activities in which creative expression can play a significant, even if not obvious, part:

- Rope bondage:
    - Particularly in forms of bondage such as Shibari where the goal is to create a work of art combining the rope itself, the knots, their placement, and the subject, and
    - Where the position or posture of the tied subject is expressive, such as being a statement of vulnerability or eroticism.

- Cutting - where the person being cut serves as a canvas on which the person doing the cutting creates their designs. The designs may be permanent, leaving a scar when healed, or temporary, healing completely and leaving no scar.

- Branding - where designs are burned, using intense heat or cold, into the flesh of your partner.

- Piercing - where patterns of needles or skewers are created in the flesh of your partner.

- Caning, whipping, and sometimes flogging - where the strokes leave patterns of lines on the back, buttocks, or thighs of your partner.

- Erotic stimulation - some see the use of various implements, BDSM or otherwise, to erotically stimulate their partner as an art form, with their partner's orgasm at the end being the climax of their particular artistic spectacular.

## 10.8 Conclusion

Perhaps the most important goal of tinkering and art is this exercise of creativity. The intensity and primality of some forms of BDSM play—such as flogging, caning, sex play, pain play, and so on—can preclude creativity and often just require strength, physical endurance, or just raw animal passion. On the other hand, tinkering, collecting, and art provide what can be an important outlet for creative juices while still remaining in a BDSM context, or while remaining within the context of a BDSM relationship with your partner.

Tinkering should be supported and encouraged. Always be ready to view what your partner has tinkered and be ready to support them and what they've done. Encourage them to show it and to try it out. Contribute and offer suggestions, and never diminish it or put it or them down in any way, even if you think what they've done is wacky.

Often the results of these inclinations aren't necessarily intended to be entirely practical or useful, but are instead simply creative expressions. Keep this in mind.

# Chapter 11

# Assembling the pieces

Knowing how to execute a BDSM activity with technical proficiency is often easy to learn. There are many books around on the practical side of BDSM. Many BDSM enthusiast groups run workshops on the most common forms of play, and if you happen to come across someone doing something new or interesting at a BDSM play party, there's a good chance that if you wait until they're finished and then ask them about it that they'll give you some tips.

But underlying these practical displays and these mechanical interactions with the people with whom we do our BDSM is often a need to have some sort of relationship with them. While there are some people who look for anonymous BDSM encounters to get simple needs met—such as for basic pain or humiliation—many of us look for something more profound, and for that we often need to have a partner who we trust, who knows us, and with whom we can develop something more than what an anonymous encounter or a quickie at a BDSM play party permits.

The nature of BDSM relationships—what goes into them and what we get out of them—is often not clear or easy to grasp, but the fact is that many of us look for a regular partner even though on the surface it looks like all we might do with them is the same sort of activity we can get anonymously at a BDSM play party or at a professional BDSM establishment or bondage parlour. The actual role the relationship has in these explorations is not something we always understand.

It can be tempting to compare BDSM relationships to vanilla relationships, but as I noted at the beginning of this book there's a fundamental difference in that in a BDSM relationship the BDSM part means that we do things *to* our partners, rather than merely *with* them as is the case for vanilla relationships. This *doing to* is what allows us to penetrate our partners, to cause them to feel something coming from us. When that goes away, so does the BDSM and we are left either with a vanilla relationship or with nothing at all.

I've tried to show in the preceding chapters that there's more that we can and do get out of BDSM when we engage a partner while doing so. When we have a foundation of trust, when we learn what our particular partners need and respond to, and when they know us, then we can open ourselves up to being engaged by them. We can also target what we do and how we react specifically to them, not just to An Average Submissive or to An Average Dominant. This means that what we share is more likely to hit the mark and be more effective than just by doing "standard moves".

Importantly in all this, BDSM is often a form of self-expression which we expose or show with our partners. It might take a primal, physical, or even sexual form, and it can be critical to recognise this when it is the case. Being able to be ourselves with our partner—be they dominant or submissive, master or slave, top or bottom—can be one of the most important things which a BDSM relationship provides, and it might be that the physical side of BDSM is just a context which allows this to occur. Focussing on the physical activities, on their technical execution, can take away from the personal and people needs which are the real purpose for What It Is That We Do.

In book two of this series, *BDSM Relationships - How They Work*, I'll be looking at practical techniques and strategies for developing and maintaining a BDSM relationship. Then, in book three, *BDSM Relationships - Pitfalls and Obstacles*, I'll be looking at many of the problems which can occur trying to keep and maintain a long-term BDSM relationship and at what you can do to avoid or overcome them.

# Book Two

# BDSM Relationships

# How They Work

# Chapter 12

# Introduction

In book one of this series, *Understanding BDSM Relationships*, I looked at BDSM wants and needs, and at how they get satisfied in the context of a BDSM relationship. It's important to note that when I talk about a relationship this can include any sort of connection between two BDSM-practising folk, whether they live together in a full-on, 24/7, master/slave household, whether they are a full-time couple who only occasionally dally in BDSM, or whether they are two friends who mainly meet up at BDSM parties and who only play together there.

One reason why I'm interested in relationships is that there's a lot of literature available about BDSM as it affects or is practised by a single person, but not so much on the role of a long-, or even short-term relationship and how it can influence the pleasure and satisfaction BDSM can provide. I think that this is a great shortcoming because when you look around at what other BDSM folk are doing, there are an awful lot of them either in, or looking for, long-term relationships, even if this is just establishing a circle of trusted friends with whom to explore. If a BDSM scene were able to be satisfying and rewarding on its own then you'd expect that there'd be a lot more one-night stands than there are. Instead, it looks remarkably as if being in some sort of relationship with someone can significantly add to or improve what we get out of BDSM, perhaps to the point where such a relationship is a necessity for many people.

In this book, I want to move from understanding to the actual doing. I want to look at how what we do, how we behave, and how we communicate affect our ability to establish and to maintain a full and satisfying BDSM-based relationship with someone. To some extent this will include what can go wrong, but I will be addressing that particular topic in more detail in book three of this series, *BDSM Relationships - Pitfalls and Obstacles*. In the what-can-go-right department in this book, I'm particularly interested to explore how what we do influences and modulates the penetration and engagement we experience with our partners. Penetration and engagement, you may recall, are two of the three pillars of BDSM relationships which I introduced in book one.

Broadly speaking then, this book is about stepping on from understanding BDSM and BDSM relationships. It's about making concrete:

- Our motivations—our wants and needs, and
- How what we do meets or satisfies those wants and needs within the context of a relationship.

To this end, I'll be going through a wide range of motivations, wants, and needs in detail, and I'll be looking at how a comprehensive list of common and not-so-common BDSM activities each work to satisfy or meet those needs.

*Introduction*

## Chapter 13

# Trust, honesty, openness, communication, and all that stuff

The success of any BDSM relationship is going to depend on communication. It never will be enough to be good at flogging or to be able to have endless orgasms if what you're trying to do is have a successful and satisfying relationship with someone.

Communication is what establishes a connection with your partner. It isn't just words, but is also actions and gestures. If you're a dominant or top then communicating can include how you strike with a flogger, how you tie knots, how you cut your partner with a blade, how you drip wax on them, and so on. Each action that your partner experiences from you sends them a message and tells them something.

If you're a submissive or bottom, then how you breath while being flogged, how you wince as you are cut, or how you kneel while serving your partner a drink, also send your partner a message.

After compatibility, communication is about the most important component of a relationship which works well, which flows smoothly, which has little or no conflict, and which is deeply satisfying and rewarding for the people involved.

## 13.1 Openness and honesty

Openness and honesty are critical to getting BDSM to work. This might sound really, really obvious—and it's something I mention often—but it's not always easy to be open and honest, either with yourself or with your partner. Many things can get in the way.

Openness and honesty are very frequently more important in BDSM relationships than they are in vanilla relationships. As I've mentioned before, vanilla relationships are about doing things with your partner. They share with you in external things which are stimulating, interesting, or rewarding. This includes going to the movies, going out to dinner, going for walks, going shopping, and even raising kids together. Little of the "goodness" in these things comes from your partner. At the movies, it's the film you watch. At dinner, it's the food you eat. While out walking, it's the weather and the scenery. And with kids, it's, well..., the kids.

In vanilla relationships you aren't so dependent on your partner to have rewarding or powerful experiences. As long as you both go to the right places or events—and as long as you don't get in each other's way—a great time will be had by one and all.

On the other hand, in BDSM relationships you are completely dependent on your partner for your scenes and activities to work. If you aren't focussed, or your partner isn't focussed, then the experiences can quickly become hollow and unsatisfying. And what you need to be focussed on is each other.

Importantly, your partner is presumably trying to push your buttons so that you get the most out of whatever-it-is that you're doing together. For them to push the right buttons they need you to be completely open and honest with them.

This is where the problems can start.

If your partner is particularly desirable and there's some doubt about how long they'll stay interested, you might be tempted to present yourself in a way that might be more attractive to them. For example, if they are a keen bondage aficionado then you might be inclined to exaggerate your interest in bondage when actually you prefer flogging. While in vanilla-land this might be an effective strategy to keep this new partner around long enough for them to find out that you're actually the greatest thing since sliced bread, in BDSM-land this is fairly devastating. Your new BDSM partner will be trying to push the buttons you've indicated you have even though you actually have other buttons. You end up faking responses, and this is not a good long-term strategy for a relationship.

Another thing which can get in the way of openness and honesty is ego. Admitting to weakness, or lack of skill, or lack of knowledge in a particular area can sometimes be hard. This can also be dangerous if your ego tries to get you to exaggerate how much experience you have in some of the more challenging areas of BDSM such as heavy impact play, cutting, piercing, mummification, or breath play.

## 13.2 Communication during play

Communication is important to let your partner know what's working and what isn't. Importantly, it's also one of the key parts of engaging your partner.

If you immerse yourself in your BDSM activities—such as soaking up the thuds when your partner is flogging your back, or focussing intently on the patterns you're creating when you cane your partner's rear end—then your partner may not be getting something they need. They may be hungering for a feeling of being connected to you. If they're not facing you and you're not making any sounds yourself, they'll probably not feel connected at all.

While forcing yourself to moan, "Oh! Baby!!!", all the time might be excessive, making noises and murmuring comments as things progress can be of immense help in telling your partner: a) that you're still there, and b) how you're feeling.

Moans are often good value in this regard, but don't limit yourself just to sounds. Wriggle, writhe, move your feet, and change position to improve the angle of attack. Say things quietly to yourself, but loudly enough for them to hear, such as, "Mmmm. That's nice.", "I love the way you turn red!", or "That's making me so hot!"

Making sounds or communicating may not feel 100% natural for you. You may even be concerned that your noises and wriggles may be a distraction for your partner. Talk to them and find out how they feel.

## 13.3 Negotiation

Some days BDSM is just not going to come easy.

You might not be in the mood, you may be tired, or some particular activity your partner is looking for really squicks you out. When this is the case, don't just shake your head and say no because this can make your partner feel rejected. Instead sit and talk with them. Look for a solution to this problem.

If you're tired, maybe something light will work for you. Alternatively, plan a session for the next day so your partner is sure you're still interested in them and so they have something to look forward to.

If the particular activity your partner has in mind really puts you off, there may be an alternative which will work for them just as well and which you'll also find satisfying and rewarding.

The important thing is to talk. Be open about how you feel. Be open to the suggestions or ideas from your partner.

# Chapter 14

# Meeting people

Before you can have a BDSM relationship, you need to meet people with whom such a relationship is possible. Finding a BDSM partner can be very challenging for a number of reasons. Firstly, very few people stroll around wearing head-to-toe latex or full BDSM leathers, nor are BDSM weekend or nocturnal escapades common topics of conversation around the average water cooler. BDSM is instead more underground and this makes it challenging to find someone with similar interests to your own.

Secondly, newcomers to BDSM—those people just discovering BDSM urges in themselves, or those who have only now decided to act on them—frequently have no idea that there are others like them "out there". They don't know about any opportunities to meet others, to get experience, to attend workshops, to get skills training, and to share ideas and thoughts with other people who have the same drives and desires.

Indeed, it's not uncommon for people to have their first BDSM experiences totally ignorant of the fact that there are many hundreds of thousands of people actively pursuing the very same things they are only just getting to know.

Because BDSM is often associated with sex, places you can look for information about BDSM activities in your geographical area include articles and advertisements in your local sex-positive newspapers, checking noticeboards, or by asking in any local shops which sell sex aids.

BDSM can also have an affiliation with the gay, lesbian, and bisexual (GLB) community, and even if you're not gay, lesbian, or bisexual, it might be worth contacting any GLB groups in your area, or checking out their newsletters or newspapers to see if they have any outreach programs or workshops which might be suitable for you.

These days, an excellent way to find out what's going on in your geographical area is to enter "BDSM" and the name of your nearest moderately-sized city into an Internet search engine. Many people mention where they are when they write about their own personal BDSM experiences online, and many social and support groups have an online presence as part of their own outreach programs.

The sorts of things you may find in your searches can include:

**Education and support organizations** - A number of groups, mostly organised by volunteers, provide training, seminars, websites, outreach programs, and newsletters both for people just getting into BDSM, and for people wanting to improve their BDSM skills. These can be great places to go for advice and other information.

Some of these groups can be quite large, some even having multiple locations spread across a number of states. A few to look at are:

- The Society of Janus (http://soj.org/)
- The Eulenspiegel Society (http://www.tes.org/)
- Masters And slaves Together (MAsT) (http://mast.net/)

**Munches** - These are regular social events often held in public cafes, restaurants, or coffee shops, where BDSM folk meet and chat. Munches are a good choice for your first steps into the BDSM world. You can go to munches anonymously and there's no ongoing commitment or expectation from you. If you like the people, you can keep going back until you're comfortable and ready to take the next step; namely, to start exploring BDSM with people you now know, but in a private atmosphere.

**Workshops** - These are organised training events where you can learn BDSM skills and techniques—such as how to safely tie someone up, or how to do fire play, or how to do flogging. If you're more into having these things done to you, go along and volunteer for people to practice on you.

**Play parties** - These are also social events, but are typically behind closed doors in premises containing well-equipped dungeons or play spaces. Play parties are opportunities for individuals and couples to meet up and engage in light and not-so-light BDSM activities in a social environment.

One of the advantages of play parties for newcomers is that there are always other people around. Most play-party organisers don't allow play to go on behind closed doors, and they ensure that there are experienced dungeon monitors keeping an eye on things. Playing alone with someone you've only just met can be risky, so a play party can be a good choice for your early outings. If you already know a few people from attending munches or workshops, then play parties can be safe and comfortable places to get your feet wet.

## 14.1 Precautions

When you think you have found a potential relationship partner and decide to get to know them better, arrange a safe call the first few times you're on your own with them, particularly if you're planning to do some BDSM play with this new person. A safe call is where you arrange to telephone a friend at a particular time to let them know that things have gone OK. Typically you give your friend the name of the person you'll be with, where you'll be, what you'll be doing, and when to expect a call from you. Your friend is supposed to call the police if they don't hear from you. You can't really be sure the first few times you meet up with someone new that they aren't Jack The Ripper, and letting them know that you've arranged a safe call can help keep you secure.

Don't be afraid to ask for references before you go off with someone, regardless of whether they're dominant or submissive, top or bottom. Talk to their previous partners and to others in your local community to see what sort of reputation they have.

If you're new to BDSM and are a submissive, ask around at munches and workshops to see if there are any more-experienced submissives who are happy to give you advice. Many larger support and outreach groups have mentoring programs where you can find someone who'll help you get to know the ropes [pun intended].

The same applies for new dominants. Playing safely can mean getting guidance on some of the more subtle points from people who have more experience than you. Don't be afraid to ask for demonstrations. Be polite though. If you're at a play party or workshop and see someone doing something interesting or new, ask them about it when they're free. Many dominants and submissives are proud of their skills and will happily share their knowledge and expertise.

## 14.2 Promoting yourself

If there are no opportunities to meet other BDSM folk near you, and there don't seem to be any people in your social circle who might be inclined to explore BDSM with you, then looking online for a partner may be a good option.

There are a number of websites where you can promote yourself and get known. At the time of writing two of the most active seem to be:

- Alt.com (http://alt.com/)
- FetLife (http://www.fetlife.com/)

When you do choose to make yourself known online, or when you look around online to see if there are any potential partners for you out there, here are a few things to keep in mind:

- You are trying to promote yourself so that you appear interesting enough to get to know. When you write about yourself, give yourself some depth. A one- or two-line summary of yourself is unlikely to attract anyone.

There are a lot of people who will write biographical information about themselves or describe their interests solely in terms of, "I need to serve you, mistress!" or "I am desperately in need of discipline!" While this makes it sound like all they want to do is take, take, take, it isn't necessarily a bad thing because there are folk out there who are really only interested in whaling into someone with a flogger. However, if you just want a severe caning, say so. If you just want sex, say so. The important thing is to be honest about it. If you want more than these things, include some personal information about yourself which makes it clear you're not just a life-support system for your cock or cunt.

- Don't include pictures of your genitals if you're serious about finding a relationship. On the other hand, if you want people to think of you as a dick or a cunt, then include pictures of your genitals by all means.

- Join online discussion groups whose topics are things you're interested in. Read what people are saying and add your thoughts. Avoid contributing comments that consist entirely of, "Me, too."

- Don't contact people privately without their permission. You'll seem like a stalker if you do.

- If you do find someone online who sounds interesting and you'd like to meet them face-to-face, ask for references and arrange a safe call. It's not very good if you drive to a secluded hotel in another state and find that this person is actually about fifty years older than they claimed online, or that they're armed with piano wire or an axe. Maybe meet in a coffee shop first.

## 14.3 Discussion

One of the big challenges to meeting other BDSM folk and finding potential partners is that BDSM is so often hidden away. In some of the more enlightened countries and cities of the world, BDSM and alternate sexualities are readily embraced. In other communities, even hearing about BDSM at all can be a rare event.

When you're new to BDSM, take the time to ask around, inform yourself about what options are available in your neck of the woods, and then get to know a few people before diving in to your first bondage, flogging, or other BDSM scenes. Even if it takes you well out of your way, when there are social events, workshops, or discussion groups anywhere near you, go along and join in. It is well worth your while.

## Chapter 15

# Build your own partner

Because there are so many different types of submissive, and because there are so many different types of dominant, getting yourself a partner can be very hard.

One of the first problems will be finding someone who is interested in the same activities as you. For example, you might be strongly attracted to bondage and all the people you meet might already have a well-developed interest in flogging, needle play, or something that you're not interested in at all.

A second problem is that the people you meet who already have some experience with BDSM might already be far more skilled or knowledgeable than you. They may not be able to, or may not be interested in, helping you to catch up to them.

One solution to finding a suitable BDSM partner is to make your own. You start out with someone who you like and who seems mostly compatible with you, and then you gradually introduce them to BDSM and see how they react. This could be someone you meet at work, at the supermarket, at a nightclub, or when out socialising with other friends.

While there are many aspects of BDSM which can be very scary and intimidating if you're suddenly confronted with them, there are many other BDSM activities which can seem interesting or fun, or just offbeat or kinky to newcomers. You can fairly safely introduce a new partner to them without having to worry that they'll think you're an axe-murderer and run away screaming. With any luck, once you've introduced BDSM to this new partner you may find that they readily embrace BDSM and are more than happy to explore it with you.

The question then is: how do you do this?

One strategy is that once you both are comfortable being alone together, invite them around to your home one weekend or evening. Then leave a well-illustrated—but not too extreme or explicit—practical guide to BDSM[1] either on your coffee table or somewhere else where they'll find it. Give them a chance to notice it and to maybe flip through it while you make coffee or while you prepare lunch or dinner.

When you know they've seen it, make a comment like, "I see you've noticed the book by Midori (or whoever). I was flipping through it the other day, and some of the things look like interesting things to try." See what they say.

---

[1] A couple of examples could be Midori's *The Seductive Art Of Japanese Bondage*, or Miller and Devon's *Screw The Roses, Send Me The Thorns*. These are both large-format books and are relatively innocuous. They should only scare away the hopelessly conservative.

## BDSM Relationships - How They Work

If you have reached the point in your relationship with this person where being naked and sweaty is not unusual, then another idea is to leave a few BDSM items lying around the bedroom and see how they react. I'd advise you to keep the scary stuff—such as your cage with the spikes on the inside, your whips, and your canes—locked away to start with, and maybe instead just leave some candles, a small pair of nipple clamps, and ONE short length of rope where your new partner can notice them.

Candles can be a gentle introduction into the sensation-play side of BDSM. Dripping a few warm drops of molten wax from a candle on the small of your partner's back can be quite sensual instead of scary or intimidating. Remember that you're trying to get them interested in BDSM. You don't want to overwhelm them and scare them away.

Another idea is to invite your potential new partner around to watch a carefully-selected movie and see how they respond to it. In particular, you want to see if they sit through it all the way, or if instead they find it so unappealing that they volunteer to wash the dishes, de-weed the garden, or re-grout the bathroom tiles while you watch the movie on your own. A positive sign is if, part way through, they start ripping off your clothes and grabbing at your crotch... We can only hope!

Here are a few movies with a distinctive BDSM flavour:

- *The Story of O* from 1975. Of course, this is a classic,

- *Secretary*. This is the 2002 movie of office perversion with James Spader and Maggie Gyllenhaal,

- *The Night Porter*, from 1974, with Dirk Bogarde and Charlotte Rampling.

*Build your own partner*

Finally, and again if you've been hot and sweaty with this person, and if there's a conveniently-timed sex fair or exposition in your city, I suggest that you go along and make a point of being obviously very interested in the BDSM stalls and exhibits.

# 15.1 Conclusion

BDSM can be very scary and confronting. Taking someone who has no experience with BDSM to a play party where they see people flogged or whipped with blood running down their back, or where they see someone having large-gauge hypodermic needles thrust through their nipples, or where they see someone being dangled upside down by their testicles, is probably not going to help your chances of ever seeing them again.

On the other hand, showing them the sensual side of BDSM, or introducing them to something exciting but not too scary—such as blindfolding them, or tying just their wrists together—may get them interested. It also may turn out that what works for them is doing these things to you. You may find that that asking them to blindfold you, or to tie you up may be all that you need to start something powerful.

Picking the activities to suggest at this delicate stage of your relationship can be helped by coming up with your own list of things which: a) you'd like to explore with this new partner and, b) won't be too scary or confronting for them the first time around. In chapter 19, *The lists*, I have lists of many BDSM activities. Check them out. Maybe discuss some of them with your partner.

# Chapter 16

# Criteria

When you're assessing someone new to determine what chance they have of being *the one*, you need criteria to measure them against. It's easy to meet someone at a BDSM party or social event and be carried away by their appearance or by their behaviour. Sometimes these outward signs can trigger deep and powerful responses in us. Are these a reliable guide to future contentment? Probably not, however they may still indicate that this person is worth a closer look.

When you meet someone and decide to give them a closer look, what sort of criteria or characteristics do you look for when evaluating them? Permanent and semi-permanent characteristics are things about them which either aren't going to change, which are going to change very slowly, or which they aren't going to lose. These are good characteristics to examine. For example, their intelligence is not going to change much over the course of their lives—at least, not until they're very old or they suffer some form of brain damage. Intelligence can be an important criteria when you are someone who likes to be mentally dominated. You aren't going to be satisfied by someone who is not able to be smarter than you.

Temporary or transient characteristics are things which are going to change, develop, or deteriorate in the short-term. These aren't going to be good criteria for considering long-term possibilities with someone. A top might have very poor mummification skills when you meet them, but a month later they may have attended an intensive workshop and now are pretty much an expert at it. Assessing them on something like this which can change quickly is not a good idea. On the other hand, if you're keen to do a mummification scene straight away then you clearly want someone who knows how to do it today, not someone who may know how to do it in a month.

Let's have a quick look at some of the most important permanent characteristics:

- **Intelligence** - how well someone can use their mind is something that is generally built-in. I'm not just talking about IQ here, but also how enthusiastically and how well someone will use their brain. If a potential partner is not too bright, or they are bright but won't use it, then that leaves the thinking to you. This may or may not be what you want. Alternatively, if they are bright and know how to use it then this could mean that either a very rich and challenging relationship is in store, or it could mean mental exhaustion.

- **Education** - what a person has learned through their lives is their education. It may be academic or may come from the school of hard knocks. Someone who is extremely well-educated may be a great choice if you're looking for intellectual stimulation or challenge, but may be overkill if you're looking for an uncomplicated life.

- **Skills** - being able to handle a relationship, and being able to engage in the sort of activities you want to explore is going to depend to some extent on the life skills, the interpersonal skills, and the BDSM technical skills of your partner. Some of these can be learned on the job, but knowing what sort of initial skill set you need your partner to have will make it easier for everyone.

- **Experience** - experience effects how well a person can make judgement calls. If you're looking for a constant and solid foundation for a relationship then go for lots of experience. If you're young, or if you're inexperienced yourself, or if you're looking to learn and grow with your new partner, picking someone with too much experience can be a liability because they've got less reason to grow and you're going to end up doing the growing all on your own.

- **Values** - these are what a person uses to make their judgements and decisions. They can include religious beliefs, family values, professional attitude, and so on. These values are generally learned at an early age and develop and mature as the person grows. Values show up in someone's sense of honour, their morality, and their ethics.

- **Emotions** - the importance of a person's emotions—how well they can express them, how deeply they feel, and how well they empathise—is going to govern the emotional depth or the emotional one-sidedness of a relationship with them.

You can usually get some idea of a potential partner's intelligence and education by talking to them. You can ask them questions about their background, mention things which are of interest to you and see if they can say something interesting back, see what interests them, and even ask them about school and university.

You can get an idea about their skills and experience often just by watching. Pick the sorts of skills and experience you're interested in so you can zoom in on them. Don't limit this just to what happens in the dungeon or bedroom. Life goes on outside of the dungeon and if you're looking for a long-term partner you need them to have other people-related and life-related skills. If they still live with their mother, for example, maybe they need some more life skills before you invest much time in them.

Values and emotions are harder to divine, and you probably need to spend more time with this potential partner to judge these. However, if they've passed your intelligence, education, skills, and experience assessments with flying colours then perhaps you can afford to get a little closer to them.

The opposite of permanent characteristics are temporary or transient characteristics. These are going to change over time, often quite quickly. Judging a potential partner on things which, by their very nature, come and go is likely to lead you either to reject perfectly suitable people, or to shack up with duds.

- **Situations** - the job someone has, how much money they have, and where they live all can change at the drop of a hat. Selecting a partner on the basis of how much money they have is, of course, shallow, but choosing someone because of their job or the suburb in which they live is not much better because these can easily change.

- **Relationships** - who your potential partner knows, who their friends are, and who they spend time with may be fascinating—particularly if they hang out with famous BDSM mistresses, awesome BDSM authors, rock stars, models, TV stars, or famous nobodies—but deciding that they'll be a good partner on the basis of these is a great way to end up with a hollow, and probably quite short, relationship. By all means check out the sort of person they like to be associated with, but the actual people shouldn't be something you judge them on.

- **Possessions** - and finally, one of the worst things to judge someone on is their possessions. Dungeons come and go, fancy floggers get lost or fall to bits, and latex undergarments get old and worn. Judge a potential partner on what and who they are, not what they own or have.

The most important way of distinguishing between the characteristics which will tell you what a potential partner will be like in a longer-term relationship is by looking at what they are, i.e., permanent characteristics, rather than what they have, i.e., temporary characteristics.

# Chapter 17

# Motivations

No one does BDSM or has a BDSM relationship for just one reason. There are always combinations of wants and needs involved, and before we can explore issues of relationships and compatibility we first need to understand our own wants and needs and those of our partners. For us to find our time with our partners satisfying and rewarding, be it for a quick scene or for a long-term relationship, we both must have our wants or needs met. If this doesn't happen, or it doesn't happen enough, then one or both of us will find our time together unsatisfying.

This chapter is a catalogue of reasons why people explore BDSM with a partner. You can read through it to help you identify what drives you and what drives your partner. It's not always obvious why we do BDSM and why we might prefer different activities and interactions with our partners at different times, but this chapter should help you nail down at least some of the things which drive you both. Armed with this information, you'll be better able to zoom in on the right things to do as the needs of you and your partner ebb and flow.

Ideally, you should go through this chapter with your partner. Importantly, be honest with yourself and with your partner as you do. BDSM isn't always socially or even emotionally acceptable and because of this you or your partner may not have even considered some of the things here as possible motivations. For example, if you like being tied up you may think that it's just because you like the feel of the rope. However, you may also have something inside you which hungers for physical surrender to the control of your partner. Liking the feel of the rope may be entirely true, but this could be a reason which is emotionally easier to swallow than admitting that you like being under the control of your partner.

When you don't know or don't admit to all the motives involved in your BDSM exploration, activities, and relationships, it makes it impossible to explore the full psychological and emotional intensity that's possible for you. In the rope example in the previous paragraph, if all you'll admit to your partner is that you like the feel of the rope when you actually want to feel them manhandling you, then when they're trying to do the right thing for you they'll be focussing on making the rope feel good. This is not what you really want. Instead, what you really want is for them to be more physical with you, but they're not going to do this because you haven't admitted this desire to them. Something similar applies when you are a top, dominant, or master: if you are hungering to feel your submissive writhing in agony on the ground as you torture them mercilessly, and all you say is that you want to give them a hard fucking, then what you'll get is only distantly related to what you really need.

Some of the wants or needs which are met by BDSM can be found in anyone—be they top, dominant, or master, or be they bottom, submissive, or slave. Often it's the case that these wants or needs are common to all humanity and that BDSM is merely particularly well placed to meet them.

Perhaps the main thing here is that BDSM often creates a context where the socially unacceptable becomes possible and even welcome. Where outside the dungeon such thoughts as hurting, humiliating, or objectifying someone are things you'd absolutely not mention to anyone for fear of getting locked away, in the world of BDSM they are things we can readily contemplate and discuss both with our partners and with our peers. Whether we do them or not is another matter. Just as we're free to talk about them, we are also free to do them... or not.

With that in mind, let's start out with a look at things which BDSM permits and which may be of interest to tops, bottoms, dominants, submissives, masters or slaves.

## 17.1 BDSM for quiet times

Although it might not seem like the highest-purpose reason for doing BDSM, when things are a little quiet around the house spending a bit of time in the dungeon with some rope can be an excellent alternative to TV. In this book I'm talking about BDSM relationships, and that means engaging your partner. Even if it's just some basic knot practice to fill in a quiet afternoon, doing these things together helps reinforce and develop your relationship with your partner.

Quiet times are also low-pressure times. If you're not trying to set a new record for pain tolerance or for the maximum number of knots tied on a single person at the one time, it means that you have time to muck about, try goofy things, and just generally experiment. Nothing is lost if what you try doesn't work out.

## 17.2 The real you

Rebellion is typically an in-your-face way of claiming ownership of yourself. It's about loud statements, such as shaving off all your hair, getting facial piercings, or riding a Harley. The act of rebellion can be very satisfying and feel very fulfilling. And, indeed, when we're talking about being loud and individual just check out your nearest BDSM play party!

Part of the story of BDSM and why it's so attractive much of the time is that it allows us to be ourselves. Many things that people do, even in the privacy of their own homes, are influenced or governed by opinions which come from outside. Despite some people's attempts to make it look like it only involves shiny leather catsuits and lightweight floggers, BDSM is rarely socially acceptable and embracing BDSM into your life means making a big psychological step towards saying, "I am going to be me, and not what the world wants me to be."

If you're looking to give yourself over to a partner who will use you in any way they want and still respect you in the morning, then this is entirely possible in BDSM.

If you're keen to have an orgy of sensations, be penetrated in every available orifice, be tied tightly while all this is happening so your struggles don't interfere with the action, then this is possible—and common—in BDSM, too.

If you're keen to be part of a relationship where the modern stuffy attitude of equality for women cramps your style, then

## BDSM Relationships - How They Work

BDSM can and does support a pairing where inequality is the order of the day.

Chapter 19 of this book, *The lists*, contains lists of many, many BDSM activities to help you find things which will work for you. In some circles, these lists might be called *purity tests* and are basically checklists of activities where you get a score based on the number of activities on the lists which you've tried. They could probably more accurately be called impurity tests because they are commonly used as a self-measure of how much you've been corrupted in such areas as BDSM or sex, e.g., by how many different sexual activities you've tried—anal sex, oral sex, sex in public, sex with a stranger, etc.

Having said that, BDSM purity checklists are actually quite useful. Many people—particularly newcomers to BDSM—have no idea of the extent of the activities which fall under the umbrella of BDSM. BDSM purity tests can provide an excellent source of ideas and I encourage you to seek them out and explore. Many times you'll find things listed which you may never have thought of but which may work wonderfully well for you.

The important thing is that you need to look honestly at the activities listed and consider which ones might be genuinely satisfying or rewarding for you or for your partner. Ideally, you should sit down with your partner as you go through these lists, discuss the activities, and talk about what turns you on or off about each one. Try not to be too quick to dismiss or move past activities which turn you off. Take a moment or two to think critically about your reaction and whether it really is the case that this particular activity is not for you.

BDSM is really about being you. When you look at the things you like about BDSM, the things you do, the things you'd like to do, and the things you don't do, think about how much they let you express what you really feel inside, and think about how your partner and your relationship with your partner fit into you being able to be you.

## 17.3 Validation

Some BDSM folk use BDSM as a tool to validate themselves. In front of someone else—i.e., their submissive, bottom, top, master, or peers at a BDSM party or social event—practising BDSM or exercising a BDSM relationship can be validating and can confirm this person's role or status in their own eyes, in the eyes of their partner, and in the eyes of their peers.

Coming out of the BDSM closet the first time and putting your BDSM interests on display AND having them be accepted by people who you think of as your peers and contemporaries can be a very powerful and important support for your identity. Being able to be yourself, talk about your interests, and have others share and discuss these same interests gets rid of a lot of doubts and uncertainty about whether you're crazy, strange, or whether you should be locked up.

## 17.4 Punishment

As a top, dominant, or master, it sometimes falls to you to discipline or punish your submissive partner. In the context of a long-term relationship, there are three important situations when this can occur:

1. It could be punishment in a D&s context where your partner has failed to perform some task or other, or where their behaviour hasn't achieved the standard you are looking for. In other words, this is real punishment being applied to motivate your partner to perform better.

2. It can be when your partner experiences feelings of guilt which are completely unrelated to you. These could be feelings stemming from their childhood, from some other part of their past, or from something they've done recently—such as inadvertently hurt someone. They may look to you to help them assuage those feelings. Even though they haven't disappointed you *per se*, you provide the uncomfortable or painful activity which they can then internally process as punishment and feel better and cleansed because of it.

3. They may have entrenched ideas about right and wrong from their upbringing which conflict with the way they live their life now. This conflict might have to do with their work, friendships, or even their BDSM proclivities, and can leave them with lingering feelings of being "bad". Your punishment helps them find or create an internal balance.

Note that what I'm talking about in the above is not play punishment. It's not about creating playful or fun excuses to give your partner a spanking. It's about real discipline.

Because we're talking about a real need—and one which generally requires a partner to impose—punishment and discipline can be a significant opportunity in relationship terms. It's often something which is quite intimate and personal to the

*Motivations*

person needing the punishment, and this can be very powerful to share with them.

We can distinguish between real discipline and real punishment on one hand, and play discipline and play punishment on the other. When you have a casual or playful relationship with your partner, you can use manufactured or forced infractions by your submissive to playfully justify a bit of spanking, flogging, or erotic play. The sorts of infractions I'm talking about can include:

- Not addressing you correctly,
- Being to slow to bring you coffee, and
- Not squirming enough when you tickle them.

Punishment can also be about creating an emotionally safe context in which to explore other activities, such as pain, confinement, or humiliation. As I've noted here and in other places, some people have trouble accepting their BDSM inclinations—possibly struggling with the idea of deliberately being submissive or dominant, or with the idea of wanting pain from or inflicting pain on a loved partner. If we mentally associate BDSM with punishment then we make it into something which we can justify by connecting it with our past, such as our time at school, and this means that the sometimes difficult idea of wanting or needing pain can be attached to the more acceptable context of discipline at school.

Recognising when you're doing BDSM to address a real need for discipline or punishment compared to other times when you're doing it just for play or for fun will help you and your partner to get the most out of what you do. If one of you is looking for a real discipline scenario and the other is just playing then it's not likely to work out completely satisfactorily for either of you.

That said, there's no reason that a punishment scene focusing on a particular need can't later flow into something different such as playful fun once the main need has been met. This is something you need to discuss with your partner.

## 17.5 Intellectual challenge

BDSM is often primal, with many activities deliberately intended to focus on primal or animalistic wants and needs. Heavy pain play and rough manhandling fall into this category. These sorts of scenes can be relatively short, sometimes less than 20 to 30 minutes.

When there's more time available, and when any animalistic or primal urges have been explored and satisfied, some BDSM folk use their time to create opportunities to intellectually challenge and to compete with each other. I've noted in other writings[1] that you don't find Scrabble™ or chess boards in dungeons because these games tend to be too cerebral and actually detract from a BDSM mindset, but some forms of intellectual challenge do fit in.

Predicament bondage[2], for example, is one such activity. For dominants and submissives, predicament bondage is a chance for a submissive to test her partner and feel reassuringly put in her place when her dominant "wins".

---

[1] [MASTERS2008, pp. 27 - 39]
[2] See page 182.

Some escapologist bottoms thrive on trying to devise ways to escape the ropes or chains their top uses on them. Their relationships can contain nightly challenges where the top tries to devise a novel form of restraint while the bottom might spend all night trying to get out of it.

In the D&s or M/s world, a master or dominant might give his partner seemingly conflicting orders, or give them tasks which involve some difficult elements of planning, or even give them commands which end up being impossible to perform. The exercise for the slave or submissive then becomes one of resolving the conflicts or solving the problems which their partner has created for them.

For example, a dominant might have given his submissive a standing order to always answer the telephone and take a message when he is away. Then, when he needs to go out briefly he might order his submissive to remain in a certain seat until he returns. A few minutes after he leaves, he rings up anonymously using his mobile telephone[3]. What is his submissive to do? She has seemingly conflicting orders. Should she simply stay seated and let the telephone ring? Should she get up and answer the telephone? Should she maybe try to drag her chair over to the phone without getting up? If she does get up and answer the telephone, what should she do when she hears her dominant's voice? This is a conundrum which her dominant has created, which she can feel intensely subject to, and which can be an intellectual, rather than primal, challenge to resolve (or not!).

Challenges provide excellent opportunities for a dominant to compel the surrender of their partner. In many cases in BDSM,

---

[3] Let's assume that the submissive can't see the telephone number of who is calling.

surrender comes just in a physical, sexual, or primal form. Intellectual challenges allow this surrender to be taken and experienced at a conscious, rational, and intellectual level as well. They add to the involvement of both partners and create vistas for experiences well beyond the bounds of a dungeon.

## 17.6 Controlling your partner

Many BDSM activities provide an opportunity to take control of your partner. While things like flogging, caning, and erotic denial can have other appeals as well, much of BDSM also involves some element of control over your partner. Just on its own this exercise of control and power can be intensely exciting and rewarding.

- Impact play allows you to use the sting of the whip or cane to make your partner move and writhe when and how you want. If you're using impact play to sexually arouse your partner then the targets you choose, such as nipples or genitals, the way you hit these targets, how often you hit them, and what you hit them with, all determine how fast and how strongly your partner gets turned on.

- Bondage involves restraining your partner in some way. It can include tying them up with rope—either freestanding or to some object or piece of furniture, shackling them or restraining them with chain, placing them in a cage, or mummifying them with something like Saran® wrap. In all cases, this restraint renders your partner under your control. You can do with them what you like.

*Motivations*

- Erotic denial is a type of sexual BDSM where you sexually stimulate and arouse your partner, but then you don't let them achieve climax... or, at least, not when they want to. You can do this as part of bondage play when you restrain them in such a way that they can't move and their genitals are exposed. You're then free to use your hand, fingers, a vibrator, or any other implement to sexually turn them on, but you always stop or slow down when they're getting close to orgasm until they beg for it.

- Predicament bondage is a variation of normal bondage where you deliberately allow your partner some limited freedom of movement. However, the position you create for them is uncomfortable. The challenge or predicament for them is that every movement they try has a cost. For example, you might tie them in a standing position with one foot attached to a rope which loops over a pulley to the hair on their head. If they put their foot down so they're standing on both feet, the rope pulls tightly and even painfully on their hair. If they hold their foot up, their leg quickly gets tired. The exercise of control here is that you get to create challenges and problems for them, and each time they find a comfortable position you rearrange the ropes to create a new and harder puzzle for them.

- Dominance and submission (D&s) is less about having particular scenes of flogging, bondage, cutting, etc., and more about control over your partner on an ongoing basis. It involves taking charge of them, setting directions or goals for them, monitoring them, giving them tasks and duties, and ensuring they perform them. For some submissives this can include discipline and correction for tasks poorly performed.

The control in D&s is explicit and often quite focussed. The control can feel more concrete because of the deliberate intention of the dominant to assert control and of the submissive to surrender to it. While there may be control in scenes such as cutting, bondage, etc., control in these situations is not so focussed and, indeed, is often merely implicit. For dominants who hunger to feel control over their partners, going straight for the jugular, so to speak, and issuing orders and requiring obedience can be far more arousing and satisfying than the unfocussed beating around the bush of flogging (pun intended).

- Mind fucks are BDSM scenes where you create a situation which, to your partner, appears more frightening, confusing, or challenging than it really is. For example, scratching a cold, blunt blade across your blindfolded partner's skin at the same time you dribble a small amount of warm water on the scratch can lead them to think that you've cut them; or lighting a propane torch behind them where they can hear it, moving the torch near their skin so they feel the heat, and then applying an ice cube to their bare skin can make them think you have burned them with the torch. In both of these scenarios you are manipulating your partner's sensations or perceptions so that they experience fear or shock and react accordingly.

- Humiliation is an activity where you criticise, humiliate, or embarrass your partner to drum home that their feelings of self-worth or value lie in your hands. You can make them stand in the corner wearing a dunce's cap, have them parade naked in front of their friends, or eat from a dog bowl. You control and challenge their confidence in themselves.

- Service is where your partner makes themselves available to satisfy some or all wants or needs you might have. This can include serving you drinks, making your bed, sexual service, running errands for you, being available when you feel the urge to hurt them, and so on. You direct them, determine the tasks they are to perform, judge their competency, set performance standards, and apply correction.

- Cutting and piercing are where you use a knife, needles, or skewers to penetrate the skin of your partner. You can use your partner as a canvas on which you might create designs of incisions, blood, or needles, or you might use the pain you inflict to control the state of mind of your partner.

As you can see, there are many direct or indirect ways of controlling your partner through BDSM activities. One of the big advantages here is that with so much choice about things to do you can control the experience of control itself. How much your partner feels themselves to be under your control is something you can vary to accommodate both your own desires and their ability to tolerate or absorb it. For example, if you tie your partner firmly to a chair then they may well be at your mercy, but how intensely they feel that is then going to depend on what you do to them. If you just leave them there then, true, they are under your control but they may find it merely to be a pleasantly relaxing experience. If, however, you take the opportunity to attach tight clamps to their nipples or genitals then that same situation is transformed into one where both you and your partner feel the intensity of the control that you can and are exercising over them.

Even D&s, where control is quite explicit, can be light or intense depending on what you do with it. For example, sending your submissive out to do some shopping may seem quite light, but standing over them as they scrub the floor under your supervision can be quite intense.

## 17.7 Symbolism

Symbolism can play a big role in BDSM.

Symbols can make it easier to enter into an appropriate state of mind before a scene. Uniforms are good examples of these sorts of symbols. For some people uniforms can be a fetish, but for others they can represent an authority dynamic which they're trying to achieve. A dominant or top wearing a police uniform can epitomise authority and can be easier and more natural to submit to than the same dominant or top wearing a sarong or a pair of budgie-smugglers[4]. A submissive wearing either a French maid's outfit or nothing at all can find it easier to get in the right mood than one who is wearing their customary jeans. And a dominant may find it easier to get in the mood when their submissive is dressed appropriately than when they are dressed in, say, a power business suit or as a tradesperson. Indeed, a top, dominant, submissive, or bottom who puts on the right clothes or who sees their partner in the right clothes can already find themselves getting into the right state of mind before they even start doing anything with their partner.

In fact, just the wearing of the clothes can be a reward in itself because, as we've noted earlier, self expression can be

---

[4]Australian slang for tight-fitting men's swimwear.

a valuable outcome of BDSM. When a BDSM relationship or even just a BDSM scene allows someone to express themselves more fully—such as with a uniform, with slutty clothes, with no clothes, or while posturing with a flogger—then this is already positive.

External physical symbols can be just as effective. A dungeon, the smell of leather, floggers, rope, and other toys are common BDSM symbols and can set the mood very well.

In addition to clothes, actions and words can also be symbolic. A diminutive female dominant can often physically subdue her larger male submissive, not by actually overpowering him, but by using symbolic actions to which he readily surrenders. These might be grabbing him by the shoulder and pulling him downwards so that he kneels, pushing the back of his head forward so that he bows, or taking his leash—assuming that he is wearing one—and guiding him to where she wants him. It's clear that this submissive is physically capable of resisting her, but the actions she takes and the force she applies often don't need to be more than symbolic. He will typically surrender to her intent and to the force of her personality. The actual use she makes of her own strength symbolises these two things.

Masters and slaves also use symbols. A master rarely needs to actually apply force to compel obedience. It can be enough that he merely shows his intent to take control and backs it up with his own strength of purpose. A master who says, "Stand up!" to his slave can be just as surely taking control as if he were to grab his slave and haul him physically to his feet.

Often this use of symbols can be as effective, or more effective, than an arduous display of physical dominance during a scene. It's true that sometimes symbolic control or symbolic adoption of a role needs to be reinforced by actual use of power or control, but it isn't the case all the time. Some scenes and activities can be just symbols and reminders of what has gone on in the past, or what may happen again in the future, and this can be a subtle but reassuring reinforcement of the relationship you have with your partner.

Finally, symbols can also be the goal, rather than just being a way of getting there. Being able to wear leather, or being able to wield a flogger are signs of achievement, and wearing a collar can be a sign of commitment.

## 17.8 Being controlled

I won't bore you with statistics, but the numbers show that a lot of people—vanilla and otherwise—have intimate relationships with their partner precisely because they want to experience power from their partner[5]. A lot of BDSM is about power and control, and there are many ways in which this desire to be controlled can be satisfied in BDSM.

- Bondage in its various forms—ropes, cages, cuffs, etc.—provides ways that your partner can physically restrain and control you.

- Flogging, caning, and other forms of impact play provide ways for your partner to manipulate and control you through sensations and pain.

---

[5] If you are keen to see some numbers, refer to [MASTERS2008, pp. 135 - 139], [HILL1996], and [MESTON2007].

*Motivations*

- Dominance and submission, and mastery and slavery, provide ways for your partner to take control of you through orders, creating rules of behaviour and standing orders, by determining what you wear and what you eat or drink, etc.

- Humiliation, mind fucks, and interrogation scenes provide opportunities for your partner to manipulate you psychologically or emotionally.

- Sensation play—with heat, cold, textures, and sensations—provides ways for your partner to manipulate your feelings and awareness through controlling or stimulating your senses, such as smell, touch, hearing, etc.

- Hypnosis provides an interesting way of going deeper into control of your mind than other BDSM techniques allow. Post-hypnotic suggestions (commands you follow after being woken up from the trance) can be effective at helping you experience the feeling of control being taken away from you.

All of these things can be explored with your partner, and it's useful when you are sensitive or responsive to being controlled, and when it's something you find rewarding or satisfying, to discuss all the options above, and any others you can think of, with your partner.

Control can appear in many forms. It can play itself out in a large range of different ways such as helplessness or surrender on your part, or by creating situations where you might resist but be overwhelmed by your partner, and so on.

## 17.9 Developing trust

Trust can be hard to earn and easy to lose. It is an important prerequisite when we're talking about engagement and penetration because these require as few barriers and defences as possible. For someone to lower their defences and be penetrated, and to allow their partner to see and engage the real *them*, they need to feel safe. This, in turn, means that they need to trust their partner.

Trust develops with experience. For your partner to trust you, they need to see you respond to difficult and challenging situations. If they only ever see you when the sun is shining, the sky is blue, and when the birds are singing happily in the trees, then they're not going to be able to trust that you'll be able to deal with things when the sky is cloudy, when the thunder starts rolling in, and when the birds have all buggered off to hide in the local church steeple out of fear of the impending lightning.

BDSM can be a tool to help develop trust because BDSM isn't always blue sky and sunshine. Many BDSM activities are challenging, and because there is often a risk of at least minor physical or emotional dents when penetration goes awry—such as when a flogger stroke hits in the wrong place, when a rope is too tight, when you or your partner experience an unexpected emotional reaction, or when a poorly-conceived order misfires—there are many more opportunities for trust to grow than there are in less confrontational activities such as a visit to the zoo or stamp collecting.

BDSM demands openness and honesty for penetration and engagement to occur. Instead of trust developing incidentally as the people get to know each other, it is something which we should actively work towards because the more trust there is, the more powerful, penetrating, and engaging our BDSM will be.

I'm not talking about some magical quality of BDSM in any of this. Both you and your partner have more to gain or lose as far as trust is concerned than in a vanilla relationship. BDSM requires much more admitting to, and being open about, our intimate wants and needs. Sometimes these are hard to talk about and this makes the sharing and opening up very precious. Many BDSM activities, such as cutting and bondage, inherently require a lot of confidence in the skill and good intentions of your partner—certainly far more than you'd look for in vanilla-land.

When used with caution, BDSM can help you find someone who you can trust with your most valuable of possessions—your body and your soul.

## 17.10   Minimising self

There are people for whom the here-and-now nature of BDSM is the key to their interest in it. In the outside world they may be high-powered, thrive-under-pressure individuals who are driven to be in control of themselves and what's going on around them. This level of mental activity can be very hard to turn off. For these sorts of people unwinding and relaxing is a major enterprise. For them a hypodermic needle tip through the genitals or pulsing electric shocks through the nipples can compel a change of focus far more effectively than sitting down in front of the television and watching a rerun of Magnum P.I., going for a run along the beach, or doing a workout at the gym.

Some forms of BDSM absolutely require a surrender to the experience and force a change of focus. This is something that is difficult to find outside of BDSM, at least in ordinary circumstances, but it's also something that's often vital when you want to turn off and simply be.

Some BDSM activities merely give you the opportunity to focus on them. Rope bondage is a good example. If there's enough stress or worry outside the dungeon it can intrude on your experience under the rope. You can even be distracted by loud noises or a song on the radio. If, on the other hand, you have hypodermic needles being inserted through your testicles or clitoris then you might not even notice a meteorite strike.

The intensity of such forms of BDSM takes a complex man or women and reduces them to their basics. It pushes aside the civilised layers of behaviour they have learned and which they are required to wear outside the dungeon and strips them down to their bare self. It compels surrender and creates a form of tranquillity. This is a very powerful result of BDSM. It is not recreation or an escape from the worries of the external world, but is instead an escape from self.

Some of the BDSM activities which can compel this sort of outcome include:

- Piercing - using hypodermic needle tips, sewing needles, or skewers to penetrate a part of the body such as nipples, belly, back, or genitals. While this might outwardly look decorative or be a way to create designs using patterns of needles, the psychological effect can often be quite profound.

- Cutting - using a sharp, sterile knife to cut into the upper arms, chest, breasts, back, or belly. Again, this can outwardly be to create designs in the flesh, but the cutting often causes intense and inescapable pain. For some people, the sight of their own blood can also be overwhelming.

- Flogging - using multi-tail floggers to create either intense stinging or heavy thudding sensations. Some floggers and how they're used can create very strong scoring or cutting sensations, while others can be heavy and pounding and their thuds resonate through the whole body.

- Mind fucks - manipulating your partner's experience so they think something intense or dangerous is happening to them when in reality they are quite safe. Triggering a fear of falling or a fear of the unknown while your submissive is blindfolded can also be quite terrifying.

If it seems that I'm talking about something which might be useful to you here, then discuss it with your partner and engage them in the search for activities which work for you.

Importantly, keep in mind that when you're looking for these sorts of intensities they tend to be very one-way things. That is, when you're lying face up having patterns carved into your breast, or when you're receiving a heavy flogging, it might be truly effective for you but it might just be work for your partner. They're there concentrating on making sure you get the pain or the intensity necessary to get you to the state of mind you need, and they're making sure you stay safe and healthy, don't die of blood loss, and so on. While they may be doing it because they care about you, be sure to make it up to them later in some way through BDSM scenes where you focus on getting their needs met, or by creating opportunities for them to do what they want.

## 17.11 Be the canvas

For some people the draw of BDSM is not so much how the different BDSM activities affect them, but is instead about surrendering themselves for use by their partner.

Surrender can be an intense and powerful act. It can be profoundly intimate, emotional and spiritual. For example, many tops and dominants use heavy scenes, such as floggings or canings, as a way to work out their own tensions or stresses. Their submissive partners may not have the need to work out their own stresses or tension at the time, but the experience of placing themselves at their partner's disposition and being heavily used, as well as the experience of meeting the demands of their partner's needs, can be very powerful and satisfying to someone who is inclined towards surrender and service.

Similarly, for someone who is not into being cut themselves *per se*, they may find that through making their body available to their partner for the cutting of designs in their flesh the surrender and service aspect becomes an intense and intimate time with their partner. The same can apply when your partner enjoys creating piercing designs with hypodermics needle tips in your skin, or when they tie elaborate patterns of rope and knots all over your body to express themselves.

This surrender can be a form of objectification, making yourself into a tool or a canvas with which your partner expresses themselves. Earlier I mentioned minimising self as a reason why some people do BDSM. Surrendering yourself to being the canvas on which your partner expresses their needs and desires can be another way of achieving this. You reduce yourself to being nothing more than an object on which your partner works out their own needs.

*Motivations*

## 17.12 Self ownership

Because BDSM is seen to be socially unacceptable in some quarters—particularly in the more conservative or fear-ridden parts of our society—actually getting involved in and embracing BDSM can be a loud and powerful statement about your identity. Instead of going with the flow or trying to conform to what society says you need to be, entering the world of BDSM is saying that you are your own man or woman and are setting your own path.

Also, some people come from backgrounds or situations where their family or social group disempowers them. Or, put another way, their family or social group applies pressure—sometimes irresistibly—to get them to behave in certain "acceptable" ways. Effectively their choices get made for them and they have no real control over their own lives. They get told what to do and are expected to do it. This can extend to the clothes they "choose" to wear and even to the job they "choose" to do. Sometimes this pressure is due to their cultural or ethnic background, but it can equally come from being born into a conservative family, or it can come from the church you attend, or it can come from the people with whom you hang out. It leads to you feeling like you don't have control over yourself or that you don't own yourself.

To counter this, engaging in activities which significantly affect your own body can make a powerful statement about ownership of yourself and can go part of the way to compensating for these feelings of powerlessness. Outside of BDSM, wearing weird clothes and getting a tattoo can be ways of compensating because they say and demonstrate that you can do what you want to yourself regardless of what other people tell you.

In terms of statements however, being involved in BDSM goes a whole lot further. For some people, just the symbolism of being a BDSM practitioner can be a powerful statement and an act of rebellion. The real BDSM itself can be merely icing on the cake.

There are a number of BDSM activities which let you get an intense feeling of ownership over yourself and which can give you a way of feeling that you're not under the control of parents and family, teachers, particular people in your peer group, or society at large. For example:

- Flogging and whipping are very symbolic in terms of ownership. Allowing someone such as your partner to flog or whip you is a powerful step in terms of deciding what can and can't be done to you. These are acts which directly enter your personal space and by allowing or requiring someone to do these things to you, you are saying that you are in control of who hurts you, who marks you, and who triggers deep feelings inside you.

- Cutting and piercing often make marks or patterns on your flesh. Allowing yourself to be used by your partner for the creation of patterns or designs on and in your skin, particularly if you have had a hand in the designs themselves, is another strong way to say that this is your body and that you decide what happens to it.

This problem of self-ownership doesn't just apply to bottoms, submissives or slaves. In many cases, folk who are naturally inclined towards being tops, dominants, masters, or mistresses feel themselves pressured to conform to other standards and can't let their natural desires see either the light of day or the dark of a dungeon.

*Motivations*

For some people, being involved in BDSM is a reclamation of themselves. It can be a taking back of control of themselves and how they express themselves. This can have a particularly strong impact on how the person or people involved feel about themselves. If they are compelled to live their day-to-day lives as something they don't feel or aren't passionate about, then letting their hair down and being themselves in the privacy of their dungeon with their partner can be very reaffirming and build up a lot of self-confidence.

This is because BDSM creates its own unique context where you can be intense with your partner. It provides circumstances and activities where you can be far more passionate and even primal than street life allows. Society tells you to be calm and sedate and not to get worked up about anything. On the other hand, BDSM is about deep feelings and intensity. It often provides a way of taking back the control of your wants and needs which society tries to take away by telling you how to behave and what's good and what's not. BDSM instead encourages you to do many of the things society says are no-nos.

The important thing about self-ownership is that it is about boundaries. When the world around you has told you, possibly for your entire life, that there are things which you can't do to yourself, or that there are things that you can't change about yourself, then this creates a fundamental boundary line inside you which can be difficult or impossible to pass on your own. Crossing this boundary and properly claiming control over yourself is an act of rebellion just as much or more than getting a tattoo or wearing weird clothes. It can be a sign that you're stepping out of the shadows which have hidden you away both from yourself and from the rest of the world.

Your partner can be a significant part in this with you, and this is something you both can usefully explore together. While it's not limited to submissives, if you are submissively inclined then this is also an important part of your own journey because before you can give yourself to your dominant or master you need to own yourself fully to begin with.

## 17.13 Expiation of guilt

Another reason why people do BDSM is because it can have a discipline or punishment aspect. Some forms of impact play such as spanking, caning, and flogging are obvious examples of things which have an association with childhood discipline or punishment. Confinement, such as being locked in a cage or being compelled to sit in the corner, are others. This discipline aspect of BDSM becomes even more apparent when the people involved enact their punishment scenes in rooms decked out to look like schoolrooms, or when the one being punished dresses as a schoolboy or schoolgirl.

Spanking, flogging, and caning are great staples of BDSM. You'll find them in most places where BDSM is practised. Sometimes guilt is a motivator for doing them because some parts of our culture are very good at instilling guilt into people and it can last a very long time. If you're one of these people with such a burden, and you were repeatedly disciplined at school then perhaps something similar in a BDSM dungeon can provide a suitable context and help you to get the guilt out of your system.

BDSM can provide a safe, supportive environment in which this expelling or expiation of guilt can occur. But again, it's important that you communicate this need to your partner. A flogging for kinky sex is very different from a flogging for guilt, and when your partner knows exactly what you're looking for they can help make sure that you get the punishment you need.

## 17.14 Self harm

One of the uncomfortable truths about BDSM is that it isn't always sweetness and light. Some people might have you think that it's only about kinky sex or that it's just about a bit of fun in the bedroom. While this may sometimes be the case, there can also be a darker side.

Self harm is one of these darker sides, and one particular form of self harm sits well—or as well as such a thing can—with BDSM. This is cutting. It bears some outside similarity to the cutting we find in BDSM and it's particularly prevalent among young women. It involves using a blade or knife to cut or scratch oneself and cause sharp pain. The cuts can range from long shallow cuts to deeper cuts releasing possibly a lot of blood. People who cut in this way will almost always do it on their own, often in the bath or shower where the blood will easily wash away. They're needing the pain, and it's this pain which provides temporary relief from what ails them.

There are many reasons why people cut. It's outside of the scope of this book to explore why they cut, but the point is that they do. While you can argue that in an ideal world no one would have the need to cut themselves, our world is not ideal and for some people cutting is the best or only option they have.

Because the need to cut is often embarrassing or is something you don't talk about with others, you are likely to do it on your own. If you're in need of pain from cutting and the need is strong, you may cut too deep. Worst case scenario: if you cut too deep there may not be anyone in the house to help you and you could bleed out and die. And if you're cutting because you have an intense need to do so, you may not pay attention to some of the more fiddly bits of cutting such as using sterile blades and making sure your cuts don't get infected.

While BDSM can't get rid of the need to cut, it can provide an environment where it's much safer. If you do have this need for pain, then having your partner cut you instead of you cutting yourself provides a number of benefits—safety being the main one.

- By having your partner wield the blade instead of you yourself, it allows you to more fully surrender to the pain. When you are holding the blade and doing the cutting, part of you has to stay in control. With your partner taking care of both the blade and your well-being, you can just feel and sink into the pain.

- Your partner will not be under the influence of your strong need for pain and they'll be able to pay attention to practical matters such as making sure they don't cut too deeply, and ensuring that the cuts are kept clean and disinfected.

- You don't have to worry about being interrupted.

- Your partner can cut areas where you can't normally reach. Commonly, people who cut themselves will use their bellies, forearms, and thighs because these are easily reachable. Because of the scarring involved it means that they have to wear long sleeves, long pants, and can't go to the beach wearing a swimming costume. Your partner can cut areas you can't reach, such as your shoulders or your buttocks, so that other more public parts of your body (arms, legs, etc.) don't need to be covered up due to scarring.

It can be hard to admit to your partner that you have such a need for pain through being cut. It can be psychologically easier to tell everyone, including yourself, that you're into this aspect of BDSM for the kinky sex or that you're simply submitting to your partner as a canvas for their designs with a blade. However, if you don't admit your need to your partner then you reduce the chances that your need will get met. You may find that some cutting scenes with your oblivious partner are not enough and that you need to retreat into the shower or bath when the need is particularly strong and do more cutting yourself.

Try being open with your partner, and even if you feel that it's something that you shouldn't be doing but you need to do it anyway, tell them and maybe they'll be ready and willing to help you out with their skills.

## 17.15 Being touched

Touching is one of the most under-mentioned aspects of BDSM. Touching your partner—especially non-sexual touching—is a vital part of any close relationship. It helps create feelings of companionship, intimacy, and caring. When we communicate with our partners, a touch can easily signify as much or more than words alone.

In BDSM, the activities we do provide many opportunities for touching, but when we discuss these activities, go to workshops about them, or read about them in books, the fact that touching is involved is often not mentioned at all. If we don't touch each other during BDSM play, the play becomes very sterile or clinical. This might be fine for the occasional medical scene, but as part of a relationship we should be looking for times when we can physically touch or be touched by our partners, either intentionally or as an important incidental part of our play.

Some of the sorts of touching which can occur include:

- Squeezing
- Caressing
- Pinching
- Biting
- Licking
- Pushing
- Pulling and dragging
- Sucking
- Face slapping
- Back-handed slapping
- Tickling
- Spanking
- Kissing
- Poking

- Blowing
- Twisting nipples
- Brushing with your hand
- Brushing lightly with your hair
- Tying knots against bare skin

Some of these might seem more incidental than fundamental parts of play, but as you're reading this, think about the things you do with your partner. How do you feel when they touch you? How do you feel when you touch them? What would it be like if the touching was missing? Think about the difference between an open-handed spanking versus spanking with a paddle. Are they the same? Do they feel as intimate and close? What about nipple torture with clamps versus nipple pinching and twisting with fingers. Do you get the same feeling of connection?

It's worth noting that we can sometimes have too much touching, just as we can sometimes have too little touching. For someone who enjoys the tactile side of things and who finds the touch of their partner during play to be reassuring, this latter can certainly be the case. On the other hand, for someone who wants or needs to sink into the physical sensations their partner is inflicting on them—such as during cutting, nipple torture, flogging, or bondage—being touched too much can be a distraction.

If there are times during play when you want or need your partner to keep their hands off you, let them know when it's good to touch you and when it's a distraction. Many people find that being touched during heavy impact play or heavy pain play is a distraction, but being held, touched, or even just having their partner nearby when they are coming down from the experience can be the bee's knees. If this is the case with you, say so if your partner hasn't already worked it out.

Let's look in more detail at a few of the ways that touching enters into BDSM play:

- Nipple torture. Touch is pretty obvious here when you're pinching your partner's nipples between your fingers, but even when you're using nipple clamps there's incidental touching as you perhaps pull on your partner's nipple to stretch it out to make it easier to attach a clamp. You might also incidentally or on purpose caress their breast as you place the clamp.

- Flogging. While the flogging itself is a hands-off activity, it's common for a top to warm up their partner with a spanking; then, as the flogging progresses, to check how their partner is going from time to time by stopping and feeling the warmth of their skin. Maybe at the end of the scene they also poke and prod a bit to check for any bruising. All of this is, of course, incidental touching.

- Cutting and piercing. These both involve a lot of touching in the form of rubbing your partner's skin with antiseptic, pressing or stretching their skin prior to inserting the knife blade or needle, touching or pressing on wounds, applying dressings, and so on.

- Physical handling or manhandling. This is often a fairly robust activity involving grabbing part of your partner's body—such as the scruff of their neck, their throat, or their shoulders—and using a modicum of strength to push them around, press them against the wall or down on the bed, or push them down on to their knees. The main

*Motivations*

goal of this is the experience for both of you of strength and physical power. But don't underestimate the role of person-to-person touching in this. Being touched at the same time you're being manipulated by your partner can be quite powerful. Would it be the same if you used a rope to haul your partner around, or would it be the same if you were hauled around on a rope by your partner instead of having the actual physical touch?

- Bondage. The focus of bondage is often ropes, knots, and chains, but along the way there's often a lot of physical touching or brushing of hands on skin as the ropes or chains are positioned. This may be quite an important part of what makes bondage work for you and your partner. Lack of touching can make bondage quite clinical and while this works for some people it's not always what is wanted or needed.

- Communication. BDSM is frequently deliciously primal. It addresses animal wants and needs, and these are best communicated physically. Grabbing someone and manhandling them, caressing them, slapping them, pinching them, and even fucking them, all communicate something via touch and physical sensation.

- Expressions of tenderness. Some BDSM is hard and heavy, but sometimes BDSM can be an expression of love or tenderness and this almost always involves some form of person-to-person touching. Light sensation play is an ideal opportunity for this, particularly when you're exploring tactile sensations with your partner. The goal needn't be pain, but do be sure to start and end the play with lots of stroking and touching.

- Reassurance. Actually being there, in physical contact with your partner, can be reassuring or comforting before, during, and after a scene. You sometimes don't even need to be particularly active about it. Just the contact with your partner or the pressure of one part of your body up against theirs can do the trick.

It's good to spend a little time talking about touch with your partner. Reflect on all of the BDSM activities you do together and think about when you touch each other. Could the experiences be improved by changing the nature of your touching and how much there is of it? Would more touching be better in, say, bondage and less in flogging? Or maybe the other way around? Or something different altogether?

## 17.16 Bonding

In terms of relationships, one of the most positive outcomes from practising BDSM is creating strong intimate and emotional bonds between partners. This bonding occurs for a number of reasons:

- More so than in vanilla relationships, successful BDSM requires openness and honesty. If you don't admit to your secret needs and desires then your partner will never know the sorts of things which are most important and satisfying to you.

    Because of this, people into BDSM need to, and do, talk to each other about important and intimate things more than their vanilla counterparts. This sharing of our intimate selves removes barriers between us and makes bonding more likely to occur.

- BDSM also allows for more intense psychological, emotional, and physical experiences with your partner. For many folk, BDSM is about affecting their partner, about causing them to feel and respond in intense ways. The feeling of being entered or penetrated by your partner—even when not sexually, such as through pain, needles, or knives—is something you don't get with the non-BDSM people in your life and this can create tight bonds between you and your partner.

- Much of BDSM is about power and control, and to fully get the benefit and to fully respond to what's happening between you and your partner, you need to open yourself up. More than just talking and saying what rocks your boat, you need to expose your intimate self to your partner and you need to allow them to affect you. This can be both very powerful and, at the same time, empowering as you let them in to touch and trigger you.

While it might sound like this is just what a submissive feels while they are receiving attention from their dominant, it actually works both ways. A dominant also needs to be open to how you respond, what you say, how you react, and how you feel. They also need to have reactions and feelings which are going to be triggered by you. They need to surrender to the possibilities of their own feelings and feel safe doing so with you.

- On a more mundane note, intimacy also can also come from the exploration and exploitation of some very private parts of your anatomy—and not just your clitoris, breasts, or penis. BDSM can leave no stone unturned in its exploration of your body. Privacy is something you need to be ready to surrender, and accept that all of you is fair game.

You may feel an intense closeness with your partner when they are completely at your mercy—perhaps when they're tied and helpless, or while you are using potentially dangerous implements on them, such as knives or whips. This show of trust on their part can be something which helps bring the two of you closer together.

If this aspect of BDSM is important for you and your partner, make sure that you create opportunities from time to time to actually explore and savour this. While other BDSM activities may also be exciting in their own ways and for their own reasons, bonding and closeness can be entirely valid, and even highly important, outcomes for an evening's or weekend's BDSM explorations.

## 17.17 Recreation and fun

Day-to-day life can be full-on, stressful, and overwhelming. It can take your mind away from happy thoughts, and even after you've finished work for the day it can leave you thinking about challenges at work, about problematic situations with co-workers or family, and about difficult decisions that need to be made. By spending an hour or three in the dungeon with your sweetie, aided by some ropes, some candles, and an array of other bits and pieces, you and your partner can flee into a BDSM world where everything outside no longer matters and is no longer relevant. This is a great way to escape and to relax.

The point of this is to unwind, to retreat into your dungeon or play space and have a seriously good time with your partner. Remember that BDSM doesn't always need to be intense. BDSM scenes can be times to play. Fun can be a necessary part of a relationship, and you sometimes need to ensure that there are opportunities for it between you and your partner. A lack of fun can have a big impact on the success of your relationship.

Fun and recreation as goals can almost be in direct contrast to satisfying animalistic hungers and passions. However, remember that fun can lead to other things which may be more primal, and just because you entered the dungeon with light fun in mind doesn't mean you can't finish up with something heavy and intense if it feels right to do so.

Indeed, for those of you who have difficulty putting your worries aside as you enter the dungeon, some serious attention with a flogger or with some needles is sure to drive other thoughts out of your mind and just leave you with the immediacy of what is happening between you and your partner *right now*.

Fun and recreation are often about distracting you from your everyday life and BDSM can be entirely suitable for achieving this goal. The vast majority of BDSM activities involve things quite unlike the outside world. Whether you're on the receiving end of drops of hot wax, or whether you're the one doing the dripping; or whether you are being tied with so much rope that you could be mistaken for a giant ball of string, or whether you're the one doing the tying; or whether your partner is carving their initials into your upper arm with a scalpel, or whether you're the one doing the carving; or whether you're focussing on getting your pony trot just right, the fact is that there's a lot of focussing on the here-and-now going on and this will certainly drive other thoughts away.

In it's own way it is relaxing, and at the end of an undistracted BDSM session both people involved can feel very relieved. They can unwind. Tension dissipates and you are left feeling cleansed.

If any of this sounds good to you, tell your partner. Some people mistakenly think that each BDSM session needs to be heavy or full-on. This isn't the case. If using BDSM for relaxation or fun some or all of the time is what works for you, pursue it with your partner. Even if you have no specific BDSM activity in mind, just going into your dungeon with the idea of being open and trying new things can be a good way to have fun.

There's a difference between this BDSM for recreation and fun and the BDSM for minimising self which I talked about earlier[6]. Using BDSM for recreation is about getting yourself into the here-and-now and pushing distracting thoughts aside. The end result is you totally focussed on what's happening.

Minimising self, on the other hand, is about actually diminishing yourself, making yourself less. It is about escaping from yourself for a short time and so while the lights may be on, so to speak, you're actually not at home.

## 17.18 Primal expression

BDSM activities and relationships provide opportunities to express ourselves primally and to get primal needs met.

A lot of the time when I talk about primal needs and primal expression I would be talking about things like physical handling and aggression, and about sex. But primal also relates to:

---

[6]In section 17.10 on page 190.

- Fear,

- Strong and deep emotions,

- Food, hunger, and thirst, and

- Social needs (i.e., being with and interacting with others)

All of these things are part of us, and when they become part of our BDSM and of our BDSM relationships we can have a powerful context in which to address them and to find release and satisfaction.

For example, our social needs can be met with fellow BDSM enthusiasts. Not just with our primary BDSM partner, but also with others who we maybe meet at BDSM play parties or at social BDSM get-togethers.

Perhaps there's a reason why formal dinners prepared and served by BDSM slaves are a real goal for some and a fantasy for others. The ideas and images of mastery and slavery aren't of sandwiches while watching the news on TV, but instead are of sumptuous, multi-course meals on long tables with candelabras. The image is normally of a feast or meal with a number of others present, some serving and some being served. Note the social context of this, i.e., it's a formal occasion for social interaction.

The need to express ourselves physically can come through heavy manhandling during BDSM play or through rough sex. Two of the three criteria I mentioned in book one for a BDSM relationship—namely, penetration and disparity of power—are clearly present here.

One of the reasons why primal expression is particularly relevant to BDSM is that our oh-so-proper society doesn't provide much opportunity or encouragement for expressing the animalistic or primal side of our natures. We sometimes have the chance to get a little bit of vicarious excitement at football games or while watching demolition derbies, but the rest of the time when we're with other people the rules say we need to be quiet, respectful of others, not to be bossy, to be sedate, calm, not to speak loudly, etc., etc. This is a bit of a bummer because we humans are animals and it wasn't too long ago that we were whacking each other with clubs as foreplay. We certainly haven't outgrown our built-in inclinations towards being physical.

Notwithstanding some of the vigorous rumpy pumpy which goes on in some households, sex itself—one of the few really primal things many people actually get to do—is often wrapped in guilt. Some quarters of society tell us it should only be done to make babies, or that it should not involve bruises or blood loss, or that it should only be quiet and gentle. Sex in perfumed rooms on silk sheets might be romantic, but it doesn't necessarily satisfy the animal inside. Embracing BDSM is one way to open the gates to powerful, immensely satisfying, and very animalistic self-expression.

A funny thing about the missionary position is that it quite literally involves one person pinning their partner down. Expressed like that, it is beginning to sound BDSM-ish. Even women not into BDSM report that the feeling of being pressed under their partner is a powerful, exciting, and desirable experience, but in missionary position sex this can be more incidental than intentional. In fact, some people engage in sex because it's one of the few socially acceptable ways for them to be physically dominated or to physically dominate someone.

Through BDSM however, you can make strength, power, and domination a planned and agreed part of what goes on in the bedroom or dungeon, and this can help make previously guilty pleasures into the main event.

Some parts of BDSM are actually all about this, and so by including BDSM in your life you get the opportunity to express the animalistic parts of you in an open and honest engagement with your partner. And when the hungers for domination and submission which you and your partner feel are particularly strong, you may find that sometimes you won't even think about the sex part because the D&s side has been so rewarding in itself.

This physical, animalistic side of BDSM appears in some, but not all BDSM activities:

- Many tops who practise flogging will often have a range of floggers in their arsenal (sorry, toybag) ranging from the small and light floggers used more for sexual titillation—such as for flogging clitorii, testicles, or nipples—through to the heavy, pounding floggers which actually do start to trigger animalistic feelings and urges both for the person receiving the rough and heavy thuds, and for the person using all their strength to wield the flogger and strike their partner.

- Physical domination, including wrestling and manhandling, can also contribute mightily where animalistic urges and hungers are in play. The actual use of physical strength, both to subdue on one side, and to resist on the other, can be extremely powerful between two people. It can create intense feelings of dominating, overwhelming, and of compelling the surrender of your partner, or it can create feelings of complete helplessness and submission.

  We need to be cautious here because some styles of physical domination are merely symbolic or cooperative rather than actual, particularly where the dominant is a small female and the submissive is a large male. Symbolic or cooperative physical domination will be far less satisfying in a primal sense than actual physical domination.

- Bondage, another very common BDSM activity, can be light-and-fluffy or heavy and intrusive. Just being tied to a chair is not likely to be very useful in terms of satisfying animal urges, but bondage involving lots of heavy handling and the opportunity or even need to resist can be very effective.

If this talk of primal passions, animal feelings, being rough, or physical manhandling triggers something inside you, you should discuss it with your partner if you haven't already. There is a strong tendency in many people, particularly in newcomers to BDSM, to not be rough or heavy because society teaches us that this is a "bad thing"... and sometimes it can be. However, many people are drawn to activities like bondage or flogging because of the possibility that a few knots may lead to some physical handling or that light flogger taps may evolve into some serious pounding. Indeed, they may hunger for this primal physicality but be uncomfortable asking for it because they might think it's wrong—such as for a big, tough dominant to forcefully take physical advantage of their small and petite partner—but this may be exactly what the doctor ordered.

Such explorations and activities need to be approached confidently, and this can only be done when you have full and open communication with your partner. Things can go badly astray when there are hints or promises of animalistic needs being explored and only a light tap of a flogger or a quick tie-up ensues, so you need to be clear about what you want or what you are prepared to do.

While I've been mainly focussing here on primal expression and feelings in the form of the use of physical strength this is only because this is one of the easiest and most accessible primal feelings which we can reach or activate through BDSM. As I mentioned at the start of this section, others things—such as food and sex—can be just as primal and should not be neglected.

## 17.19 Surrender

To fully and completely surrender to something can be a transformative experience. It means lowering all of your barriers and allowing something to enter you, or allowing yourself to experience something completely without resistance. Surrender differs from submission in that submission often simply means moving some—but not all—barriers aside temporarily and then putting them back when the scene or activity is done.

Surrender works to create change in the person who experiences it. This change might be a deeper understanding of self, a greater awareness of what you are capable of feeling, a more open attitude to what goes on around you, and perhaps more honesty and trust in regards to your partner.

Surrender is powerful and frequently very intense. Because it means opening yourself up, what happens to you while you are surrendered will often reach deeper inside you and affect you more strongly than when you simply submit to what's going on. Surrender is also sometimes hard to identify, but many people into BDSM are actually looking for it regardless of what specific activity they do.

## BDSM Relationships - How They Work

Many BDSM activities compel surrender. That is to say that surrender is a requirement, not an option. This is because the activities themselves are so intense that they force barriers to come down. For example, strong pain play such as heavy flogging or caning can do this. Indeed, some people seek out heavy or intense BDSM activities precisely because they are looking for surrender and these sorts of scenes guarantee it. On the other hand, some sensation-based activities, such as wax play, may not get anywhere near intense enough to compel surrender and may be merely sensually pleasant or erotic.

Surrender is one of the most powerful and transformative experiences in BDSM, and yet it is also one of the one's least mentioned and least explored. But understanding surrender, and understanding how and where it fits into your life and into the lives of people around you, is a fairly critical factor in getting yourself into the sort of relationship which will be effective and satisfying for you.

One of the difficulties of coming to grips with BDSM relationships is that there are labels we use to describe ourselves which have differing meanings. These terms include:

- Top
- Bottom
- Dominant
- Submissive
- Master
- Mistress
- Slave

*Motivations*

- Switch

The terms themselves have widely different meanings depending on who you ask, who they're with when you ask, where you ask, how you ask, which country or city you're in when you ask, the time of day when you ask, the weather conditions when you ask, and practically anything else you can think of. However, the terms do hint at the place surrender has for that person.

Surrender is not submission. While they may look the same on the outside, surrender is more profound than submission. It is the process by which we open ourselves to an experience and allow it to enter into us completely and without resistance. There is an air of helplessness to surrender because it means that we must open the door and completely step out of the way.

Submission, on the other hand, is frequently just acceptance or tolerance. We can see this where bottoms and submissives retain the option of saying no; whether this is no to continuing a scene, no to getting a drink for their dominant, no to dressing in a particular way, no to their partner's wish that they fuck someone else, or no to anything in general that their partner would like. In submission, you stand at the door ready to close it at any time.

In reality, there are many doors. A submissive or bottom may have one door that they keep open all the time for bondage experiences, another that they open occasionally for personal service to particular partners, one that they keep firmly closed for anal sex with strangers, yet another which they open from time to time for cutting scenes, and so on.

We can call BDSM slaves the people who seek to surrender as much as possible to their partner. Continuing the door analogy, a slave seeks to step away from their doors, or from as many of their doors as possible, and let their partner—their master—completely and unreservedly control the doors instead.

## 17.20  Catharsis

Emotions and nervous energy sometimes build up during the course of our lives. This often happens when we don't have the opportunity to safely get these emotions or this energy out of our systems. When the office retard traps us at the water cooler and begins to regale us with boring stories about his life, social custom tells us to listen for the shortest time possible and then make a polite escape. Unfortunately, in this situation we're left with some frustration or irritation at the minutes of our lives which have been irretrievably lost. In a perhaps ideal world, as soon as the bore started talking we would have grabbed the nearest heavy object and begun educating him with it in regards to wasting our time. This would have provided a release for us. However, the use of heavy objects in this way is generally frowned upon and so the frustration stays with us, at least for a time.

It's not only negative feelings which build up inside us. A parade of deliciously attractive members of an appealing gender at some event may leave your loins keen for some action while all you can do then and there is maybe clap quietly and say in a restrained voice, "How very nice!"

Any powerful emotional or sexual experience which we can't express due to either lack of opportunity or due to social constraints can also leave us emotionally or sexually charged and can linger inside us until we get a chance to get rid of it.

*Motivations*

One process for cleaning out these emotions and nervous energy after the events which caused them is called catharsis. It's a purification or release of these emotions through intense or powerful experiences. Some people might use a run along the beach, heavy exercise at the gym, or some martial arts practice as a way of achieving this. However, working out this energy with your partner in the dungeon can be a better way to go because you can direct that built up tension and energy towards having a powerful scene with your partner. Putting that energy to use with your partner is going to do a whole lot more for your relationship than if you burn the energy solo, such as at a gym. To my mind this is a good way of doing things. Using BDSM scenes for catharsis provides benefits for both you and your partner rather than just for you alone.

Heavy handling, pain, being strung up by rope, humiliation play, and a whole range of other BDSM activities can be intense enough and powerful enough for catharsis. Just as with BDSM practised for recreation, cathartic BDSM can leave you feeling relieved and cleansed.

This catharsis is something BDSM folk may be achieving without actually thinking much about it. For some people—particular those who have had BDSM in their lives for a long time—scenes can be their best and most familiar way of discharging all this accumulated nervous energy and emotion. If they can't do scenes this energy will just keep building up. When this happens, the most obvious signs are that the person may become irritable or restless, sometimes without knowing why.

When someone doesn't recognise or realise that they use BDSM in this way, they may not give their BDSM scenes the attention which they should. As a result, BDSM scenes sometimes don't happen or aren't intense enough, the result being the irritability or restlessness which I mentioned above, or worse.

"Worse" can be when the people involved aren't consciously aware of the connection between their BDSM activities and the release of this pent-up energy. Instead of controlling it or finding other avenues to let it out—such as a visit to the gym—or by just simmering through it until it dissipates, they may start acting out. Without knowing why, they may start trying to goad their partner—perhaps behaving badly so that they get punished and, hence, get the pain or intense experience they were needing. This is not ideal and will put a strain on the relationship.

When a serious need for catharsis arises, the scenes which provide it need to be planned, time needs to be allocated, and whatever is required to make sure it comes off needs to be done. When they aren't given the priority they deserve, these BDSM scenes can easily fall off the planning wagon and not happen at all.

They can also fail to happen, or happen but not be satisfying, because:

- Your new partner doesn't like the same things your last partner did and so doesn't do the things which customarily lead to your catharsis,

- Your new partner prefers to do BDSM less frequently than you need,

- One of you is focussing on something else—such as kinky sex—and neglecting what needs to be done for their partner to feel cleansed,

- Medical reasons—broken bones, illness, etc., or

- Other things happening in other parts of your lives which leave you or your partner too tired or too distracted to scene.

## Questions

1. Do you or your partner feel cleansed after some or all of your scenes?

2. How important is this experience of feeling cleansed? Is it a great relief? Do you feel like a weight has been taken from your shoulders? Do you feel more free after scenes?

3. What is it like when you can't scene or when you can't get this relief?

4. If scening isn't possible, how can you or your partner get catharsis?

# 17.21 Super-hot sex

While it's a topic that I'm cautious about discussing in terms of BDSM, sex just can't be avoided. The reason why I'm cautious talking about sex is because there are a lot of people who think that BDSM is only about sex. I'm concerned that if I talk about it too much it'll encourage them not to look any further than the bits between their legs. There's more to BDSM than sex, much more, and I'm hoping that through these books you're seeing just that.

That said, many people look at BDSM as a way of making sex more exciting and powerful than it would normally be in a vanilla context. This is an admirable goal and one which I fully support. There are a few ways this can work.

Firstly, even though we live in a liberated society, there are still some things which you generally don't talk about with your parents. BDSM is one of them. Because of this, BDSM acquires a sort of secretive or illicit feel to it. Mixing a hint of BDSM into your bedroom games might therefore add a little thrill from doing the forbidden. Even for those folk who limit themselves to fluffy handcuffs, or those who use silk handkerchiefs to tie their partner's arms and legs to the corners of the bed, this can be quite exciting. It can add an extra charge to sex. It may be that the buzz comes from fulfilling a secret fantasy, from actually or symbolically opening yourself up to your partner more than you might normally do, or it may come from doing something risque, something which you know that your parents or closest friends would disapprove of.

Secondly, sex is often an opportunity for you and your partner to intimately share each other's bodies and feelings. An important part is them being able to feel you, and you being able to feel them. Sex, of course, provides this in abundance.

Cocks and cunts have an enormous number of nerve endings all waiting to really make your day and sex makes them get up and dance. But in vanilla sex this is about all that happens. BDSM adds to how much you can penetrate your partner, to how much they can feel you, and to how much you can feel them. This is not necessarily about sticking things into your partner—though you could argue that the BDSM activities of cutting and piercing fit this description. Instead, I'm talking about our ability to use BDSM to create intense experiences and feelings with our partner beyond mere sex.

In vanilla sex for example, foreplay might consist of fondling, massage, soft music, dirty movies, an expensive dinner, or some combination of the above. These are nice, but they're not really that powerful.

Compare them to stringing your partner up to a bondage frame, tying them so tightly that they can't move, then teasing or torturing them with pincers or clamps on their sensitive bits, and exploring their genitals without them being able to move to stop you; or imagine starting out with a gentle caning and working up to an intense and heavy hammering of their butt; or imagine stripping your partner naked, pushing them around roughly, and wrestling them to the ground. Consider what it's like when you're on the receiving end of these things. There is power and intensity written all over these activities. Whether you're a dominant or a submissive involved in scenes like this, the scope for having a deep and penetrating awareness of your partner is much higher than, say, by sharing a dirty movie and some popcorn.

And then you add actual sexual intercourse on top of it.

Of course BDSM sex is hotter than vanilla sex!

## How to enhance the experience

- Put aside your fears. Fear is one of the main things that gets in the way of fully immersing yourself in the experience you have with your partner. It creates barriers and limits how much they can penetrate you. That doesn't mean that you should be careless or take unnecessary risks. But once you and your partner have looked at the risks, made the right preparations, and taken the right precautions, then do allow yourself to be in the moment with your partner.

- Open yourself up. You can open yourself up physically by perhaps undressing and spreading your legs. However, there's much more to it in BDSM than that. BDSM can be a very intimate, shared journey, and when it is this makes sex much more powerful and intense. But for it to be intimate and shared you need to let your feelings, your desires, your hungers, and your lusts out where your partner can see them. When you feel something, don't hide it. Talk about your feelings and lusts. Demonstrate them. Show them. By doing so you create opportunities for your partner to go places with you, to explore you, and to see you as never before.

- Communicate more with your partner before, during, and even after sex. Use words, facial expressions, and gestures. Some people hold back from letting their partner know how they feel either during BDSM scenes or in the course of an ongoing BDSM relationship. In a scene they may be too caught up in ecstasy to speak, or they may not want to distract their partner when their partner seems to be having such a good time. But by holding back you prevent your partner from experiencing you. They don't know and can't feel you unless they get some sort of message such as an occasional grunt, wriggle, or groan; or even the occasional, "That is soooo HOT!"

- Likewise, encourage your partner to let loose with grunts, groans, and expressions of amazement at the feelings you're giving them. This will help you to feel them more.

Vanilla sex can be limiting as its focus is often mere genital-on-genital friction. Adding in BDSM, actively exploring dominance or submission before or during the act, or adding in intense physical feelings through bondage, torture or impact play, can double or triple the feelings, closeness, and responsiveness. Rather than just limiting the action to the area between the hips and thighs, BDSM lets psychological play and other forms of engagement take place at the same time.

I've noted that much of BDSM in the context of a relationship is about penetration, about you and your partner deeply and deliberately experiencing and feeling each other. By combining BDSM and sex we get penetration occurring not just sexually—i.e., cock-in-cunt—but psychologically, emotionally, and maybe even elsewhere physically on your bodies. This means that instead of the focus mainly being your dick or your cunt, your whole body and mind, and those of your partner can be and are fully involved.

## Questions

- For you, what is the next step up from vanilla sex?

- Which aspects of combining BDSM activities with sex do you find hot?

- If you're already an experienced BDSMer, do you ever engage in sex with a vanilla partner? How is it different to BDSM sex?

- Do you find it difficult to let yourself go? Why?

## Chapter 18

# Dominance and submission

The most visible style of BDSM has to do with physical pain, physical sensation, and physical restraint. It involves activities such as cutting, bondage, cages, gags, hoods, caning, whipping, wax play, spanking, and so on. For many folk, these physical activities are the tools they use to achieve their own particular outcomes. Causing intense pain might lead to catharsis, tight rope bondage might lead to a physiological release, sensual flogging might lead to heightened sexual arousal and then to hotter sex with partners, etc., etc.

There are other people for whom the exercise of power or the experience of power are the tools. Instead of using physical sensation, we could say that they use psychological or emotional sensation. For them the exploration and the exercise of power, authority, and control are the most interesting, powerful, satisfying, and rewarding parts of their BDSM. What they do to and with each other physically is less important than the opportunities which their activities give them to express and experience power. The physical results of these explorations—such as the red butt, the bruises, or the tangle of rope and knots—may simply be icing on an already satisfying and delicious cake.

It can sometimes be difficult to separate the physical side of BDSM and the psychological. I might order my submissive or slave to her knees and firmly push her head down as she does so. The main part of this for us both might be the effect of the exercise of my authority, but pushing her head down adds a physical aspect which reinforces the psychological. If I just told her to kneel and pushed her head down without having underlying power or authority the effect and the outcome for us both would be very different and certainly far less satisfying.

The deliberate exploration of power, authority, and control is the realm of dominance and submission (D&s) and mastery and slavery (M/s). While this might not be discussed much in vanilla or conservative company, as I've noted earlier[1], research shows that exploring and experiencing power motivates many people's intimate relationships with as many as 20% or more of men and women saying that this is significant for them. Even so, because of the common focus on the physical side of BDSM, many people don't realise the extent to which power and authority are being actively utilised in their relationships because it is obscured by the physical activities which go along with them. This may be because they simply don't notice or

---

[1] Section 17.8 on page 187.

are too busy with the physical aspects of their play, or it can also be because accepting that they enjoy taking control of their partner or that they enjoy being controlled by their partner may be uncomfortable thoughts.

Understanding the role of power and authority can help you with your relationship. If authoritatively pressing your submissive to their knees, or if being pressed to your knees by your dominant is effective for you beyond the mere physical force which is used, then there may be a significant D&s component involved. Recognising that this is so lets you focus on and use this in addition to any physical BDSM you practice, potentially multiplying the satisfaction and penetration for you and your partner.

Power is like the electricity you get out of a wall socket. You might have a reassuring feeling that it'll be there when you need it, but it's not actually providing you with any benefit until you plug something in and start using it. Likewise, just having power in a BDSM relationship is not enough. Actually using power over your partner or feeling your partner using their power over you is what makes D&s or M/s effective for both of you. The physical aspect might still be rewarding, but taking away the exercise of power and just leaving the mechanical or physical side of BDSM may not be enough.

Power comes in many different forms. Physical strength, intellectual superiority, and diabolical cleverness are three examples. But something like the ability and readiness to inflict pain can also be power. It is something which can be used to control your partner. It is also something which many people don't have. That's not to say that it's sadism *per se*, but actually using pain or inflicting pain are not things which are very common or supported in our society, and being comfortably able to do so is another tool in your BDSM toolbox.

Anyway, there are many forms of power which are relevant to BDSM. Below is a list of activities or scenarios in which different forms of power or authority can be exercised. When you're reading through these, try and separate out in your own mind the difference between the power itself and the activities which make the power felt. Note that in many cases the activities involved aren't the flogging, caning, or bondage which are typically associated with BDSM.

## 18.1 Different types or forms of D&s

- Physical domination - Many people respond positively to being physically manipulated or manhandled, dragged by the hair, choked, pushed to the ground, and so on. This sort of domination can include erotic wrestling and even lightweight activities such as taking your partner's arm and guiding them to where you want them to go.

  It isn't always necessary for the dominant to be physically stronger than their submissive. In many cases, the fact that the dominant attempts to use strength or force is enough for the submissive to surrender.

- Domination through pain - This is the use of pain to manipulate feelings and behaviour, or to cause reactions. Pain is a powerful tool in a dominant's toolbox because it is difficult to resist. It can be sharp or thuddy pain, such as from some types of floggers. Dried peas in shoes can be quite effective, as can grains of uncooked rice under the knees while kneeling. Many submissives will not be able to stop themselves responding to the pain or discomfort.

On the other hand, for some submissives the act of resisting is what they need. The pain they receive from their dominant is what they can struggle against in a similar way to how some bondage enthusiasts will struggle against their ropes once they are tied.

- Intellectual domination - This is dominating or overwhelming your submissive by knowing more, by having more experience, by being able to think more quickly, or by simply having a higher I.Q. than they do. For some submissives this gives them a reassuring feeling of being put in their place, while for others the use of intellect to dominate them gives them a way of challenging their dominant by struggling to compete against it.

- Emotional domination - Manipulating emotions, such as by creating and using fear, can also be an effective way for a submissive to feel the power or skills of their dominant.

- Humiliation - Manipulating the feelings of self-worth of a submissive—such as by insulting them, revealing their weaknesses, criticising their abilities, or by exposing embarrassing past or present behaviour—is another way in which a dominant can bring their submissive to feel both helplessness and an inability to resist.

- Objectification - Reducing someone to less than a person—such as by making them serve as a table or chair, or by treating them as merely a life-support system for their genitals, i.e., as a collection of bodily organs which keeps their cock or cunt alive—decreases their ability to value themselves and compels them instead to feel valued as much or as little as their dominant chooses. Again, this is an exercise in control and power. The dominant decides when, where, and how often to use this object, and decides the value of the object, i.e., the submissive.

- Military interrogation - This is a form of role play where the submissive or slave is typically tied or handcuffed to a chair. The dominant or master then uses pain, fear, or torture to get them to reveal certain secrets. In reality the dominant already knows the secrets, and the submissive knows this. The exercise is for the submissive to resist the dominant, and for the dominant to attempt to use whatever means necessary to get the submissive to yield. Note that sometimes the desired outcome is that the submissive successfully resists, rather than is broken.

- Manipulation of sensations - A dominant can take control of what sensations a submissive can experience by means of blindfolds, earplugs, or by wrapping them in soft material so they can't feel either with their fingers or with the rest of their skin.

- Manipulating situational awareness - Going further, blindfolds and earplugs can limit your submissive's ability to determine what is going on around them. You can cause your submissive to think something dangerous, confronting, or shocking is happening to them through misleading them, misinforming them, and through manipulating what they see, hear, or feel. This can be called a mind-fuck.

- Service-oriented domination (personal) - This is directing and controlling how your submissive performs different types of personal service. We can define personal service as something which has to do with a dominant's intimate or immediate wants and needs. These can include preparing or providing food, drink, or sex; acting as a personal assistant; providing entertainment in the form of singing, playing an instrument, or dancing; and so on. The important thing is that they directly involve the dominant. These sorts of interaction allow the submissive or slave to get instant feedback on their performance, and allows the dominant to retain fine control of their partner, or even to micromanage them.

- Service-oriented domination (impersonal) - Some submissives and slaves also respond to serving their dominant or master at a distance. This sort of impersonal service is where the actual service is performed away from the dominant, such as by doing household shopping or running other errands, attending training, performing household maintenance, editing master's literary creations, cleaning the car, and so on. The dominant initiates the service but then the submissive completes it on their own.

When we compare the personal and impersonal variations of this type of domination we can see that there are some parallels between these and physical BDSM activities which involve, on the one hand, a lot of physical interaction between the submissive and dominant (personal) and, on the other hand, those where the submissive is left to "soak", such as with mummification or longer-term static bondage (impersonal).

- Scene-only domination - The above two types of domination involve the submissive or slave performing useful service for their partner. The outcome is that something has been achieved—such as the shopping done, time saved for the dominant, or some pleasure has been given—such as sex or a yummy dinner. For some couples, simply spending time together with the dominant exercising his submissive by ordering her around—such as directing her to sit, stand, adopt particular postures, leading her using a leash, and so on—is satisfying on its own. In this case, the exercise of power is immediate and only lasts as long as the exercise period or scene.

- Role play-based domination - Scene-only domination can be combined with role play to create a context or style for the domination and submission. When the submissive adopts the role of a puppy for example, this allows the dominant to use their control and authority to train the submissive in that context. In this example, it could include toilet training, learning to sit, fetch, and so on. Mischievous behaviour can be tamed, discipline can be applied, and correct behaviour as defined by the dominant can be taught in this style of domination. Age play or infant play can also be used in this way.

- Hunter / prey domination - One aspect of D&s which is not often discussed is where the submissive actively attempts to evade or resist their dominant partner. This typically involves a form of challenge from the submissive and can be combined with one or more of the above types of domination.

It can involve the dominant physically or symbolically pursuing, capturing, and possibly defeating the submissive. The use of diabolical cleverness is common from both the dominant and the submissive.

For example, in straightforward military interrogation the interrogator (the dominant) might just impose gradually increasing levels of pain or suffering on their submissive partner. In response, the submissive might try to mislead or distract their dominant, try to exhaust them, or lead them to believe that they, the submissive, are close to breaking when they aren't. They might also try to deflect any pain—such as by turning or twisting during caning—or may try to escape the ropes when their dominant is looking away. Instead of the submissive being a willing and receptive target for the dominant, the submissive resists and effectively challenges their dominant to defeat them. It can become a hard game of D&s-flavoured cat-and-mouse.

Physical domination can often be symbolic. A small woman may be able to physically dominate a much bigger and stronger man simply by pushing or exerting nominal strength. For both, it may be the symbolism which is important. However, physical domination can become a genuine battle which the submissive may not always be guaranteed to lose and where the dominant needs to actually overwhelm their resisting partner, pin them down, and force them to yield.

Predicament bondage is a challenge-based style of bondage where the top or dominant ties their partner in an uncomfortable position but leaves some leeway to allow their partner to find a better or more comfortable position. Often though, the options available to the submissive are designed by their partner to only allow an exchange of one sort of discomfort for another. Should the submissive manage to temporarily find some bodily contortion which gives them some unexpected comfort—and thus defeat their dominant—their dominant ups the challenge by adding another rope or knot to remove the solution the submissive found.

It is not uncommon for a submissive to challenge their dominant anyway, just in the normal course of things. Submissives who like or need to be dominated by their partner often look for reassurance that their dominant is still up to the task. Rather than going through the motions, sometimes they try to challenge or resist in small or large ways to experience their partner's reaction, which could be to correct their submissive, discipline them, or whatever.

All of the above provide opportunities for domination and submission to occur. They create a context in which the outcome—the feelings and experiences of the people involved—is heavily influenced by the power and the authority the dominant uses, and by how the submissive responds to these. This is different to scenes and activities which are primarily physical, such as flogging or cutting, where the actual execution of the physical activity is far more important than the power or authority behind the execution.

Not all of the different types of domination I listed above will be effective for everybody. Which ones work and which ones don't will depend on your needs at the time, on your past experiences, and on other factors. It's worth sitting down with your partner and asking yourselves:

- Which of the activities are attractive to you?
- Do any of them scare you?
- Are there times or moods in which some activities would be more appealing or satisfying to you than others?

- Would the range of activities be different when you're horny? Whey you're tired? When you're just home from a stressful day at the office? At the beginning of a long weekend? Any time?
- Which of these activities work for your partner? When?
- Which of your partner's needs can they satisfy?
- What is the role of physical domination for you? Is physically overwhelming or overpowering your partner satisfying for you and them?
- What is the role of intellectual domination for you? Is being outwitted or out-thought important?
- Is the role of pain important to your explorations of dominance and submission?
- Do you want to maintain the feeling of dominance over your partner outside of the dungeon or away from where you play?
- Do you want to be constantly aware of your partner's dominance over you?
- Do you want to limit the dominance and submission to strict times when you play together?

While you're considering all of the above, another important question is:

- Which of the above types of domination or ways of using power definitely won't work for you or your partner? Which of them would be counterproductive to the goals and motivations you and your partner have for your BDSM?

Some expressions of power and control can cause bad or negative feelings. For example, physical domination for some rape victims, intellectual domination for people who lack self-confidence, or manipulating sensations combined with a blindfold for someone afraid of the dark. You need to discuss with your partner the ways of using power which push your buttons, the ways which cause problems for you, and the ways which are simply uninteresting.

From the list above we may notice that some D&s can be conflict-based. The dominant has power and the submissive resists or fights against it. Hunter/prey is a case in point, as can be intellectual domination, military interrogation, and even some forms of predicament bondage. Where conflict or resistance is a key factor, where resisting and then being overwhelmed is a possibility, you need to recognise that the idea of defeat has now entered the picture. For some submissives, giving their dominant a good run for their money is important and empowering, while for others the need to be actually and fully defeated is a vital component. Likewise, many dominants like or need the thrill of the chase and don't necessarily want an easy victory. Indeed, some just want the chase and aren't interested in victory. Knowing when and if you should actually defeat your partner, or be defeated by them, is something you should discuss with them.

When there is this element of conflict or resistance to your D&s, a good way to ensure that your submissive is not defeated, and that they don't appear to have gotten the better of you (which is a bad look), is to constrain your activities to a time limit. When your military interrogation, for example, reaches the time limit, you stop and congratulate your partner on being one tough cookie and not having given in. They then applaud your clever ways of torturing them.

All of the things I listed earlier are ways of making power and control felt. This can either be the feeling of being controlled by your partner, or the feeling of power over your partner. In an earlier book of mine, *The Control Book*[2], I looked at the mechanics of control in a BDSM-style relationship, at the taking of control, at the use of control, at reinforcing control, at releasing control, and so on. If you want more detail, please look there.

It's important to note that controlling your partner or being controlled by your partner need not have anything to do with the standard array of BDSM implements—such as floggers, whips, leather catsuits, needles, hooks, and so on. Indeed, some people can have control-based relationships with their partner and there's hardly a BDSM implement in sight. It can simply be enough for one partner to be willing to take charge and the other to follow.

This sort of subtle power difference between two people can manifest itself in the bedroom by who prefers to be on top and who prefers to be on the bottom. Other times it can be hinted at by who predominately chooses restaurants, who walks in front, and who asks whom which clothes look best (i.e., seeking approval from their partner).

If you do want or need control to be an important part of the relationship you have with your partner, there are some things you need to do.

---

[2][MASTERS2009]

## 18.2 Determine why

### For dominants

You need to have a clear idea of which of your wants and needs are going to be met by dominating or mastering your partner. These can anything from the prosaic to the rare and unusual:

- You might find that grabbing your partner by the scruff of the neck, tearing off their clothes, and then having your wicked way with them turns you on sexually. Sometimes surprisingly, this can also be exciting and satisfying for a variety of partners.

- You may find it cathartic at the end of the day to simply bend your naked partner over a table, flog them to release your tensions, and then fuck them.

- You might find that it feels exciting and empowering to have your partner trained up so that they act almost as an extension of yourself, being tuned in to your priorities and values, and able to participate in and contribute to your projects almost as if you were doing them yourself.

- You may find it powerful and exciting to see your highly-talented, smart, and attractive partner surrendering themselves willingly to your directions as you make choices for them, give them orders, and set tasks for them.

- You might also find it intense and stimulating to use your personal authority and power to compel your partner's helpless obedience in anything from trivial exercises in micromanagement to complex choreographed scenes of behaviour.

- Dominating your partner might create opportunities for fun and playfulness, such as teasing, tickling, or taunting your partner.

Some submissives and slaves really do blossom when they have a strong and effective dominant or master in their lives. Be cautious about this being a one-way thing. You may get an initial rush out of seeing your partner respond to you, and you may feel motivated to put in a lot of effort to achieve this, but if all you really get out of it is that you see them blossom and then they pack up and leave, then you've received the short end of the stick.

This is all about having a good relationship, not being sucked dry. On the other hand, if having your partner blossom enriches both your lives and creates new and exciting possibilities, go for it.

## For submissives

As a submissive, you also need to have a clear idea of why you want to be dominated by your partner. Some submissives seem to have the idea that being dominated means endless orgasms, and that the good times roll on without them having to do very much at all except make their genitals available. If you can find someone who calls themselves a dominant and who is happy to go along with this, then by all means proceed full steam ahead.

Otherwise, if you want or need control over you by your partner to be a part of your relationship, then you need to work out why. What's in it for you? At this point don't worry about what your partner gets out of it because this is something they need to work out for themselves.

- Are you looking for hotter sex?
- Do you enjoy the feeling of being physically handled by your partner?
- Do you find it empowering to surrender to their personal needs? In other words, is providing personal or intimate service to them—such as serving them food or drinks, attending to their needs at home, or serving them sexually—a strong motivator for you?
- How strongly or strictly do you want them to control you? Do you want them to be strict with you? Lenient? Tolerant? Playful? Turn a blind eye?
- Do you respond strongly to being a servant or by doing menial or simple labour for them such as cleaning duties, gardening, errands, etc.?
- Or do you want to be a co-worker in their lives, contributing to their projects or community causes?
- Are you looking for a partner who will create a framework of rules and standards in which they expect you to operate? In other words, do you want or need your partner to set standards of behaviour and boundaries for you? Do you want them to shape how you behave, how you speak, etc.?

## 18.3   Determine the scope of the control

### For dominants

It can be easy to say that you want complete control, but do you really want to be involved in deciding what size underwear they buy? Or which way they drive to the supermarket? Or which particular salad they have for lunch? Or how many of those little plastic soy sauce fish thingies they use on their sushi?

You need to realistically look at what will be useful and productive for you to control and what will be a burden.

- Are you just interested in a bit of heavy-handling of your submissive one or two evenings per week, perhaps with some oral sex (performed by them, of course), and the rest of the time they make up their own mind about things?

- Do you look forward to sitting them down at your feet each evening, discussing their day with them, and giving them directions for the next day(s)?

- Do you like choosing your partner's clothes for when they go out?

- Do you enjoy having them serve you meals when you're at home?

- Do you enjoy having them serve you in other ways at home—doing the housework, doing the cooking, doing the cleaning, doing the shopping?

- Do you want to keep them naked and available for you sexually when you're both at home?

- Do you want to involve your partner in your projects and have them work alongside you?

This is one of the big parts of being a dominant. You need to have a clear idea of what you want. Your submissive partner is going to respond to your decisiveness and determination. This comes

*Dominance and submission*

from the strength of your feelings and needs. Merely wanting them to do something, like lick or suck your genitals 24 hours per day, is not enough. You have to have the determination and drive to take control and compel their obedience. Otherwise it's not really dominance, and it can descend into mere asking or even begging.

So, make a distinction between what you just would like, and what you are prepared to pursue and take.

## For submissives

Saying that you want your dominant to have complete control may sound good and feel right when you are in the throes of passion in the dungeon, but in real life there are frequently areas where your partner should absolutely not have any influence. At the same time, for D&s to work for you there probably need to be things that definitely do need to be controlled.

- What's off-limits?
    - Finances?
    - Your job, such as being required by your dominant to wear clothes to work which are inappropriate?
    - Your family, children, and other dependents?
    - Your pets?
    - Your insurance policies and retirement planning?
    - The house or property you own?
    - Your car?
    - Your health and medical treatment?

- What do you definitely want them to control?
    - Your pink bits?
    - All the activities which aren't determined to be off-limits?
    - What and when you eat?
    - Who you socialise with?
    - When and how you speak?
    - Your use of alcohol?
    - Your choice of clothes, perfume, and deodorant?
- When do the above apply?
    - Is this just in the dungeon?
    - Just on dungeon nights?
    - Just when you've discussed it and agreed to it?
    - Just outside the dungeon?
    - All the time?

## 18.4  Determine how

For a dominant, having someone available 24/7 to whom all manner of nefarious things can be done, or who may be called upon to bend over backwards to serve you in various ways, is a tantalising and often powerful thought. Similarly, for a submissive, the idea of having a master or dominant who is always ready with a rope or an authoritative word can create deep and powerful sexual or emotional stirrings.

How do you make this happen though?

## For dominants

Dominants and masters need to have an idea about what they're after from their partner. There are many dominants and masters whose goals seem to consist exclusively of getting their partner horny and "giving" them orgasms, perhaps as a leg-opener. This may seem to be the reverse of the way things ought to be done, i.e., with the submissive or slave serving their partner rather than the other way around.

Dominance is about establishing, maintaining, and using authority and power over your partner. Once you have established this authority then the quick fuck, or the cooked dinner, or the help with a personal project become a natural part of that framework.

Authority and power become manifest, they become felt and tangible, when there is a goal or when there is an intensity of purpose behind them. If you have no goal then neither of you will feel anything. If your submissive has agreed to anything you want and the best you can come up with is, "I order you to do what you want!", or "With all the authority vested in me I don't particularly command you to do anything much at all!", then you might just as well not have the power or authority at all.

What you need to do is read through the list of types of D&s earlier in this chapter[3] and see whether any of these seem powerful to you. I deliberately used the word "powerful" here because power is generally what you need to feel for D&s to work. If you instead find the things in the list only arousing, intense, exciting, profound, cleansing, or anything else, then

---

[3] Section 18.1 on page 228.

perhaps D&s isn't what you should be working on. But, if the adjective "powerful" applies to what you feel then maybe D&s is where you should be focusing more or all of your energy.

### For submissives

As a submissive you also need to work out how D&s will work for you. The same list of different types of D&s earlier in this chapter may be a help to you in at least crossing out the things which you are sure aren't going to be suitable for you, and may help you find some things which you're sure will be.

Reflect on things you have experienced—both in BDSM and in vanilla experiences—which seemed to trigger something inside you. Do you find that visits to the doctor where you have to undress or be probed are "interesting"? Is being directed by a burly man in a policeman's uniform a turn on? Is being tortured by your partner powerful just because they like seeing you in that situation? Is being treated as a table or footstool rewarding? In sum, how important is power to you?

## 18.5   Purpose and conviction

### For dominants

I can't stress this enough: when you're the dominant or master in a 24/7 relationship then the things which are going to give you the most mileage are purpose and conviction.

If you think that owning a slave or having a submissive is a really great idea... well, maybe it is. But if this idea comes first, or if all you have is the idea and that's what turns you on then you've probably put the cart before the horse. Acquiring a slave or submissive and then working out what to do with them is not the way to go.

Instead, you need to have a goal, a purpose, or an intention which requires two people, and then you find a submissive or slave who can be a part of making that goal into reality.

Many dominants and masters fall into the trap of looking for a submissive or slave with the hope that they'll then get inspired, or that the needs and wants of their new submissive partner will set them and the new relationship off in some useful direction. Perhaps we should call this submissive-driven dominance because the submissive is the one who ends up determining what happens. For a submissive who likes to top from the bottom, this might be a good thing.

However, there are many submissives and slaves who are going to respond to the strength of purpose of their dominant or master. Indeed, they may need this. Instead of being the ones who are doing the driving, these are the ones who need to be driven, who need to submit or surrender to the strength and power of their partner. In D&s, this strength often comes from the purpose or goals of the dominant.

When you have a dominant who looks for inspiration from his submissive partner, or a master who directs his slave based on his slave's wants, then you can end up in serious conflict when they're matched up against a slave or submissive who needs to surrender to their dominant or master. Neither partner will get anywhere because each will be waiting for inspiration or direction from the other.

There are many different sorts of uses to which you can put your submissive or slave, but the key things are that there's some passion or drive of yours involved, and that they get to feel that you are putting them to good use. Many submissives are delighted to be useful, and while you shouldn't try to just create work for them, recognising opportunities where they can do the things you might ordinarily do yourself can be quite effective for you both.

For example:

- You direct your submissive to assist you in preparing or cleaning the dungeon for the night's activities.
- Send them out to buy you something you need when you are busy with something else.
- Put them in charge of some aspect of running the household such as making the bed, or preparing breakfast each day. You set the standard of work and supervise them, or check up on them at intervals (e.g., weekly).
- Have them assist you in running some personal project such as a web log, BDSM dating website, or newsletter. You should be chief editor, and they would be your assistant editor, researcher, or whatever.
- Have them be your driver when you go places together.
- Of course, sex is a common theme in many people's BDSM and there's no reason why sex can't be a purpose or goal, such as daily oral sex.
- If you really like tying them up, then require your partner to be your bondage bunny.

When you are planning on having a D&s or M/s relationship, before you even start looking for someone to have it with, you need to work out what you are wanting to achieve with them and the relationship. Especially in D&s and M/s relationships, your partner will be needing you to know where the relationship is going, and to have some idea of how to get there. If you don't know these things then it means that either the relationship is going to be a dud or that your submissive/slave partner is going to have to take over to some extent and provide direction... and this is probably a poor outcome for you both.

So, determine your goals, how strongly you feel about them, how long it'll take to achieve them (if they are goals with an end), and the sort of slave or submissive you'll need to get there.

Once you know these things, you need to ask yourself whether what you're looking for is something that is part-time or full-time. If it is strictly related to needs-meeting then maybe a part-time or casual relationship will work. If it's something ongoing or that needs more frequent interactions then maybe a full-time, live-in relationship is in order.

In any case, once you know these things—and not before—you're ready to find a submissive or slave to be your partner in this. They also need to know up front what the goals are and how you're going to achieve them because they need to know whether all this is going to satisfy their own BDSM wants and needs.

## For submissives

While it might seem that purpose and conviction are characteristics of a dominant, a submissive or slave also needs that sense of purpose. If you're hoping that your dominant is going to take charge and make everything wonderful then think again. You too have an important and active part in this.

Your purpose is to surrender to your partner. You need to be physically, psychologically, and emotionally available for this to happen. If your partner grabs you by the scruff of the neck and you don't surrender then they may still get their way, but it may not be that rewarding for you. Whenever you dig your heels in and reject their use of their power—maybe because you feel rotten, have had a fight or a hard day at work, or because you have a headache—then the good times will certainly not roll. Digging your heels in is your choice. I'm not saying here that you should necessarily force yourself to be available, but you do need to recognise that a big part of being a submissive or slave is being ready, willing, and able, even when the time is not right for you. To dominate you, your partner needs to choose the time that is right for them. If they always choose times which are right for you then they're not dominating you or compelling you at all.

## Self-focussed and other-focussed

Another way of considering this is by determining where your focus lies when you're engaging your partner. If you're focussed on the feelings and experience you are having, then you're self-focussed. If you are instead focussing all of your attention on the feelings and reactions of your partner then you are other-focussed.

If you're a dominant or top flogging your partner and the action is making you so horny that you can barely keep your hands off your partner then you're self-focussed. If instead you're paying very close attention to the twitches and moans of your partner as you work them up into a lather of rhapsodic ecstasy then you're focussing on them—you're other-focussed.

From the other side, if when you bring your partner a drink it gives you butterflies or makes you feel all gooey inside then you're self-focussed. If you're paying keen attention to what your partner is doing so that you can anticipate their needs before they even realise them themselves, then you're other-focussed.

There's nothing right or wrong about being self-focussed or other-focussed. Both are powerful and potentially very satisfying and productive for your relationship. One is neither better nor worse than the other. It is important though, that when you're being self-focussed that your partner is being other-focussed or vice versa. Self- and other-focus are complementary. Two people who are only other-focussed are not going to have a lot of joy, and nor are two people who are only self-focussed.

Focus changes frequently. A dominant might easily be self-focussed most of the time during a scene, but switch his focus to his partner from time to time and at the end of the scene to make sure she is OK while still staying dominant the whole time. A submissive also might switch her focus back and forth between herself and her partner as they interact. It is often the case that a particular person will be primarily one or the other—i.e., self-focussed or other-focussed—in their preferred style of play or engagement.

## 18.6 Service

Earlier in this chapter, where I listed different types of D&s[4], I mentioned personal and impersonal service. Service in BDSM can be a complex thing to appreciate. In any relationship between two people, wants and needs must be addressed on both sides for the relationship to meet its goals of contributing to the satisfaction or pleasure of the two people involved. This is a type of exchange where each person both contributes something to the relationship and also takes something out of the relationship. The end result is that both are happier, more satisfied, more complete, or more content than they would be flying solo.

In this sense, both people—be they dominant, submissive, master, or slave—serve. They both make an effort to satisfy the needs of the relationship and consequently their partner.

Any personal or impersonal service in this context is very different to what you might find in a professional service relationship such as with a butler, housemaid, cook, or valet. Firstly, and obviously, there is no salary for a BDSM submissive or slave; they're not there for the money or the job. Secondly, although what they do and how they're treated may have some superficial resemblance at times to a butler or housemaid, the wants and needs behind this service do not. Because we're talking about BDSM, the motivations behind service—either serving or being served—include just about all the motivations I listed in the previous chapter. Minimising self, recreation, hotter sex, catharsis, and so on are all possible through service. Indeed, the sort of profound surrender to service which is sometimes

---
[4] Section 18.1 on page 228.

found in BDSM can be an amazing, beautiful, and humbling thing.

If service is of interest to you, to get the most out of serving or being served, you should know the answers to these basic questions:

- What do you want to get out of service?
- What are you giving in return?

The above questions, by the way, apply equally to dominants, submissives, masters and slaves. Don't expect your own answers to these questions to be either short or simple. BDSM is often about multiple wants and needs rather than just one, and so what you or your partner are looking for may involve any number of motivations, and these motivations may vary depending on circumstances.

For example, consider a master and a slave. What service wants or needs might be involved for the slave? The answer may be a combination of things:

- The master may use the slave as an outlet for the master's own sadistic drives, or as a part of their own catharsis. As they whale into their slave with a heavy flogger or whip they are, at the same time, releasing nervous energy or stress which might have built up inside them. The slave might be using this same flogging in their own way:
    - As a means to achieve their own catharsis,
    - As a way of experiencing deep surrender to the wants or needs of their partner by suffering the pain their master needs to give them, or

- As a way of demonstrating their devotion to their partner/master by their stoic endurance of whatever their master can quite literally throw at them.

- The slave may use service partly as an expression of their devotion to someone they admire and respect, ie., their master. It's important to note that the master earns this devotion both by their previous behaviour—such as by being a respected teacher in the local community, a ready support for others in need, etc.—and by how they behave towards the slave ongoing.

- A significant aspect of being a slave is that of supporting or creating situations in which a master can be a master. For example, an important part of BDSM is the disparity of power. By being more assertive, more authoritative, more passionate, or more intense, the master can express this power difference and help the slave surrender to it. At the same time though, the slave is serving the master by being the tool they use to express this power difference.

If the slave has wants or needs which are best met through some particular BDSM activity—such as cutting, bondage, whipping, etc.—then the master can exploit his skills in these areas so that the slave feels that he is at the master's mercy in regards to having these needs met. Again, in this situation the slave is also serving as a tool which the master uses to feel "masterly".

If the master is far more experienced than the slave in matters relating to BDSM, the master can continuously challenge the slave in areas to do with service, obedience, and surrender. Again, this allows the slave to feel the power and superior skills of the master and allows the master to express himself as a master.

And if the master is more knowledgeable, or even more intelligent than the slave, the master can use this to compel the slave's surrender to the master's greater knowledge and understanding.  It's important here to note that this isn't about diminishing or humiliating the slave and making them feel less important or less valuable.  It is instead about the master using his skills to explore power over the submissive.  Remember that this is also rewarding for the master who should [hopefully] see the slave as a valuable partner and critical component in this mutually-satisfying exercise in power.

## 18.7 Service dominants

While it's common to think of service being provided by a slave or by a submissive, we can also have *service dominants*.  They often make their appearance in scenes involving the submissive or slave having orgasms.  This is something I occasionally find weird because the dominants involved seem to think they are in charge when they're actually being completely guided by their slave's or submissive's own sexual responsiveness.

If you find it exciting that you can play orgasm-denial games with your partner to such an extent that when they finally come they can be heard across half the country, isn't it really your slave's or submissive's sexual abilities which are controlling you? If they needed their clitoris wiggled in one particular way to get them more horny then aren't you compelled to obey the clitoris? There's nothing wrong with actually doing these sorts of shenanigans and, in fact, they can be enormous fun, but I like to call a spade a spade and say where the control really lays. This is because one of my themes here is engagement, and you get the best engagement when you're recognising the reality of what's going on. The point is that what you do with your partner, and what they do with you is rewarding, fully engaging, and satisfying to you both.

No matter how dominant or authoritative a dominant or master is, if the goal is to bring his slave or submissive to orgasm, or to have her cry out in agony from a heavy whipping, or to send him into blissful sub-space, then the master or dominant must provide what the submissive needs so they react that way, i.e., so they come, yell, or whatever.

The dominant or master may be the one who decides that service is to occur, but when it is the slave's or submissive's needs being met, it is the slave or submissive who determines what has to be done.

## 18.8 Discussion

Dominance and submission come in a variety of flavours—such as physical domination, mind fucks, and so on—and some people will have their own preferences. But just as some days I prefer lemon gelato, there are other days when I like strawberry or vanilla or chocolate. The various flavours of dominance and submission each satisfy particular hungers and desires. There is no need to identify yourself with one particular style or flavour of D&s. More you should consider how well each one works for you and your partner in different circumstances.

Even when one particular style of D&s works for you and your partner most of the time, changes to your own circumstances, changes to why you are doing D&s, and even jadedness from over-familiarity can mean that it's time for you to try something new. The lists and discussions in this chapter should give you some ideas.

## 18.9 Questions

- How do you differentiate between artful domination and psychological abuse[5]?

- What can you do casually with someone (e.g., someone you meet at a party) which can be exciting, rewarding, or satisfying in a D&s sense? Something service-related? Training? Physical handling? Sex? Something else?

- Things to do or not do:

    – What things should a dominant do in a D&s relationship?

    – What things should a dominant NOT do in a D&s relationship?

    – What things should a submissive do in a D&s relationship?

    – What things should a submissive NOT do in a D&s relationship?

- Does fear have a role to play in D&s relationships? If so, fear of what? How does it contribute?

---
[5]While I'm just posing this as a question here for you to think about, if you're interested in more of my words on the topic I did devote a whole chapter to abuse in another of my books, *This Curious Human Phenomenon* [MASTERS2008, ch. 21, pp. 209 - 223].

- Can fear be an indicator of an abusive D&s relationship? For the dominant? For the submissive?

- Activities:

    - Which activities, behaviours, and attitudes (either in you or your partner) have helped develop and reinforce the experience of D&s for you? Where does the feeling of power come from?
    - Which activities, behaviours, and attitudes have worked against or diminished the experience of D&s for you?
    - Are there any styles or flavours of D&s which definitely don't work for you or your partner? Why?
    - Are there any styles or flavours of D&s which only work at certain times for you and your partner such as:
        * When you don't have much time?
        * When you're on holidays and completely relaxed?
        * When the day has been busy or stressful and you're unwinding?

# Chapter 19

# The lists

One of the challenges of BDSM can be finding ways to express each of your BDSM feelings, desires, and needs when you're with your partner. While rope bondage and flogging are common, just because they work for some people doesn't mean that they're going to work for you, or that there won't be times when they're not enough and you're needing something else.

In this chapter I have listed some 200+ BDSM activities and sorted them into different categories. These lists can help you in a couple of ways:

- Firstly, they can serve as inspiration and a source of ideas. As you read through these lists with your partner, you may find activities which neither of you have thought of exploring before.

  There may be activities which you prefer, but doing the same thing all the time can sometimes become a bit stale, even when it is exciting, satisfying, and fun most of the time. Having a rich BDSM repertoire can help you make sure that you're ready for the times when you and your partner want something new, something different, something particularly intense, or just a little fun.

- Secondly, as you read through these lists you may start to see patterns in the sorts of things which appeal to you. This might help you understand what you want out of BDSM, different ways in which you might be able to get it, and what this means for the sort of BDSM partner and relationship you need.

  For example, you may discover that impact play is a common factor in all of the activities which push your buttons, or you might find that you like your BDSM to be strictly limited to scenes involving chains, or you might find that anything involving having your partner helpless at your feet is what rocks your boat. Knowing these things helps you target what you do so that you get the most out of it.

Keep in mind that this book is about relationships rather than being a how-to guide of super kinky things to do with your partner. For this reason I haven't attempted to explain how to do any of the activities I list here, but if you are keen to find out more about them, or to try them and don't know how, then have a look at the practical guides on my own web site[1], or check out your local kinky bookstore or Amazon.com[2].

---

[1] http://www.peter-masters.com/
[2] http://www.amazon.com/

Revisiting the lists in this chapter from time to time can also be useful. As you get more experience in BDSM, and as your own skills and abilities develop, some activities which were once uninteresting, unappealing, or even impossible, may become the most exciting things since sliced bread. Changes and growth in your relationship with your partner also change what is possible, exciting, and satisfying. And if and when you move on to a new partner, you will probably need to explore an entirely new spectrum of possibilities.

# 19.1 Yourself

When you read through these lists, think about your own reactions to the things I talk about. You may find some things intriguing, some disgusting, some terrifying, and some just plain boring.

For example, some people find blindfolds scary[3]. Blindfolds can take them well out of their comfort zone and even if they're happy to be dangled upside down while their tits are flogged, they really, really like to be able to see what's going on otherwise they start shaking or even panicking. If you find blindfolds scary, ask yourself why? Is it that seeing helps you stay in control? Is it that you don't trust your partner? Is it that you do trust your partner, but you're afraid to let go because of where it might take you and your relationship?

---

[3] Particularly bottoms tied firmly to an A-frame who discover that their top, who is warming up with a nine-foot single-tail whip, is the one wearing the blindfold!

Before I go too far with this, it's important that you realise that because something doesn't appeal to you or you find it scary, you don't have to do it just to prove something. If you are not attracted to asphyxiation, which is one of the riskier BDSM activities where your partner deliberately prevents you from being able to breath, this may simply indicate that asphyxiation isn't for you.

However, if your goal with your partner is to have a profound and intimate relationship and you realise that you avoid all BDSM activities where you'd have to completely put yourself in their hands—such as those involving mummification, blindfolds, cages, sensory deprivation, suspension bondage, etc.—then trust, or lack of it, is definitely something which is going to shape your BDSM relationship.

On the other hand, if you really enjoy being tied up but don't enjoy having sex at the same time, then possibly you are looking for some sort of emotional or physiological release rather than the actual nookie. Sometimes this might mean that explicitly non-sexual activities—such as cutting, piercing, or no-contact bondage or flogging—will be more up your alley, or whatever body part you play with, than play involving genitals.

The same person doesn't always do the same BDSM activity for the same reason. A bondage top might tie their partner one day because he feels like being creative with the restraint he imposes on his partner. On another day he might tie her up because he feels an urge to claim her and take control of her. These are very different motivations, but the same activity—namely, rope bondage—can be the way both of these different wants and needs get met. This is something to keep in mind because as you look through the activities here, there could be some which might work for you and your partner on some days or in some circumstances, and which won't work on other days or in other circumstances.

If you can't stand being given orders, perhaps you have an issue with being controlled. In this case, you might find yourself more comfortable with physical BDSM activities—such as bondage, flogging, nipple torture, etc.—than with things like humiliation, interrogation, service, and so on. Or if being of service is important to you and it's the orders themselves which don't work for you, maybe you need your partner to be clear about what they like you doing and what they don't like you doing and then you fit into that framework rather than take direct orders.

If you like serving your partner and having tasks to do for them, but only while they are in the room, then perhaps you are less a service submissive and more one who needs to feel directly and actively handled by your partner. Perhaps being on a leash, or being corset-trained, posture-trained, or micromanaged might be things which will work well for you.

If you classify yourself as a dominant but only like doing your BDSM in the form of scenes that have a clearly-defined start and end, perhaps you are more a top than a dominant.

If you are on the dominant side of the equation and you also want a profound BDSM relationship with your partner but limit yourself to light-and-fluffy BDSM games, then perhaps you either don't want or aren't ready to take responsibility... or perhaps you aren't that keen on it all anyway and are taking control just to keep your partner happy.

And if you just enjoy having your submissive partner entertain your nether regions with their tongue, then perhaps you are just a horny guy and aren't really into BDSM at all.

*The lists*

These are all very important reflections because what you're looking to do is have a satisfying and possibly quite profound BDSM-based relationship with your partner. Being utterly honest about what needs and wants drive you is going to go a long way towards helping that happen. If instead you let ego or pride get in the way and find yourself making a supreme effort to convincingly portray Super Dom or Supper Subbie when that isn't really what you are, then you're dooming both you and your partner to something that'll never be fully satisfying.

## 19.2   The lists

When you look through the lists below you will probably find many things which are limits or boundaries for you. Some people argue that you should try everything, but this is—as far as this author is concerned—a pile of doggie doo-doo. Limits are entirely reasonable things to have because the goal is not necessarily to try everything, but is instead to find those things which satisfy your own particular wants and needs. You don't need to be super kinky to be super satisfied and, in fact, if you do feel the need to try absolutely everything then it might be worth asking yourself whether this is just because you want the variety or if there's something else inside you which is preventing you from finding satisfaction.

### Impact play

Impact play is where the top or dominant strikes the bottom or submissive with something. This can be with their bare hand—such as face slapping, breast slapping, or butt spanking.

Using your hand has a sense of immediacy and intimacy, particular when it's an over-the-knee spanking. There is no distance between the top and the bottom. It's up close and it's hand-to-body contact.

Many other types of impact play—such as flogging, whipping, caning, and so on—have a sense of distance associated with them. Any intimate contact must be performed separately to the main action with the whip, flogger, or cane. It's quite common for a top or dominant who is administering a flogging or caning to pause from time to time, step up close, and then touch or caress their partner, either to reassure them or to get feedback about how they are enduring the strokes.

Physical distance can be important for bottoms and submissives who use the regular, repetitive strokes to achieve a particular state of mind such as sub-space. When this is the case, personal contact can be distracting for them and can prevent them from reaching the state of mind they're after. Thus, the fact that their partner must stay out of arm's reach to use the cane, whip, or flogger is quite necessary for them.

Most forms of impact play have emotional or psychological associations which makes some types more suitable than others in particular situations. For example, if you and your partner are looking to explore impact play for a punishment scenario then caning or spanking would be good choices. On the other hand, if you're looking for some sexual overtones then breast slapping or pussy whipping would probably be more suitable.

Face slapping, whether forehand or backhand, can be associated with humiliation or with putting someone in their place, and it's definitely a statement saying, "I am in charge! Now get back to where you belong!"

*The lists*

BDSM RELATIONSHIPS - HOW THEY WORK

When you're looking to explore or express physical domination or control then using heavier implements will be more effective than, say, slapping. Physically striking, kicking, or manhandling your partner can also carry the feeling of physically overwhelming them.

The choice of implement you use will determine the feel of the strokes and the amount of pain involved, if any. Floggers come in a range of weights with varying tail lengths. They can sting or thud, or be heavy or light. Canes often sting and then leave a burning feeling. Whips, when wielded well, can actually cut the skin and this is a very sharp pain.

Finally, heavy or intense impact play can be cathartic both for the person receiving the strokes and for the person administering them.

Some of the more common forms of impact play include:

- **Caning** - striking with a cane, or with a stiff plastic or fibreglass rod, usually on the buttocks or backs of the thighs.
- **Cropping** - striking with a riding crop.
- **Flogging** - striking or applying a multi-tail flogger, often to the upper back or buttocks. Can be sharp or dull pain.
- **Paddling** - striking a wood or leather paddle on the backside.
- **Spanking** - using your hand.
- **Spanking** - using a hairbrush.
- **Strapping** - striking with a leather belt or strap, typically to the buttocks or the backs of the thighs.

- **Whipping** - using a single-tail whip, typically to the upper back.

More specific or particular forms of impact play include:

**Face slapping**. We often regard our face as one of the most private parts of our body. Although we display it for everyone to see, very few people actually get to touch it. Being slapped in the face is something we usually experience as quite invasive. It can be very effective as a control-taking move by a dominant or master. Be careful not to slap near the eyes.

**Back-handed face slapping** is usually harder or stronger than a forehand slap, i.e., slapping with the palm of the hand. With a forehand slap the hand is extended and strikes flat with the soft, inner part of the hand. A backhand slap is usually done with the hand relaxed and the fingers curled. This allows the boney finger joints and nails to strike. A back-handed slap can be symbolic of putting someone in their place and can carry more emotional impact than a forehand slap.

**Pummelling**. Many forms of impact play are specific to certain parts of the body. Some people look for an assault-style of impact play, perhaps as a form of forced subjugation, and this is more of an all-body thing. It includes **kicking**, **punching**, and general **beating**. This can sometimes be combined with **wrestling**.

**Pussy whipping**, **breast slapping**, and **CBT** (cock and balls torture) all focus the impacts on bits of the body which we normally consider to be sexual. This can be highly symbolic and the effects quite powerful. The person doing the striking needs to be careful because these bits of the body are generally quite sensitive and damage easily.

*The lists*

**Corporal punishment** and **over-the-knee spanking** can carry with them a feeling of punishment or of being disciplined. Some people do them in a schoolroom setting or while the person being punished is in school-uniform. There can be an element of **role play** in this which can help create the right mood for this to work.

**Breast slapping** is, as the name suggests, slapping one or both breasts with a hand or with a paddle. This is most effective with someone with ample breasts and can be quite sexual. It can also cause bruising, and it can be quite painful due both to the impact itself and to the consequent violent bouncing of the breasts stretching the skin and pulling against ligaments.

# Role play

Role play is where the two people in the scene act out roles different to their normal everyday ones. This is done for two reasons.

Firstly, the roles almost always involve a difference in authority or power. If we're talking about something like kitten play—where the submissive acts like a playful or mischievous kitten—then we have opportunities for the submissive to act up and then be chastised or punished by her master. Even when no mischievousness or punishment is involved, a kitten's owner is in an inherently more powerful position than the kitten and can choose the kitten's food, require the kitten to eat from a bowl on the floor, direct the kitten's house training, and so on.

When the two roles are human this authority or power difference can come from the age differences being played—especially when the submissive or bottom is playing an infant. This creates opportunities for humiliation such as having your diaper changed with accompanying colourful comments, having food and drink choices taken from you, being dressed or undressed, etc.

A difference in power or authority can come from other roles such as doctor and patient, police officer and prostitute, soldier and commanding officer, etc. Even though the two people involved are normally able to consent, one of the factors of many forms of role play is that consent is removed by the role. For example, in a scenario where a police officer pulls over an inebriated but pretty driver, the police officer is empowered to do things without the consent of the driver such as arrest them and handcuff them.

The second reason why role play can be effective is that it removes the two people in the scene from their normal lives and from their normal standards of behaviour. This allows them to do things, such as hit their partner, which they might not be able to readily consider when being themselves. Role play takes them away from themselves for a brief while so they can be "bad". When the role ends they feel separate from the "bad them" in the scene. This means that role play can be an effective tool to help bypass inhibitions, particularly inhibitions to do with inflicting pain on, being rough with, or disempowering your partner. Military interrogation[4], for example, is a form of role play in which you deliberately create an environment very distinct from normal life where a bottom or submissive can be tortured.

- **Age play** - adopting the role of someone much older or, more commonly, much younger. Even though the person

---

[4]Which I will mention again a little later.

*The lists*

playing the role is above the age of consent, the role is commonly of someone below the age of consent such as a schoolboy or schoolgirl. See below for *infantilism*.

- **Animal play** - adopting the role of an animal. Common animals are cats and kittens, dogs and puppies, and horses and ponies. There may be an element of utility in this with dogs or ponies pulling carts, being dressed up, or being trained to perform tricks.

- **Castration fantasy** - what's on the box, though some people have actually gone so far as to do it for real (in which case it can only be done once... or possibly twice).

- **Doctor and nurse** - role play of an illicit nature between consenting adults in adult roles, though with the doctor being in a position of authority over the nurse.

- **Doctor and patient** - also role play of an illicit nature between consenting adults in adult roles, though this time the doctor has an implicit rather than explicit authority to which the patient can surrender. The patient can sometimes take the dominant or initiating role by attempting, for example, to seduce the doctor. On the other hand, the doctor can also dominate and penetrate the patient with something like a catheter or other probing instrument.

- **Dressing up** - adopting the role of another person, perhaps a king, a dancing girl, a French maid, and so on.

- **Fantasy rape** - is role play where one partner is taken "against their will" and violated. See also *kidnapping* below.

- **Incest play** - adopting the role of the son or, more commonly, daughter of the dominant. Typically the son/daughter role will be in their teens to very early twenties. Might also be called **daddy/daughter play**.

- **Infantilism** - involving diapers, dummies, cots or cribs, prams and strollers, etc.

- **Kidnapping** - role play involving abduction. This can be quite complex and involve abduction from the street, bundling the victim into a car with the aid of masked friends, and so on.

- **Kitten play** - a type of *animal play* often involving a mischievous kitten which might need to be toilet trained or disciplined.

- **Pony play** - play including saddles, small carts, bridles and mouth bits, grooming, dressage, feed bags, etc.

- **Prison scenes** - role play scenes involving prisoners and warders. Might include cages, "watering down" (hosing the prisoner), and possibly escapes. Can also provide a context for *fantasy rape*.

- **Puppy play** - a type of *animal play* which can have a lot in common with *kitten play*.

- **Religious scenes** - organised religions often involve power hierarchies and/or sexual repression. Both of these are ripe for exploitation in role play. Could be a priest taking advantage of a local parishioner who has come to him or her because the parishioner has sinned, or could be something to do with a nun, etc.

## Sensation play

BDSM is often about control, and while pain can be a tool for control it isn't the only physical sensation which we can inflict. Sensation play is about controlling what your partner can see, hear, feel, smell, and even taste. This can include exercises of sensory deprivation where you cover your submissive's eyes so they can't see, cover their ears so they can't hear, and wrap them in soft cloth or cotton wool so they can't feel. This can create a very powerful sense of isolation and powerlessness.

At the other end of sensation play, you can use ice or flame to create feelings of cold and heat, use scented oils and perfumes to stimulate sense of smell, use fingers or feathers to tickle, pin wheels (Wartenberg wheels) to create pricking sensations, and violet wands or T.E.N.S. units to create sparks and electrical currents in your partner's skin.

- **Abrasion** - using sandpaper, rough cloth, or coarse rope to rub against and lightly tear or abrade the skin.

- **Blindfolds** - can also be useful for someone who can't keep their eyes closed on their own, such as when they constantly want to see what's going on.

- **Ear plugs**

- **Fire cupping** - based on traditional medicine and uses round glass cups and fire. Using a small amount of volatile, flammable liquid, a small flame is lit in a cup pressed against the skin. The flame burns briefly and consumes some of the oxygen in the cup. This creates a suction effect which then holds the glass cup in place on the skin.

- **Flame/fire play** - brushing a small amount of volatile, flammable liquid on bare skin and then igniting the vapour to produce a brief flash of flame and warmth.
- **Hood** - to cover the head, ears, eyes, nose, and mouth.
- **Hot oils and spices** - applied to the body or on the genitals. Can produce pleasant or strong scents. Can also create feeling of warmth or even burning.
- **Hot wax** - dripping molten wax from candles onto the skin.
- **Hot wax** - for removing hair. The tearing-off part can hurt.
- **Ice** - can be sensual when rubbed on some parts of the skin in small amounts, such as on nipples. Can also be used to tickle or to torture someone who is tied up and who can't escape.
- **Isolation tanks** - these are closed tanks containing warm water at around body temperature. Most physical sensation is removed due to the skin's lack of contact with clothing or hard surfaces. The closed tank also minimises air movement and muffles any external sounds.
- **Lotions, potions, salves, and creams** - create sensations as they are applied, such as by massage. They may also have their own scents.
- **Padded gloves** - limit the wearer's sensation via their fingers and hands. They can also be tools to disempower the wearer because they can't effectively use their hands any more, even to remove the gloves.
- **Perfumes**

- **Scratching** - using fingernails, pins, or wooden skewers to rub against, scratch, or poke the skin.

- **Scented candles**

- **T.E.N.S. unit** - this is a device used to stimulate muscles through the skin using electricity. It is more fully known as a *Transcutaneous Electrical Nerve Stimulation* device. It creates twitching, buzzing, and pulsing feelings in the muscles.

- **Tickling** - can become torture when extreme and when combined with bondage.

- **Violet wand** - this is a device which passes high-voltage electricity at safe and low currents through a gas discharge tube (which typically glows violet, hence the name). This creates mild to strong electric shocks via sparks which jump from the glass tube to the submissive's or bottom's skin.

- **Wartenberg wheel** - a neurological testing tool consisting of a spiked wheel which is rolled across the skin. The spikes are extremely sharp, and as well as the sensation of tiny pricks these can inspire a certain amount of fear.

# Bondage

Metal bondage refers to restraining someone using metal chains, cuffs, cages, and so on. The point about metal is that it's hard, cold, and immovable. Rope and leather bondage are very different because rope and leather have some flexibility and can be stretched, twisted, bent, or folded. Metal can't. This makes it attractive to people who want that feeling of inflexibility, of knowing that they can't wiggle out of the cuffs you put them in, and of knowing that they stay in the cage until you unlock it.

Here are some other points about bondage:

- There's always a bit of looseness in metal bondage. Metal cuffs are rarely snug and they allow the person wearing them some movement without the cuffs biting into them. Metal cages may even have enough room to allow moving around.

- Because of the flexibility and stretchiness of rope, some submissives see trying to escape from rope bondage as part of the exercise. In fact, for some submissives you can completely spoil the bondage experience for them by placing them in metal bondage instead of rope because metal can feel escape-proof.

- Bondage can be full-body. You can use chain or rope to tie someone head to toe. Mummification is a powerful variant on this. It uses kitchen wrap or similar to bind arms, legs, and torso into a mummy-like package.

- Bondage can also be applied just to part of the body. Hands and feet can be bound or cuffed together. Breasts and cocks can be bound with rope. You can gag your partner with cloth or tape, or you can stick a dildo in their mouth and hold it there with a strap.

Bondage can be used to control your partner. Tightly tying them, particularly when they're naked, can cause them to be helplessly sexually available and unable to resist what you do. Spreader bars, which attach to their ankles or knees and hold them apart, are also good for this. Slings and swings are webs of connected

*The lists*

leather straps which allow you to tie your partner with their legs apart and have them suspended at your waist height so you can do very naughty things to them while comfortably standing over them.

You can tie or cage your partner and then control when they drink, when and how they go to the toilet, and what else they can do. You can suspend them upside down, put them in a straight jacket, and you decide when they get out.

Finally, in part because it uses the human body, bondage can be artistic. In the right hands, rope and chains can be placed to accentuate the shape of different parts of the body, such as the breasts, or to create intricate patterns of ropes, knots, and colours.

- **Arm/leg sleeves** - are long sleeves into which both arms or both legs are placed. The sleeves usually have laces which can be used to pull the arms or legs tightly together. Arm sleeves are often used behind a bottom's back and will hold their arms straight and rigid.

- **Breast bondage** - often used more to squeeze or press breasts than to actually restrain movement. In other words, most other forms of bondage are used to stop a person moving in some way. Breast bondage is more for sensation and is used to press the breasts in place when wrapped tightly over them, or to squeeze them when wrapped around them.

- **Cages/confinement**

- **Chains**

- **Collars** - are leather or padded steel collars typically with a number of anchor points or D-rings which can be used to attach a rope or leash, or as anchor points for a more complex bondage tie.

- **Cuffs** - handcuffs, ankles cuffs, and leg cuffs.

- **Decorative bondage** - is a type of rope bondage where there is a focus on the colour, symmetry, or pattern of the ropes and knots. The actual restraining ability of the tie may be secondary.

- **Finger bondage** - restraining just fingers. For example, spreading out the fingers of one hand and then tying each individual finger to the one chopstick. Also the Chinese finger trap.

- **Gags** - cloth gags, inflatable gags, phallic gags, rubber gags, tape gags, or underwear or stockings stuffed in the mouth.

- **Genital bondage** - typically used for guys, for obvious reasons. Can be used to squeeze or as a way of stopping them running away[5] in the manner of a leash. Some forms of rope bondage, particularly those involving a rope harness (see next item), have a rope passing between the legs of the bottom, in which case an opportunely placed knot can be very effective for both males and females.

- **Harnesses** - these are made of leather or tied with rope and are typically used as anchor points for further bondage. A harness usually doesn't restrict movement, but like on a horse or other animal a harness gives you places to which you can attach other things. A full-body rope

---

[5] As if they would!

harness, for example, is often a prerequisite for suspension bondage because it can give good body support and provide multiple points to which you can tie the ropes or chains to suspend the bottom.

- **Hog tie** - for complete immobilisation. Be careful doing this on someone with flexibility problems.

- **Intricate bondage** - a variant on decorative bondage where the fine detail is important. Finer ropes and cords may be used in intricate bondage.

- **Japanese rope bondage** - more specific type or subset of decorative bondage often using particular ropes, stances or positions, and knots.

- **Manacles and irons** - heavy and onerous to wear around. These really give the feeling of being restrained.

- **Mummification, plastic wrapping** - using plastic kitchen wrap to bind arms, legs, or the whole body. Overheating is a serious risk, as is suffocation if the wrap is too tight over the chest.

- **Nipple bondage** - specifically on nipples only and completely separate to breast bondage. Uses fine cord, shoe laces, string, fishing line, etc.

- **Posture frames and braces** - these hold a submissive's head or back firmly in one position while still allowing them to move around. High heels for someone unfamiliar with wearing them can have a similar effect (such as on some guys).

- **Slings** - these are webs of leather straps, often suspended horizontally or near-horizontally, to which a submissive or bottom can be tied and then explored (i.e., sexually) or flogged.

- **Spreader bars** - rods which attach to cuffs on the ankles or knees which hold the legs apart to expose the genitals.
- **Stocks** - two pieces of hinged wood which, when closed and locked, have three holes. One large one in the middle for the head, and two on either side of this for the wrists or, with someone flexible, the ankles. Stocks can be fixed, such as being on a heavy stand, or "wearable".
- **Straight jacket**
- **Suspension bondage** - tying someone and suspending them above the ground. Can be horizontal suspension bondage (i.e., body horizontal, face up or face down), upside-down bondage, or vertical bondage.
- **Thumb cuffs** - miniature metal, lockable cuffs which fit around the base of the thumbs. Very similar to handcuffs, though obviously much smaller.

## Objectification

Controlling your partner, if that's what turns you on, isn't just ordering them around or forcing them to kiss your feet. An important part of some people's BDSM is the objectification of their partner. This controls the partner's feelings of self-worth or even their feeling of being human. Lending your submissive to another dominant without asking your submissive first is treating them as a possession or as an object. Likewise, requiring your submissive to pose as a statue, or using them as a toilet, is dehumanising them. These are all strong statements that you control your submissive's value.

Sometimes objectification is an attempt to humiliate or dehumanise, but some submissives can find it an exciting and powerful opportunity to serve their partner by being, say, the best candleholder in the room. For some this might sound funny, but it is a difficult goal to achieve as it requires staying motionless for long periods. There are submissives who relish such forms of challenge posed by their partner.

- **Being auctioned** - this is sometimes a BDSM party game where submissives are auctioned off for the evening to the highest-bidding dominant. This can be simply a bit of fun because usually what happens in such a situation is that the submissive gets tied up or flogged in front of others at the party by the winning dominant. It becomes more serious, and more penetrating, when the winning dominant gets to take the submissive for a day or a weekend with few limits.

- **Being given away or loaned** - similar to being auctioned, but in this case the owner dominant gives or loans out his submissive to another dominant. This reinforces the idea that the submissive is property and has few rights.

- **Being inspected** - treating a submissive like a car or horse and inspecting her ("it") as if they were an object whose feelings do not need to be regarded, particularly when the dominant performing the inspection comments or rates different aspects of the submissive to another dominant as he does so. This can be very objectifying.

- **Being used as furniture** - as a chair, table, candleholder, door prop, towel holder, etc.

- **Serving as art** - posing as a statue or modelling.
- **Being used as a toilet or chamber pot**

## Pain play and torture

In BDSM, pain is used to achieve a goal. This goal could be sub-space, catharsis, an assuaging of guilt, increased sexual arousal, or greater intimacy. We can distinguish this from true sadism which, depending on the definition you use, has to do with sexual fantasies, urges, or behaviour; or which has to do with simply getting a thrill out of seeing someone else in pain. There's typically a sense of selfishness in true sadism where the goal is to hurt for one's own pleasure. In BDSM, apart from it often not being about sex at all, when pain is used it is usually more about healing than hurting, and it's about being mutually beneficial and satisfying as opposed to being just selfish.

It's notable that when we're looking at activities where you directly seek out the experience of pain, one of the key ideas is suffering. The pain needs to be suffered or endured to be effective. This is the case with catharsis, for example, or with assuaging guilt. One of the problems with pain though, is that many bottoms and submissives will reach a certain pain level and will then either slip into sub-space or else their body will start releasing endorphins and the pain becomes muted. The pain stops being felt. In particular this can happen when the pain is spread over a large area and becomes overwhelming, such as when the whole of the back is used during flogging.

There's nothing wrong with sub-space, of course; it is often a desirable outcome. But when the goal is to suffer the pain and sub-space occurs instead then the aimed-for goal simply isn't

*The lists*

achieved. You might have been on the road to a fine catharsis, but then your body and mind swerved, and you ended up in subspace or a neurochemical high instead.

The list here is about directly causing pain and suffering. In all cases, for pain or torture to be effective it needs to be and remain focussed. Physical pain needs to focus on one part of the body. Nipples are always excellent because they can be quite sensitive. A woman's clitoris or a man's cock or testicles are also localised enough to be effective. Using a knife and cutting patterns into the skin will be most effective when only a small area is cut rather than if you were to cut designs all over your poor submissive's entire front or back.

Suffering can also come from forced lack of sleep or from forced sexual deprivation (the well-known "blue balls").

- **Biting** - nipples or other loose flesh.
- **CBT** (cock and ball torture) - ball stretching, clamping, piercing, pegging, nailing, or crushing.
- **Clothespegs or clamps** - attached to different or interesting parts of the body such as testicles, nipples, lips (on the face, and lower down on the ladies), the back, earlobes, and so on. Don't leave on too long because they restrict blood flow.
- **Cutting** - using a scalpel or hobby knife to cut into the skin.
- **Nipple clamps** - applying special clamps to one or more nipples. There are a variety of clamps specially designed for this. The amount of squeeze pressure usually can be adjusted.

- **Nipple torture** - inflicting pain on nipples using tight clamps, pins, pinching, or twisting.
- **Nipple weights** - attaching clamps to nipples and then hanging weights from the clamps. Best done while the submissive is tied and leaning forward.
- **Pinching**
- **Scratching** - using sharp fingernails or metal objects with sharp points to scratch sensitive skin. The belly is good for this.
- **Sexual deprivation**
- **Sleep deprivation**
- **Water torture**
- **Whipping** - the tip of a well-cracked whip can be travelling at supersonic speed. It can cut or sting.
- **Zipper** - an exercise involving a line of clothes-pegs clipped to the pinched-up skin of a submissive. Through the line of pegs is threaded a string. When the string is quickly pulled, the clothespegs are pulled off the skin in rapid succession, hence "zipper". Fun for all ages.

## Control and authority

Exploration of power—either using it on your partner or having them use it on you—is a common desire or need for people into BDSM. It can be done through physical activities expressly intended to create a feeling of one person having more control or power than the other such as bondage or pain play. You can also cut straight to the chase and simply take control of your partner during everyday activities regardless of where or when they do them. In some ways this can be more intense than BDSM scenes involving rope or dungeons or floggers. Anything done in a scene is going to be effective only for the duration of the scene. There's a built-in escape clause—when the scene ends, the control ends. Instead, when you take control of everyday activities, there is no sense of when the control is going to end. There is no possibly-reassuring feeling that it's going to end soon and that you can go back to being in full control again. This sense and awareness of control can become a constant all-day part of life. Indeed, for some this is, in fact, quite comforting and reassuring.

Any part of life is fair game for this sort of control. It can be what clothes to wear—which can be as simple as before dressing the submissive or slave must lay out the clothes they think they should wear that day and wait for their master to change or approve their choice; or it can be what food to eat and when—such as being required to wait until master has taken his first bite of food or first sip of drink before the submissive can do the same; or it can be how the submissive cuts or wears their hair, what make-up they wear, how they speak to or address their master, and so on.

Importantly, this is not a one-way exercise. It requires the dominant or master to claim the authority and use it. It isn't sufficient to give an order just once and then expect the submissive to feel happy and content forever more without any further contribution from the dominant. This is unsatisfying for both. Meaningfully having authority involves wielding that authority, making choices, and ensuring compliance.

Some areas of control have to do with self-expression and identity. It's useful to recognise that these can have markedly different effects on both the submissive and dominant when compared to more impersonal control. For example, directing how a submissive should wear their hair or what clothes they wear is going to have more of a personal impact than if you direct them to always walk on your left or to order the salad instead of the burger. The former has to do with identity, while the latter is behaviour.

Anything to do with controlling or restricting someone's opportunities for expressing themselves sexually, or for satisfying themselves sexually, can also strike deeply at their sense of self. This can be particularly powerful.

- **Asphyxiation** - also known as breath play, this involves restricting or controlling the breathing of a submissive. One way this is done is to use a mask similar to a World War II gas mask which has valves to control the air flow. Asphyxiation can also include strangulation. Sometimes asphyxiation is used to intensify orgasm, but is obviously quite dangerous and, at times, deadly.

- **Code of behaviour** - this is when a dominant or master imposes standards or rules of behaviour on their submissive. This can include how they address their partner, how they dress, how they behave in public and in private, and so on.

- **Chastity devices** - these devices are used to control when someone can have sex. For females, these can be like lockable metal panties which prevent anything substantial entering their cunt, while for males they will be lockable enclosures for their cocks.

*The lists*

- **Collar and leash** - this involves leading a submissive around like a pet.

- **Competitions with other submissives** - such as the famous peanut race where a row of naked submissives are each compelled to push a peanut pod or shell (still containing the peanuts) along a course with their nose. Imagine the view from behind! Also, competitions for who can kneel the smoothest, who can remain stationary the longest, etc.

- **Dress code** - setting standards of dress (or undress) for a submissive or slave.

- **Eye contact restrictions** - these are restrictions imposed on a submissive by their dominant, typically that the submissive must keep their eyes lowered to the floor when they are addressing their dominant unless told otherwise.

- **Food or eating control** - restrictions or limits on what a submissive or slave may eat and when. As well as affecting choice of how much to eat, sometimes this is used when a submissive dines with their dominant partner to determine when the submissive may eat or drink (e.g., only after their dominant has begun to eat or drink), or when they must end their meal (e.g., when their dominant lays down his or her cutlery or napkin). A submissive may also be sent to bed without their supper as a punishment.

- **Following orders**

- **Forced feminization** - a male submissive or slave being compelled to wear women's clothing, underwear, or makeup.

- **Forced homosexuality** - for entrenched heterosexual submissives.

- **Forced heterosexuality** - for entrenched homosexual submissives.

- **Forced masturbation** - particularly in front of an audience, this can be quite effective for a timid or self-conscious submissive of either gender.

- **Forced nudity** - in private, or in the presence of others, e.g., at a BDSM party or social event.

- **Forced orgasm** - often with the submissive bound so they can't escape the stimulation.

- **Forced servitude**

- **Hair pulling** - grabbing a submissive by the hair, particularly the hair on the back of their head, can be a powerful way of taking control of their head. This can then be used to manipulate them, or to push them into particular positions such as onto their knees.

- **Having clothing chosen for you** - for a submissive this can involve not being allowed to dress in the morning until their dominant has chosen the clothes they will be wearing. The submissive doesn't get to choose at all, including not choosing their underwear (or lack of it).

- **Having food chosen for you** - it's important to distinguish between controlling the manner in which a submissive or slave eats, as mentioned above in *food or eating control*, and controlling or choosing what they eat or drink. At restaurants, for example, the dominant may choose what the submissive can order or, more generally, may claim overall control over the submissive's diet.

- **Manhandling** - is a very primal expression of dominance and of claiming and asserting control at a very base, animal level. Grabbing someone, pushing them to the ground, manhandling them into a position, physically undressing them, dragging them by the hair, and so on, are all very primal acts.

- **Mouth soaping** - as a punishment this is a classic. It can bring back memories of childhood. It can also be humiliating.

- **Orgasm control** - this usually refers to limiting when and where a submissive can orgasm. It can also extend to control over masturbation.

- **Orgasm denial** - this is a more scene-oriented and immediate form of orgasm control, typically physically arousing a submissive to near the point of orgasm but not letting them get there for an extended period of time. This is usually combined with bondage.

- **Partner swapping** - when combined with sex this can be a powerful statement of authority through the dominant choosing who can have sex or play BDSM-wise with the submissive, and by the dominant allowing themselves additional BDSM or sexual partners. The sex need not be actual sexual intercourse, but anything intimate which is normally associated with sex—such as fondling, masturbation, digital penetration, or oral sex—can be fair game here.

- **Posture training** - this can be a form of bondage, but in the control-and-authority context it has more to do with the dominant directing how the submissive or slave walks, stands, kneels, or serves, with a particular focus on posture and movement.

- **Sexual deprivation** - is different to orgasm control or denial which allow the submissive or slave to become sexually aroused but usually don't allow them to climax until the frustration is painful. Instead, sexual deprivation is not allowing them any sexual stimulation at all. Chastity devices can help with this, but denying them access to porn, not allowing them to see their dominant naked, cold showers, and other strategies also help keep that particular genie in the bottle.

- **Slave name** - giving a slave or submissive a new name different to their civil name can be quite objectifying. In their mind, it can establish a slave or submissive identity separate to their day-to-day life. Because the dominant gives the slave or submissive this name they also own and control the name.

- **Speech restrictions** - limiting when and how a submissive or slave may speak can be an effective form of control. One common technique is to require the submissive or slave to refer to themselves in the third person, e.g., "This girl is very tired, master." Other rules can include that the submissive may not interrupt their dominant or must not speak until spoken to.

- **Standing orders** - these are orders from the dominant which the submissive or slave carries around with them, even when their dominant is not there. For example:

*The lists*

- Always ensuring that the car is filled with gas when they bring it home,
- Making sure the refrigerator is always stocked with the dominant's favourite drinks,
- Ensuring that the beds are always made before 9am on weekdays,
- Making sure that the apartment is always dusted twice per week,
- The submissive must always have their shoes shined, or
- The submissive must always greet the dominant at the door.

* **Wrestling** - like manhandling, wrestling can be a primal expression which signals the dominant's dominance over the submissive (especially, of course, if the dominant wins).

# Worship

Many BDSM activities involve one person—such as the dominant—doing something to create a change in feelings or sensations, or doing something to restrain or impose pain on their partner. These are concrete changes caused by the interaction of the dominant with the submissive. On the other hand, some forms of BDSM play are more symbolic or ritualistic and the pleasure comes less from the actual interaction between the two people involved and more from their internal reaction to it.

Worship is one such form. It is often highly symbolic and can require specific posturing by one or both partners, a specific context, and can even require specific clothing. It can be a ritualistic enactment of a difference in power involving the submissive or slave lowering themselves in some way—from bowing down or kneeling, to kissing or licking the boots of their partner. Boot cleaning, even in the absence of the partner's feet in said boots can also be included here. This lowering or abasing can be in relation to the whole dominant or in relation to some specific part of their body, such as their foot, or especially their cock or cunt.

- **Cock worship** - kneeling or lowering oneself in front of the dominant's cock, or lavishing attention on the dominant's cock.

- **Foot worship** - kneeling and possibly kissing the dominant's foot or shoe.

- **High heel worship** - ditto, but for high heels. High heels often have a special symbolism. Beyond sometimes being fetish objects, they are often perceived as powerful statements of being female and so the worship can be both of the dominant (or their shoes) and of femaleness in general.

- **Kneeling** - lowering and abasing oneself at the feet of your partner. The posture can be important in this because lowering your head completely to the ground, e.g., forehead on the ground, is different to kneeling upright. The latter might be an attentive position of readiness more than worship.

- **Licking boots** - this can involve symbolism in a number of ways. Firstly, boots can be seen as trampling tools. They press down or squash what's beneath them. Secondly, they usually aren't sexual. Instead, they are strictly, and often brutally, utilitarian and everyone is equal before them. Thirdly, licking can be symbolic of taking the boots into oneself, of being penetrated by them physically. Finally, they are the lowest part of the dominant and, as with any form of worship involving feet or shoes, they require lowering one's self to the level of, or below, the lowest part of the dominant.

- **Pussy worship** - like cock worship... well, not exactly like, but the intention and the result can be similar. It is worth comparing pussy and cock worship which are specifically genital-focused, and something like high-heel worship which is gender-focused.

- **Rituals** - such as bowing the head when entering the room, backing out of rooms so as not to turn your back on your dominant, etc.

# Sexual play

Sexual play between two people provides many opportunities for one to do various things to their partner to arouse, stimulate, objectify, make them feel vulnerable, humiliate, or sexually control them in some way. In BDSM, this is often done in combination with other activities such as bondage. Sex itself is often a very intense and powerful experience anyway, and adding in BDSM elements can make it more so. All of the activities listed here lend themselves to being given a BDSM twist, as well as most of them being potentially very sexually arousing in their own right.

- **Anal beads** - a string of beads inserted where the Sun don't shine. Rather than their presence creating interesting feelings as with something like a dildo, it is more the sensations as they are inserted and, specifically, removed which make them interesting.

- **Anal plugs** - these are devices which block up the rear passage. These can range from small to quite large, the latter requiring some training to accommodate. They are usually shaped so that once in they tend to stay in place. The part which remains outside the body is commonly flat, and the person with the anal plug inserted may be able to sit or walk around with it in place.

- **Anal sex**

- **Breast fucking** - cock-between-tits sex. Of course, this requires large-ish breasts. For the owner of the tits, this can also be objectifying.

- **Chastity devices** - making them wait until you get home.

- **Dildos**

- **Double penetration** - two holes for the price of one! For threesomes, or for two people where one has a possibly-vibrating friend.

- **Fisting** - using a suitably lubricated hand to go in orifices not originally intended for it. As well as creating strong feelings of penetration objectively, there can be a lot of surrender associated with the process (which typically takes a fair while to perform to achieve stretching rather than tearing).

- **Fucking machine** - electrically-powered thrusting devices. Never get tired. Always in the mood. Don't roll over and go to sleep before you've climaxed. These are sometimes used as devices of sexual torture by dominants who want to overload their submissive sexually while remaining in control of the action more than if their own genitals were also involved.

- **Gang bang** - one submissive, many dominants. Or, one female, many males. The singleton is the target of the sexual attentions of the others.

- **Genital sex** - one on one, genital-to-genital sex. This is not exciting AT ALL and is just mentioned here for completeness.

- **Group sex** - multiple submissives, multiple dominants. Or, multiple females and multiple males. No holes barred.

- **Hand jobs and masturbation**

- **Oral sex** - there can be some overlap between oral sex and cock or pussy worship. E.g., the "benefit" for the receiver can be straight sexual pleasure while for the giver it can be worship.

- **Outdoor sex**

- **Phone sex**

- **Rimming** - using your tongue to explore and stimulate your partner's anus.

- **Rough sex** - sex involving lots of physical force and manhandling. This can be an expression of dominance and submission, and of asserting control. See also *Manhandling* on page 288).

- **Sex during menstruation** - there can be a lot of symbolism here, particularly to do with femaleness.

- **Strap-on dildo** - a power statement by a female allowing her to sexually dominate a male or female partner. This can also include an aspect of cock worship.

- **Swinging** - also known as partner swapping. Switching back to a discussion on relationships for a moment here, partner swapping and swinging are often more about penetration (often literally) than engagement.

- **Talking dirty**

- **Triple penetration** - three holes in play at once. Usually only women are qualified for this.

- **Vibrating egg** - a type of vibrator which is used internally. There are two ways for women to use this, and one for men. One interesting advantage of these is that they are applied internally and so can be used in public. In D&s terms, a remote-controlled vibrator can allow a dominant to sexually stimulate his submissive silently and from a distance, leaving them to deal with the arousal. Can be a type of sexual torture.

- **Vibrator** - the externally-applied variety. These can get quite powerful, in which case they require habituation (getting used to).

In a lot of cases, the activities and devices mentioned above are suitable for one partner (the dominant) to use on their partner (the submissive) with the intent of expressing control over them, dominating them, and objectifying or humiliating them.

*The lists*

## Medical play

With penetration—namely, the importance of you feeling your partner and their reactions, and of them feeling yours—being a vital part of actually having a relationship, the ability to open yourself up, let down your barriers and defences and allow your partner in is key. While actual sexual intercourse and some types of BDSM play—such as cutting and piercing—do involve physical penetration, medical play can take this to the maximum extent possible by using medical equipment and procedures to physically penetrate the body of a submissive profoundly and intimately.

- **Blood play** is any form of BDSM play where blood is intentionally released. This can apply to heavy impact play, cutting, piercing, and so on. This can be very symbolic.

- **Catheterization** - this is really, seriously, and definitely an activity which should only be practised by people with the appropriate medical training such as doctors and nurses. It involves inserting probes into such places as your urethra. Inserted far enough the person holding the catheter has control over your peeing.

- **Dental or oral play**

- **Dilation** - making little body holes into big body holes using stretching devices. Oral, vaginal, and anal. As well as being symbolic, these can cause strong physical sensations of being penetrated.

- **Douches**

- **Enemas**

- **Examinations** - medical-type examinations can be both objectifying and humiliating, depending on how they're done. Treating a submissive like meat, or by performing a protracted examination in very fine detail (with verbal comments), particularly of some part of their body about which they are sensitive, can be very effective. Don't forget to keep your speculum in the refrigerator before use!

- **Injections** - also inadvisable for people who don't have medical training. However, when injections are done in BDSM they are often a saline (inert) solution which has no medical effect. They can cause pain depending on the needle bore.

- **Lactation** - play involving milking breasts.

- **Speculums** - for probing bodily orifices.

## Service

Service is where a submissive or slave attends to the wants, needs, or orders of their partner. In terms of disparity of power, it is highly representative, with the dominant providing the wants, needs, and orders without which the submissive will have nothing to do and no way to find satisfaction or pleasure.

Service can be personal or impersonal. In BDSM it is most commonly personal because many submissives get a large part of their satisfaction from directly interacting with and pleasing their dominant, i.e., from seeing their dominant being pleased.

Running errands, going out and paying bills, doing shopping, and so forth, are not particularly personal and there isn't much opportunity for the necessary feedback for those submissives who need it.

Different forms of service can have different amounts of personal-ness in them. Sexual service can be highly personal. Attending master's table as a waitress is less so, while being master's chauffeur can be almost completely impersonal.

- **Chores** - housework, washing dishes, cleaning, vacuuming, dusting, washing and hanging out clothes.
- **Home handyman(woman)** - household repairs, changing tap washers, painting, oiling squeaky hinges, carrying heavy objects, replacing light bulbs, minor electrical repairs, minor carpentry, minor car servicing duties (changing oil, charging flat battery, etc.)
- **Errands** - shopping, carrying parcels, delivering messages, paying bills, fetching things.
- **Massage -** sexual or non-sexual.
- **Chauffeur** - driving master or mistress around, cleaning and polishing the car, carrying parcels to and from the car, delivering parcels and letters, taking the car to be serviced.
- **Serving as waiter or waitress** - setting the table, taking food or drink orders, serving food and drinks, waiting attentively during meals, taking away dishes, glasses, and cutlery at the end of each course, serving dessert.
- **Serving as cook** - planning meals ahead of time, preparing or cooking meals.
- **Serving as gardener** - gardening, weeding, mowing the lawn, potting, fertilising, planning and maintaining a vegetable garden, planning and planting seasonal flowers.

- **Serving other dominants** - providing any of the above to other dominants under the direction of your dominant.

## Psychological play

Much of the time in BDSM we use physical activities such as flogging, bondage, service, and so forth, to create changed awareness or sensations. This allows one person to control or direct the experience of the other. This experience is then used internally to achieve some productive outcome, be it a feeling of security, catharsis, orgasm, or whatever. This is a little indirect because while we might inflict a painful flogging, it doesn't guarantee that we'll get the desired outcome such as sub-space, but may just get instead howls of pain and cries of, "You bastard!"

In psychological play, the goal is not so much to create a situation which the submissive or bottom uses to achieve a state of mind, but is instead to go directly towards the desired state of mind or goal via specially chosen activities. This can put the dominant in the driver's seat instead of them being simply the engine as is the case sometimes.

- **Exhibitionism** - being exposed in front of others. This could be by being partly or completely naked, or by having some hidden aspect of the submissive exposed such as wearing a BDSM collar in public or in front of friends who previously didn't know about this BDSM proclivity.

- **Outdoor scenes** - doing BDSM in the outdoors, such as in a secluded or not-so-secluded forest location, in a city early in the morning or late at night, in public under the

*The lists*

cover of darkness, and so on. The fear of being seen or discovered can be quite penetrating.

- **Golden showers** - being pissed on.
- **Humiliation** - public and private, verbal humiliation, insults. The exhibitionism mentioned above can be a source of humiliation.
- **Hypnosis**
- **Interrogation** or, especially, military interrogation. This can be a time when the submissive is actively supposed to resist either their dominant, or the pain or torture their dominant is inflicting on them. For some submissives this can be about being taken to and beyond their breaking point, while for others it can specifically be about resisting and not being broken.
- **Wearing lingerie** - particularly if a butch or a guy.
- **Public exposure**
- **Standing in the corner** - punishment after being bad.
- **Teasing and mocking** - a variety of humiliation.

# Marking

Usually, the way we look and the way we present ourselves to others is something which we use to express ourselves. It is one of the ways we say, this is who I am. When someone else, a dominant or master, takes control of an aspect of this it can be a powerful surrendering of oneself. You can find very deep surrender in the situation where someone else has the power or authority to decide when or if you get a tattoo, how to have your hair cut, what clothes you wear, and any body markings you'll have through scarification, piercing, cutting, or even branding. And when the body changes or marks are permanent—such as with a tattoo or a brand—this is a powerful statement about your commitment to the relationship or the lifestyle.

Having said that, it's clear that some forms of body marking are temporary and can be effective in scenes between two people. For example, wearing make-up can be very short-term and is a useful tool in forced feminization. Longer-term body changes can include haircuts or shaving (or not shaving), and can include dye or henna tattoos—which may last for days or weeks. Some forms of cutting can also leave scars which will heal completely over time, though this can be a bit unpredictable and will vary from person to person.

Piercing the flesh with a needle and leaving jewellery threaded through the holes is a permanent form of marking which can later be removed. Common areas for this include the ears, lips, eyebrows, tongue, nipples, navel, cock, clitoris, and labia.

- **Body decoration**
- **Branding** - this can be hot branding, typically with a red-hot wire, or cold branding with a metal template chilled with dry ice or similar. This is permanent marking. It is also quite dangerous to perform and requires a lot of skill to avoid burns which may need hospital treatment.
- **Haircut**
- **Makeup**
- **Piercing**

- **Scarification** - deliberately creating scars, often in particular shapes or designs, either through burning or through cutting, and then ensuring the wounds won't invisibly heal, such as by using tape to hold them open.
- **Shaving**, particularly the pubic area.
- **Tattooing** with ink (permanent).
- **Tattoos** with henna (temporary).

# Fetishes

Strictly speaking, fetishes aren't BDSM because they're typically done solo. In any case, this book is about relationships and someone who gets turned on by the stockings or shoes that another person is wearing isn't engaged in any sort of relationship with that person. They're being turned on by the stockings, shoes, or whatever.

However, BDSM is often about power or the use of power, and fetishes can be quite powerful. Because of this, fetishes can find a place in a BDSM relationship as a tool which a dominant can use to control their fetish-susceptible partner. For example, a woman dominant whose male partner has a stocking fetish can wear stockings and let her partner touch them as a reward for good behaviour, or not wear them as a punishment for bad behaviour. Likewise, a boot fetishist can be rewarded with a fine pair of their master's or mistress' boots to polish, or can be punished by being forced to leave them uncleaned.

**Material - cloth, texture, smell**

- **Lace**

- **Latex**
- **Leather**
- **Nylon**
- **PVC**
- **Rubber**
- **Satin**
- **Silk**
- **Spandex**

**Clothing**

- **Corsets**
- **Panties**
- **Pantyhose**
- **Underwear** - clean or soiled
- **Boots**
- **High heels**
- **Cross dressing** - wearing clothing typical of the opposite sex

**Parts of the body**

- **Feet**
- **Elbows**
- **Hair**

**Miscellaneous**

- **Lactation**
- **Pregnancy**
- **Small people** - dwarves and midgets
- **Uniforms** - can be associated with power, such as nurse, doctor, or police officer

## 19.3 Conclusion

When you're considering any BDSM activity, and especially when you're looking through the lists above, try to think about each one from the following perspectives:

- Engagement. Is this something which will be better, more exciting, or more satisfactory when your partner is actively involved? Maybe. Contrariwise, many people like to lose themselves in their BDSM experiences and trying to engage them too much (or even at all) can be distracting.

- Penetration. How penetrating does it need to be? Too much pain, too many sensations, or even too many ropes can be overwhelming at times. Sometimes being subtle is the right approach. On the other hand, for someone looking for a lot of pain, hitting them with a small flogger can just be annoying.

- Effect on your relationship. Is this activity something which is going to help build your relationship? Is it going to help you and your partner be more intimate together? Is it going to build trust? Is it an act of sharing?

- Which wants or needs do these activities satisfy? They don't need to be profound needs such as surrender, but can be something you do just for fun, a bit of variety, or as foreplay for something else (which need not be sex). However, if the needs or wants being addressed are important, such as surrender or catharsis, then treating them lightly or as just a bit of fun can mean they don't get met at all, or that you or your partner will put up defensive barriers, and that can have a major impact on the longevity of your relationship.

# Chapter 20

# Maintaining balance

Before continuing, I think it's worth reflecting for a moment on balance.

The names we give to the different roles in BDSM—such as top and bottom, submissive and dominant, and master and slave—suggest that these roles are complementary. The idea is that one completes the other, that each gets their wants and needs met through their relationship with their partner. It's implicit that when they get together that they each do their thing, and when they're done all is right with the world and everyone's happy. For example, when a dominant flogs his submissive he may be satisfying his need to control and arouse his partner both through his choice of implements and through the pace and strength of the strokes he applies. Simultaneously, his submissive is surrendering and opening themselves up to the handling, the control, and the manipulation of their sexual feelings by their partner. These are entirely different needs being met, but the fact that they can be satisfied in one particular scene or activity makes them complementary. Each partner gets exactly what they want and need, and they get it in the right amount.

Well... that's the theory.

This balance isn't always the case. Sometimes the needs of a top, dominant, or master won't be in proportion to those of their submissive, bottom, or slave. When one is fully satisfied, the other may still be "hungry". This lack of balance may be a matter of degree, such as a top being satisfied after inflicting a certain amount of pain while their bottom is still wanting more pain than they have so far received.

Sometimes this lack of balance has nothing to do with degree. What one person wants or needs may have no complement for their partner. For example, for some submissives the tight embrace of the rope in bondage can give them a powerful physiological release. This has nothing to do with their partner. All these submissives need is that they get tightly tied up and then are left quietly to "soak" for fifteen minutes or so. They can't do this on their own for practical and safety reasons and so a trusted top or dominant needs to do it for them. The top then sits back, has a coffee for 15 minutes while keeping an eye on the submissive, and then comes back and unties them.

Another activity which may have no complement is cutting. Some bottoms and submissives simply need the sharp pain from cutting without any form of engagement with their partner. Like the bondage example above, this tends to be a very one-way activity, with the person being bound or cut getting their needs met while their partner simply serves as a source of knots or as a wielder of the blade.

Because of this lack of balance, it can be that one of you sometimes doesn't get out of a scene what you put into it. In a longer-term relationship this can be OK because even though you might not get your own needs met in every single scene, over time you do as you each take turns to focus on what the other needs.

Lack of balance is neither a good thing nor a bad thing. It simply is. All relationships will have times when one person's wants or needs are stronger or harder to satisfy than their partner's. What is important is that you and your partner talk openly about these times and come up with strategies to handle them. This need not be or become a big issue, but it is a useful topic for discussion with your partner. Ask them how they feel about what you do together and whether their needs are getting met as part of the natural exchange of effort and energy which occurs between you both. If not, or if you feel your needs aren't getting properly met, talk about it and see what can be done.

*Maintaining balance*

## Chapter 21

# Online BDSM

From the earliest days of computer networks, even before The Internet, BDSM enthusiasts have used their computers to communicate with each other. Early bulletin board systems were accessed using dial-up modems which allowed people within the same geographical area, such as the same town or city, to post notices or announcements, or to contribute to discussions with like-minded BDSM folk.

As the reach of computer networks became regional, then national, and then international, the software and communication protocols expanded to allow this same sharing at national and international levels and distances.

In the 60s, 70s, and 80s, BDSM was very much a taboo subject and so the anonymity of both distance and screen nicknames allowed BDSM folk far and near to comfortably and safely get together electronically in huge numbers.

## BDSM Relationships - How They Work

Early communications were in a form similar to email which could take up to a day or longer to arrive. Interactive chat soon followed which allowed people to type messages on their computer, and these would then show up on the screens of other enthusiasts within seconds of the ENTER key being pressed. This has led to "chat rooms" and on-line communities where people meet and move from one discussion to another entirely via their computer. In more recent times, this has been augmented by the ability to see and speak with others via the Internet using webcams and microphones.

Because of these new opportunities for people to interact via their computer, and because BDSM is a type of interaction between people, it should not be surprising that some people have BDSM relationships or engage in BDSM activities entirely on-line, frequently without ever having met their partner in person.

There are advantages and disadvantages to these sorts of relationships.

For people who are living in isolated areas, such contacts allow them to stay in touch with what's happening in the rest of the world, to have chats and discussions with other like-minded folk, and even to express themselves as a submissive or dominant and for their long-distance correspondent to openly respond to this.

With the addition of a little imagination it's possible to have deeper BDSM engagements. Where the communication is text-based, this sort of interaction frequently takes the form of each person describing how they are responding, or how they imagine themselves to be responding, to what their partner is writing. At the same time, the partner is also reacting in turn, and they write that back.

For people who have little or no experience with BDSM, or for those lacking the opportunities to find like-minded others in real-life, on-line BDSM can provide a safe, exciting, and anonymous environment in which to begin experimenting with BDSM.

A big disadvantage, of course, is that you're on your own when all this is happening. Real human touch is missing. Also, because the person at the other end of the computer connection is often only words on a screen, some fairly heavy imagining might be needed to create the whole picture—such as what they look like, what they're wearing, how they sound, how they move, what they say, etc. This can be difficult, both to achieve in the first place and to maintain in the longer term.

Online BDSM is also usually anonymous so you won't really have a chance to get an intimate awareness of the other person. And because it's anonymous they may disappear at any time and you won't have any idea of where they went.

## 21.1 Making it work

The more you have to imagine, the less satisfying it is than interacting with someone actually in front of you. The solution is to communicate a lot. Don't just send messages back and forth though. Make an effort to fill in any gaps so that less imagination is required by your partner. Likewise, ask them questions so you need less imagination to "see" them. Perhaps send pictures, not just of you, but of the room you're in, the computer you're using, the rest of the house or apartment, the area near you, and even the clothes you wear. Discuss the things that are going on in your life, talk about your friends.

Consider meeting up. This can be risky, of course, but if they're somewhere you can visit—even if just for a day—it might be worthwhile. The risk is that when you meet there won't be any magic. Or they may have been lying to you and instead of looking like Mr or Miss International they look more like Mr or Miss Short-'n-Ugly.

Ultimately, if all you and your Internet partner have together is the ability to imagine almost anything then even you are irrelevant to your partner because they can easily imagine a new partner. To engage each other—your real selves—and to be significant to each other there must be an effort on each of your parts to extend the relationship so that more than just what happens on the computer is involved.

So, talk and share. Otherwise, what you have is likely to be unsatisfying in the long-term.

# Chapter 22

# Here's the thing

One of the things I've noticed about many BDSM folk is that when they start talking about BDSM they'll conclude by saying something like, "Every BDSM relationship is different," or "If you take a hundred BDSM couples, you'll have a hundred different relationships." Rather than stating these simply as facts—which they are, by the way—they're using them as excuses so they don't have to look any further, effectively saying that if all these relationships are different then there's no point in trying to understand them, categorise them, or find things they have in common because they're all *different*.

This is another pile of doggie doo-doo. It may well be that understanding BDSM relationships is hard, or challenging, or maybe just not particularly obvious, but as we've seen in this book—particularly in chapter 17, *Motivations*, and in chapter 19, *The lists*—when we detach ourselves and step back enough so we can see what's actually going on, then *what it is that we do* starts to come into focus as part of a single big picture rather than as fragments of hundreds of little ones.

It's tempting to say that the point of this book is to demystify BDSM and BDSM relationships, but that's not really it. I like the mystery and I like the surprise in BDSM. I certainly don't want either of these to disappear and then find in their place only clinical analysis and mechanical execution of scenes.

What I'm trying to do here is illuminate the journey but still leave the destinations and waypoints to be just as surprising or mysterious when you get to each one. To use an analogy, if you can clearly see the road then it's easier to choose a good path at each fork than it is in the gloom. When you know the choices you're making are founded on sure knowledge then your anticipation for your next destination builds. If instead you're fumbling in the dark, then disillusionment can easily set in because you don't know if you're making forward progress or whether you're just going in circles.

Understanding the BDSM relationships we have with our partners and with other BDSM folk has to do with understanding the philosophy and psychology of BDSM, and with seeing how what we do fits in with this philosophy and psychology. What we're doing in this second book of this series is taking the theory of book one and seeing how it applies in practice. By couching the practical aspects in good understanding and theory we can dramatically increase the effectiveness of what we do and make it targeted to what we want to achieve.

In a sense, combining the theory and the practical let's us make BDSM less of a hit-and-miss affair[1] and means that we reach

---
[1] Pun intended, of course!

*Here's the thing*

those surprising and mysterious destinations by design instead of by accident.

# Book Three

# BDSM Relationships
# Pitfalls and Obstacles

# Chapter 23

# Introduction

Having a successful BDSM relationship isn't just about the times when things go right. Just as in any relationship, there are times when things don't go right. The range of challenges which can confront you as you wrangle your relationship from one critical point to the next is extensive. These can be the same sorts of issues which beset any relationship such as communications breakdowns or external stress. Or they can be problems and challenges which are unique to BDSM, or they can simply be vanilla issues with a BDSM twist.

One difficulty in all of this is that in BDSM we often don't have any role models. Our wider society perhaps tolerates BDSM, but it certainly doesn't promote it. In movies, on TV, and in the press we might get to see both the light and dark sides of vanilla relationships, but the weekly TV dramas with perennially happy endings and the midday chat shows with dysfunctional couples don't give us BDSM folk any hints at all. We simply don't see any constructive attempts to portray BDSM. Chick flicks don't deal with romance in rope, home-renovation reality shows never include dungeon makeovers, men's magazines don't show you how to turbo-charge your BDSM toy-bag, and dating advice columns don't talk about the best places to go to pick up a partner who likes pain play.

A consequence of this is that we can first enter into BDSM more ignorant than a pimply-faced youth on their first date. What happens on a first BDSM date? Do you kiss? What is the BDSM equivalent of foreplay? Who provides the rope? What do you say?

In earlier books of this series, I explored the nature of BDSM itself, why we do BDSM, and what we get out of having a BDSM-rich relationship with a partner. I also looked at what goes into a BDSM relationship and at what gives it its shape. In this book, I want to begin looking at what can go awry when you are trying to establish or maintain a BDSM relationship with someone.

Because of the lack of role models, many people try to press-gang vanilla role models into BDSM service. This is often like fitting a round peg into a square hole and is, at best, a poor fit. Because there often aren't friends, family, people in the local community, movie characters, TV stars, talk-show hosts, or newspaper columnists who live the dream and show us what BDSM can be like, many people try to take something or someone they do know from their vanilla experience, dress them up in BDSM leathers, and then use them as their model.

The problem with this is that the same expectations which we might have in a vanilla relationships can very rarely be applied to a BDSM relationship. That's not to say that we shouldn't find our BDSM relationships as happy and rewarding as any

## BDSM Relationships - Pitfalls and Obstacles

vanilla relationship might be, but the road to getting there is often entirely different. If you try to use the same road—the same behaviours and attitudes—in a BDSM relationship as you do in a vanilla one, then you risk creating just a vanilla relationship in BDSM clothing, and that's not likely to do anyone much good.

In book one I listed three characteristics, or pillars, which define BDSM and BDSM relationships. In short they are:

1. Disparity or unequalness of power. This is where what we do with our partner is driven in its effectiveness by one of us being in a stronger or more motivated position than the other,

2. Penetration. This is not sexual penetration, but instead is designing what we do so that it deeply affects our partner, regardless of whether sex is involved or not, and

3. Engagement. This is where what we do to and with our partner is based on what we know about them intimately and personally so that our actions are targeted at them specifically. This is as opposed to just doing things which most people like hoping that our partner will like them also.

Pitfalls and obstacles to BDSM relationships have to do with one or more of these three things breaking down. While such a breakdown doesn't necessarily mean that the two people in the relationship go their separate ways, it does mean that the nature of the relationship changes. Instead of being a BDSM relationship, it might become a vanilla relationship. Of course, if BDSM was the main "glue" holding the two people together in the first place, it may mean that they actually do go their separate ways.

## BDSM Relationships - Pitfalls and Obstacles

Because BDSM relationships are about disparity of power, penetration, and engagement, this book is about what can prevent these pillars developing, or what can cause them to crumble.

Communication, of course, will be a major factor, as will trust. I'll get to these in upcoming chapters. Ignorance and fear can also play a surprisingly important role in BDSM relationships falling over. The intensity of feelings which BDSM can engender can be quite scary. It can be easy to unconsciously avoid this fear by enacting certain behaviours which limit engagement and penetration. Later I'll be looking at examples of both common and unconscious behaviours which do precisely that.

For now, and before moving on to the next chapter, I'd like to ask you to reflect on the nature of your own BDSM relationships and experiences.

1. Is what you do with your partner deeply and profoundly satisfying?

2. Do you feel completely satisfied at the end of the scenes you do together?

3. Do your scenes end with you feeling as if something were missing, but you don't know what?

4. In your wider relationship, is your partner doing what seem to be all the right things and yet you don't feel that all your needs are being met?

# Chapter 24

# The False Self

I'd like to now tie one of the three characteristics of a BDSM relationship, engagement (which I mentioned in the last chapter), to something I wrote about in an earlier book, namely the False Self[1].

The False Self is a persona which we create and which we present to the world to help us be accepted. For example, you may really enjoy BDSM, find it deeply satisfying, and outside of the office it may be one of the most important things you do, but at work or in the office this side of you stays hidden. How you behave at the office is conventional and conservative. Often it needs to be this way because showing up in your best leathers may not be the right way to get a promotion or keep your job. This persona you present at the office is not your real self. Or,

---

[1][MASTERS2008, pp. 93 - 96]

at most, it's just a subset of your real self with many bits hidden away.

A consequence of this is that you generally can't get your BDSM wants and needs met at the office in the same way you can when you are in your leathers or when you're tied up and being flogged. Because the real you can't be there in all your BDSM glory at the office, your real BDSM needs can't be met there. In terms of BDSM wants and needs this is, of course, unsatisfying, and this same sort of unsatisfying situation exists any time the BDSM part of us must be hidden away, such as when we're with vanilla friends, with family, with other parents we meet at preschool, in parliament, and so on.

Just because your BDSM side is not on display doesn't mean it's not there, and it doesn't mean that it's not there in other people as well. But because where you are compels you to suppress or hide your BDSM interests, it means that those around you can't engage that aspect of you, even if they were similarly inclined. The self you present in these circumstances isn't the real you. It is a false you which you display to suit the situation and to lubricate your interactions with people. When wearing your leathers or wearing nothing more than a rope harness might introduce friction with those around you, a more socially acceptable (and partly false) image can remove that friction.

Compare this to a situation where, for example, two friends—one dominant, the other submissive—are out somewhere together. Even if they don't have an intimate relationship or don't usually play together, they can still recognise their BDSM natures and engage each other in ways that are much more satisfying than if they were compelled to wear vanilla personas.

Sometimes society, ego, and other pressures can push us to create a persona which isn't just a subset of our real self, but is instead part us and part invention. Young vanilla guys, for example, might puff themselves up physically or tell exaggerated stories about their adventures to attract the ladies. The same thing can happen to someone in BDSM if they're competing for the attention of a submissive or a dominant. They might try to present their best side or, if that doesn't work, telling a little white lie or two about their experience might get them the attention they desire. Their slightly-elaborated presentations might get them the acceptance that they're looking for where their more actual and ordinary selves may not.

More extreme are the people who don't just try to convince the world that they're a little bit shinier or a little bit better than they are, but they instead try to convince themselves that they are as well. In their BDSM world, they might convince themselves that they like more pain than they do, or that flogging is more exciting for them than it really is, or that they love tying or being tied up more than they actually do. They might convince themselves that having their partner crawling at their feet is the right way for them to go when, in reality, they would be much better off the other way around. The motivations to do this creative self-deception can come from all sorts of sources. For example, the misplaced dominant I just mentioned might have been brought up in a family where he or she was exhorted to step out into the world and take charge of his or her life. It might simply not enter their mind that being submissive would be better for them.

Regardless of how such a false self comes into existence, when it's there it has a very big impact on engagement. What your partner does with you, how they behave and how they react, is going to be based on what they think you are and what they think you need. If they have the wrong idea then everything they do is going to be based on this wrong idea and will never completely hit the mark.

*The False Self*

Likewise, if you're not being totally honest with yourself then you could easily be looking for the wrong thing for yourself. Our non-dominant from two paragraphs back is an ideal example of this. Convinced that they are (or should be) a great dominant and have submissives aplenty crawling at their feet, he or she may be constantly setting themselves up for relationships which never work out because they should be the one on the floor, not their partner.

All of what I am talking about here has to do with engagement which doesn't quite connect. It leads to dissatisfaction, sometimes niggling dissatisfaction like sand in your shoes, and sometimes to profound dissatisfaction of the "What the hell am I doing here?" type. Engagement is only going to work when you and your partner are engaging your real selves—not just at a superficial level, but deep down. The most technically excellent flogging is not going to be completely satisfying if it's not aimed at the right person for it. Dominating your partner and putting them in their place means you have to know exactly the right place to put them. If you don't know the real them, then you don't know their real place. And when you want to stand over your partner it has to really be you that's standing over them, not just someone wearing your body.

In sum, this engagement problem can occur a few different ways:

- We can have the wrong idea about ourselves,
- Our partner can have the wrong idea about us,
- We can have the wrong idea about our partner,
- Our partner can have the wrong idea about themselves, or
- Any combination of the above.

## BDSM Relationships - Pitfalls and Obstacles

A lot of the time this can come from not knowing ourselves, and then from communicating our uncertainties or wrong ideas to our partners.

It can also come from wishful thinking, such as excessively hoping that this vision of BDSM delight before us actually is a good fit for what we need. When we don't know this for sure and are filling in the gaps in our knowledge about this person with our own imagination, then what we end up engaging is going to be partly our own imagination instead of the real person, and this will certainly not be satisfying for them.

Regardless of where the wrong ideas come from, when you are actually in a BDSM relationship with someone, engaging them and interacting with the real them is vital to satisfaction and to the success of the relationship. Without this reality, what you do and share with them will not be completely satisfying. All your efforts and all their efforts will be focussed on the wrong things.

There's a key difference here between vanilla relationships and BDSM relationships. As I noted in book one, BDSM relationships are more about doing *to* your partner while vanilla relationships can be more about doing *with*. In vanilla relationships there is often much less need for engagement. If you go to the movies with your vanilla partner, or to a fine restaurant, or if you go para-sailing together, there isn't that same need to engage as there is in a dungeon. In vanilla, it can be enough that you both enjoy the activities you are sharing together. In BDSM—at least to have an actual relationship with your BDSM partner—you must be doing to, not just with. And to do to, you need to know your partner, what triggers them, how they respond, and so on.

*The False Self*

## Chapter 25

# Trust

Trust has a number of aspects, but in terms of relationships the main thing which trust can effect is engagement.

Trust is sometimes superficially thought of as simply doing what you say you'll do, but it's not just about showing up on time for appointments or respecting your partner's use of their safeword. It's more about consistency and predictability. Your BDSM play partner can still have the deepest respect and trust for you even though you show up 15 minutes late for every single appointment, quite possibly because you are consistent.

This sort of trust is about you and your partner knowing how you each respond in a range of situations (and not just the ones where things go smoothly). When the going gets tough and your partner heads out the door, you aren't going to be able to trust that they'll be there for you during the hard times. That means that you won't expose yourself as much to them, you won't do anything particularly challenging with them, and that you'll keep your own barriers up more. The chance of them actually engaging all of the real you drops accordingly.

On the other hand, when they are reliable and when they do make an effort to do their best for both you and the relationship when things are difficult, shocking, or just plain hard, then you open yourself up more and there's increasingly better engagement.

Even in the face of good intentions and a commitment to do the best they can, trust can be hard to come by if they're inconsistent or unpredictable. If their priorities constantly change—perhaps due to work—or when the decisions they make affecting the relationship and you are constantly being influenced by external factors, you begin to perceive them as inconsistent and you can't trust them as much as you might otherwise.

Of course, when I'm talking about your partner I am also talking about you. For your partner to be able to trust you, to open themselves up, and to allow you to see the real them, you need to be consistent. When there are external factors—such as work or family—which conflict with your ability to commit and to be consistent—then your partner is going to limit their trust in you.

## 25.1 False self

Following on from my earlier discussion of false selves and their effect on engagement, we need to add trust into the mix because it's one of the things which determines both how much of our true selves we show to our partners and what sort of false self we might construct in their regard.

That last bit of the last paragraph is quite important. When we don't trust someone and we still want to be with them then we *may* create a false self which we present to them. For example, a dominant who finds mentally dominating a partner to be quite profound and intense may end up hiding this aspect of himself if he is with a submissive partner who is more into physical domination. He may find when he tries to mentally dominate her that she doesn't respond, doesn't even recognise what's happening, and may even make light of it. This might be painful for him, humiliating (in a bad way), or even embarrassing. In future, he might hide this part of himself either in similar situations or with similar submissives and this means that he has actually created a false self, one which he can display to these people, which is safe for him. In other words, this false self doesn't have an interest in mental domination, even though his real self does, and this false self is a way of protecting himself in situations where his passion for mental domination is not going to be appreciated.

There are two aspects to the sort of trust which I'm talking about here:

1. How much we trust our partner, and

2. How much we trust ourselves.

When we don't fully trust our partner, when we have doubts about whether they will accept us in all our kinky glory, this is when a false self starts to creep into existence. Instead of showing them our real selves, we show them an edited excerpt, with some bits of ourselves hidden away, and maybe with some extra bits which we don't really think or feel but which we hope will go down well with our partner.

Whether we don't trust our partner because of something they've done or haven't done, whether we don't trust them because of how previous partners have behaved, or whether we're simply afraid to trust doesn't matter. When they don't see the real us, they can't engage the real us.

The level of trust we require can be very deep. When we meet someone in vanilla-land who we really like, even talking about an occasional spanking risks potential rejection by them. If this person is someone we meet at a BDSM party, telling them we like spanking is not going to be a problem, but telling them that we like being dangled from meat-hooks by our nipples might be. And even if they are into what we might call a heavier side of BDSM, imagine that you find it immensely satisfying to have carrots which are hand-carved into the shape of religious icons inserted into your rectum, or that the most exciting bondage scenes for you are when your bottom is made up like Chucky from Child's Play and where you dangle them upside down and torture them with badly-played violin solos. How much trust is needed to let these cats out of the bag?

The trust we're talking about here is trusting that we will be accepted, that our partner won't suddenly become our ex-partner and run off into the distance screaming hysterically, and that they won't think less of us.

If we don't trust ourselves we can be saying we don't trust that what we are is sufficient or adequate to attract or keep our partner. It may well be that with a few tweaks to our behaviour or to our looks our partner will be hooked, but what is the price of this? If we need to behave differently than how we really feel because of our own doubts about ourselves then we are beginning to architect a false self to present to our partner and to the world, and as we've already discussed this leads to unsatisfying BDSM.

Again, it comes down to acceptance, but this time it is acceptance of ourselves. If posterially-inserted, hand-crafted carrots is the way you need to go and you convince yourself that it's just too kinky (or plain weird), you aren't accepting yourself. Settling for some easy rope play, a bit of slapping around, and then some basic horizontal hula is OK sometimes, but if you find yourself getting hot under the collar passing a grocery store and you don't do anything about it then you are denying both you and your partner some deep and possibly quite rewarding experiences.

## 25.2 Superficiality

One type of behaviour which is sure to trigger trust and false self problems is being superficial. This applies from both sides of a relationship.

As we've seen throughout this series of books, there are often powerful, intimate, and sometimes hidden motivations involved in our desires or needs for BDSM. While it may be about a bit of fun, relieving boredom, or about hotter sex some of the time for some people, believing that what we ourselves feel is only light-and-fluffy, or assuming that what our partner is feeling is just light-and-fluffy, may be avoiding real and profound needs.

When there are serious or profound needs involved which you don't communicate to your partner for whatever reason, then you are creating a false self for them to see. This false self doesn't have these profound needs. If all you are comfortable showing your partner is a happy-go-lucky BDSM fan then as far as your partner is concerned your profound needs don't exist and, therefore, they're not going to make any effort to help you satisfy them.

In addition, if all you're prepared to accept is that BDSM is just a bit of fun, or that it's just a bit of slap-and-tickle involving fluffy handcuffs, then your partner isn't going to show you any more than that because they know that you either don't understand or that you can't cope with anything more serious.

Even if BDSM is light-and-fluffy all of the time for you, it may not be for your partner and you need to be ready and open to accepting that.

## 25.3 Expectations

Trust is also about fulfilling our partner's expectations. We might create some of these expectations ourselves through what we say or do. For example, we might always be 10 minutes late for any appointment. While you could argue that our partner might then not be able to trust us to show up punctually, they still do know *consistently* when we'll show up and they'll be able to base what they do on that certainty. This certainty, even if it is that we'll always show up late, that we're hopeless with knots, or that we get bored with wax play, is what works to create trust, to let our partner drop their defences, display their real selves and to let us truly engage the real them.

Our partners will sometimes have their own expectations of us which we don't know about and which will influence how much they feel they can trust us. Their own expectations will come from the way they think things should be, not just with us, but often with anyone. This can be a problem with people new to BDSM because they don't know how BDSM or BDSM relationships really are and they may have ideas more inspired by the fantasy novels of Anne Rice than by reality.

The big tool for managing expectations is communication, about which I have more to say in the next chapter. Sitting down with your partner and discussing all the things you do together in fine detail can help reveal unrealistic expectations and create realistic expectations. For you both to be happy, expectations—both of what you and your partner are going to do and what you're not going to do—need to be met.

# Chapter 26

# Communication

In almost all cases, communication plays a key role in relationship problems—both in creating the problems in the first place, and then in resolving them. Communication is a major topic and I can't hope to completely do it justice here, but I'd like to at least touch on some areas to do with communication problems to highlight the sorts of things we BDSMers can face.

One of the first things to realise about communication between two people is that it's never, ever going to be perfect. For a start, when we try to talk to someone we may have an idea or image in our minds which we want to transfer to theirs but the means we have to do this basically come down to words and gestures. We might have a great plan for some suspension bondage and in our mind we can imagine the texture of the rope, the clanking of the winch as we hoist our partner into the air, the smell of sweat and fear emanating from them, the pattern of rope and knots which we have laid out across their body, the colour changes in their skin where the rope and knots begin to press in, and so forth. But regardless of what we say, be it, "I want to tie you up and dangle you from on high," or be it something more colourful like my description earlier in this paragraph, the words we say may not conjure up in our partner's mind exactly what we are thinking. And even if we were the most skilled writer or poet in the world, words will never exactly express what we think.

This means, of course, that there's room for misinterpretation. Our partner might think A when we mean B. We might mean we're going to do this suspension out in a forest, and they might have in mind that it's going to happen in a private dungeon space. We might be thinking of using rough hemp rope and they might be thinking of something softer, like cotton. We might be thinking of this scene as a 30-minute warm-up before some energetic, hot-n'-horny horizontal action, and they might be thinking of it more as a 2-hour tranquil meditation followed by a quick nap and then some coffee.

Engagement can also enter into the discussion here. If what we know about our partner is just what they'd like us to think— i.e., when they show us a false self of some sort—then when we talk to them to explain our ideas and visions, the words we choose are going to be aimed at that false self, not at their real self. We all know from experience that what we say to someone can be misinterpreted, and we all learn to adapt what we say to the person we're saying it to. We do this so that they have a better chance of getting the right message. We choose the words which we think are right for that particular person. If we were to try to communicate the same idea to a different person we might use different words. We adapt our communication style and choices from person to person. But, when we don't really know the person we're talking to, or when what we know about them is not quite true or is incomplete, then the words we choose will not be right. There's a greater chance that this other person will get the wrong idea of what we mean.

Communication also acquires its own BDSM-specific problems which we need to recognise. In particular, one of the pillars of BDSM—namely disparity of power—often means that communication becomes one-sided. One way this manifests is when a submissive or slave relinquishes authority to their partner. Along with this, they may think that they relinquish the right to comment on or be critical about the things they have relinquished authority over. So, for example, a submissive who lets their dominant decide how a rope scene should play out is often more reticent to comment during a scene than, say, a bottom who hasn't relinquished any authority and who retains the idea that both they and their partner have equal say in what goes on.

For a slave or submissive in this situation, their reluctance to communicate can be:

- Because they don't want to be seen as stepping on the authority they have handed over,
- Because they don't want to feel like they are taking over control,
- Because they don't want to appear to be interfering or meddling, or
- Because they don't think it is their right to comment any more.

One case of this I came across was when a submissive woman contacted me about a conflict she was experiencing. She was deeply committed to serving, obeying, and being useful to her master but she was finding that her own needs weren't being met. She felt that it was not her place to be any sort of burden on her master. She only wanted to serve and be useful, and to her it seemed that it wasn't her place to be looking for him to satisfy her own needs when it should be she who was satisfying his. As a result, she was experiencing significant conflict. On the one hand she felt it inappropriate to talk to him about these needs, while on the other hand she had these same serious needs which weren't being addressed.

Another difficulty can be with a master and slave where the slave is only allowed to speak at certain times and in certain ways. Clearly, in such a situation communication is constrained and this increases the chance that problems or issues, which might otherwise be aired, remain unspoken, then fester, then break out in a burst of unpleasantness.

The above examples are of situations which generally don't exist in vanilla-land, except perhaps in the military. These communication problems, or potential problems, crop up due to the exercise of disparate power and we need to take steps to mitigate them without compromising our ability to use, experience and enjoy power.

Here are a few ideas:

- If you are a master with a slave who you keep under speech restrictions most of the time, set aside regular periods—maybe one hour once per week—where they can speak their mind without fear of punishment. Alternatively, allow them to request to "speak freely" along the lines of the military. However, to preserve authority do make it clear that at these times you only guarantee to listen, not to change your mind or do what they want.

- Similarly, when you are a submissive or slave and you want to express a desire but also don't want to feel that you're pushing or trying to tell your partner what to do, try agreeing that whatever you say is just information for your partner and that it's up to them whether they act on it or not.

- Have a journal in which you write everything down and keep it in a known place for your partner to read when you're not around.

- Leave notes where your partner will find them.

More generally, communication problems are often standard problems which exist just as much in vanilla-land as they do in BDSM-land and which require the same sorts of strategies to solve or prevent:

- Don't assume that your partner will work out, know, or guess something. Ideally, when you don't tell your partner something they need to know they'll ask you about it, but if they don't know that you've left something out—such as the fact that you already have another submissive, that you're allergic to nylon rope, or that you have no visual depth perception when you are proposing to use a single-tail whip on them—then they may not ask and things might go askew.

- Send each other email... even if you live together.

- If there are certain activities during a scene which you feel embarrassed requesting, agree on a set of signals beforehand so that you don't actually have to say the words.

*Communication*

- When you explain something to your partner, get them to explain whatever it is back to you to make sure they understood.

- Keep in mind that a lot of communication is non-verbal. Facial expressions and gestures add to the message, such as having your arms crossed while talking usually indicates either that you're feeling defensive or that you're not being open.

  Facial expressions and gestures are missing completely during telephone calls, SMS and email, and so you need to be particularly careful when using these mediums to make sure the right message gets across.

- Lots of people have unconscious drives which might be conflicting with their conscious ones and this can make communication confusing. Fear, in particular, is often a culprit here.

It is always better to say something than to say nothing. I have come across some tops and dominants who don't talk with their partner because they feel that it takes away from their authority. Or, if they have strong feelings or emotions, they feel it weakens them to display these emotions to their submissive.

It might be fine to not tell your partner what you're about to do in a scene so as to create suspense or to surprise them. It also might be fine to not talk to them about some things simply because they don't need to know, such as that you had to throw one of your many floggers away because all the tails fell out. But, they do need to know about things that affect you, them, or the relationship because these have to do with engagement. If you don't communicate with them about these things then engagement suffers and you create distance.

I'd like to return to the submissive I mentioned earlier, the one who felt it was her place to serve and be useful, and not be a burden to her master to such an extent that she felt it wrong to tell him about her own needs. I gave her a car analogy. If you are service-oriented and think that being a burden on your master or asking him for something is inappropriate, then consider a car. A car needs fuel and regular maintenance, and this is something we all accept. A car without maintenance will eventually stop providing service. When the fuel gauge needle points to "E" or the fuel warning light starts flashing, it isn't the case that the car is begging for fuel, or that it is whining or whinging, or even that it is demanding that we put fuel in it. The warning signal which our car gives us is neutral communication, and if you're strongly service-oriented then you can think of what you say to your master the same way. You let them know the state of things, warn them of imminent problems with your service. Then you let them deal with it. The same as in a car, if the fuel runs out in spite of a warning from the fuel gauge, the car owner needs to deal with it. When you regard yourself as property and if you have a need which doesn't get met in spite of warnings to your master, then it's his problem to deal with it.

*Communication*

## Chapter 27

# Surrender versus submission

Surrender is vital to being able to fully experience something. If you are busy standing by the "experience door" waiting for the time—which may or may not come—when you decide to close the door because you've had enough, then you'll never be able to fully experience what happens to you. Part of you will always be detached and devoting itself to acting as doorkeeper. Not all of you will be available to actually *feel*.

Needing to act as a doorkeeper is not necessarily a bad thing in some situations, but it is a problem when you want to fully immerse yourself in your BDSM. For example, when you have a well-developed set of skills and are flogging a very experienced partner, then you can pretty much go to town knowing that they are capable, competent, and are going to do the right thing.

Likewise, if your partner is carving designs into your upper arm and you know and trust them and their skills completely, you can surrender yourself to the experience and just let go.

But if you are doing something with someone and don't know their skill level, or you don't know how they'll handle intensity or potential difficulties, or if you just don't know them well enough to fully trust them, then you submit to what they're doing instead of surrendering, and you make sure that part of you is standing aside and is consciously keeping track of what they're doing.

When you are in a relationship with someone and you find yourself holding back during play, or you find you are limiting yourself in some particular aspects of the relationship, particularly where D&s is concerned, then perhaps you're having trouble surrendering. As I mentioned, trust can be part of this. Importantly, it may be that your partner is doing everything right and that it's something in you that is preventing full surrender on your part. Maybe it's something from your past, or maybe it's because you are entering BDSM territory which is confronting or for which you're not ready.

The difference between surrender and submission when engaging in something is typically this doorkeeper aspect. Surrender is the giving up of yourself completely either to your partner or to the experience you are having. Submission is when you leave yourself a way out beyond that which happens naturally.

Surrender is vital to penetration, to feeling or experiencing your partner, and to getting the most out of what you do together. There are many reasons why surrender doesn't happen, or why some people consciously or unconsciously avoid surrender.

## BDSM Relationships - Pitfalls and Obstacles

- Some see surrender as an indication that they're weak or that it makes them vulnerable. Well, being vulnerable is the purpose of surrender! Actually fully opening yourself—whether you are a top, bottom, dominant, submissive, etc.—is critical to getting the most out of your BDSM. If you put up barriers to surrendering then the most profound experiences will pass you by.

- When trust or fear are factors, my experience suggests that it's mostly:

    - Because you don't trust yourself,
    - Because you are afraid of how you might change if you do surrender,
    - Because of a fear of losing control,
    - Because of a fear of finding out something about yourself that you have been keeping hidden away, or
    - Because your partner might discover or see something in you that you have been trying to keep hidden.

- It could also be that you don't trust your partner. You may not trust them to respect and be gentle with what you reveal when you do surrender. You also may know that they're a stupid asshole and will deal with your surrender poorly. They may be an unstoppable gossip and you need to keep some sensitive parts of you private. From a purely physical perspective they may have really bad aim and letting them loose on your ass with a cane is never going to end well, or they always tie knots too tightly, and so on.

*Surrender versus submission*

- Some people engage an archetype or an imagined figure in their mind during scenes instead of engaging, and being penetrated by, their partner. This is a way of avoiding surrendering. What they are surrendering to is an image in their mind, but it's in their mind (which they control!) and so it is not really surrender at all. Eventually, the thrill will fade and the person doing it may end up dissatisfied and go looking for a new partner without realising that they themselves were at fault.

## Chapter 28

# Dominance and submission

Dominance involves claiming authority over, and then controlling or directing, your submissive partner. Complementally, submission is about relinquishing authority and surrendering yourself to the control and direction of your partner. In book two of this series I listed a number of areas in which you can assert control over a submissive such as directing their sensations, controlling their emotions, inflicting pain on them, restricting their movement, directing how they serve, reducing their sense of identity, and so on.

D&s is a tool we can use to engage and penetrate our partners. As I've noted elsewhere, experiencing control—whether it is being controlled or being the one doing the controlling—is a common motivator in BDSM and can be quite powerful. It can be what is behind many of our BDSM activities such as flogging or bondage, and making it a focus can enhance our BDSM.

D&s also has its potential problems, pitfalls and obstacles. They fall into two main areas:

- Controlling things which shouldn't be controlled, and
- Not controlling things which should be controlled.

## 28.1 The knight in shining armour

Almost by definition a dominant likes to take control or to be in control. They can feel uncomfortable when they're not. This leads to a significant trap, namely thinking that you can solve your submissive's problems by taking control. You might be tempted to do so because:

- Your submissive seems indecisive,
- They seem easily mislead and fall prey to others, or
- You have more knowledge and experience than they do.

You may think that everything will be more wonderful once you take over.

This is you being a knight-in-shining-armour saving a damsel-in-distress. Unfortunately, many such damsels merely look good. Often, they are constantly in distress and constantly need saving[1]. What you may end up doing is burdening yourself with someone who is chronically either unable or unwilling to take care of themselves. They aren't going to "get better" under your attentions, and what you might be walking into is a relationship with a submissive who has specifically set out to find someone who will take responsibility for their lives. This is a very bad place to be. You end up enabling them to continue to be immature and to avoid responsibility.

Some people think that a submissive or slave is that way because they want someone to take charge and make all the decisions. To a limited extent this is true, but personal responsibility tends to increase for a slave or submissive when they enter into a relationship with a master or dominant rather than decrease. This is because to be of use to their partner they first need to be handling their own lives well, and then they can serve their partner. This means that they already shoulder the responsibility of caring for themselves and then take on additional responsibility given to them by their dominant partner. The responsibility they carry goes up, rather than down, when they are in a relationship with a dominant.

In terms of penetration, this additional responsibility is something the submissive or slave can feel. Indeed, for some slaves and submissives, this form of penetration or feeling can be what they want or crave from their BDSM.

A "slave" or "submissive" who consciously or unconsciously heaps their own crap onto their dominant partner becomes a burden to their dominant and is actually using their dominant

---

[1] I don't want to suggest that it's only women who play the part of the perennially-distressed damsel in need of saving. Some so-called submissive guys can also play the same part just as well as women, or better.

to serve them rather than the other way around. Some of these "vampire submissives" are very skilled at sucking the life out of dominants and oftentimes the dominants don't recognise what is happening. These submissives are, to put it kindly, poorly adapted to being a submissive. It is not a dominant's job to fix or repair a submissive. It might be a dominant's job to give their submissive advice or training, but being a crutch is not.

Just as BDSM can appear superficially attractive to those who are simply looking for opportunities to harm others because it's "obviously" about pain, BDSM can also appear attractive to those who don't want to take responsibility for themselves because it's "obviously" about people (i.e., submissives) not taking responsibility for themselves and letting dominants take charge.

So for a dominant it's important to tread very carefully in any areas of personal responsibility of your submissive. How they take care of themselves, their work, their financial future, and their medical needs are areas of personal responsibility. While there can be some very difficult choices to make in all of these areas at different times of our lives, unless you're looking at long-term profound ownership it's unlikely that you should be making decisions in any of these areas for your submissive. On the other hand, training and education as it impacts your goals for them, what they do on a day-to-day basis, and specific instructions regarding their behaviour can be entirely yours and rightly so.

For a submissive it's important to manage responsibility so that you are a support, rather than a burden to your dominant or master. Particularly when your dominant is more experienced than you, or more mature, or more intelligent, it can be tempting to lean too much on their decision-making ability, and being decisive can certainly be a highly attractive and natural ability in some dominants. However, both for dominants and submissives, a BDSM relationship—or any relationship, actually—is an opportunity to grow, rather than shrink, and if you find yourself or your world becoming smaller instead of larger due to the nature of your relationship with your partner then you should do something about it.

## 28.2 Dominance or submission as duty

Just as much as control sometimes shouldn't be asserted or claimed, at other times it should be. There is often an implicit understanding between a dominant and a submissive that the dominant will dominate and that the submissive will submit. This sounds obvious, but many D&s folk get together more because of their personalities, their hopes, and their dreams rather than their abilities to actually and actively dominate or submit. Let me clarify this: if a guy meets a girl, gets her in the sack, and demonstrates amazing vigour, she might be quite impressed. If she's particularly randy on an ongoing basis she might think that this guy can satisfy her clitoral and vaginal needs on an ongoing basis as well. However, maybe he just came off an extended dry period and being that vigorous was a one-off performance. Maybe, as he gets acclimatised to the increased attention his dick receives his vigour trails off and she finds herself unsatisfied.

The same can apply to D&s. When a dominant and a submissive set up shop together it is because they have BDSM wants or needs which they want to satisfy within that relationship. There can be an expectation that this will occur. Because it takes the two of them to make this happen, if one looses steam and the

D&s or BDSM stops happening then the other may quite rightly feel poorly done by.

In casual BDSM encounters, say at a party, this problem doesn't exist, but for each person in a long-term relationship helping to ensure their partner's needs are met probably should rise to the level of being a duty or obligation. If one partner starts running out of puff, they should talk about this and work together to find a solution.

In book two of this series I listed a number of ways in which dominance and submission can be experienced and expressed—such as hunter/prey, emotional, service, intellectual domination, etc. When reviewing a D&s relationship and what makes it tick, it's vital to recognise that there is probably more than one type of domination involved and it may well be that a combination of D&s styles is necessary. If one partner runs out of energy for one style it may not be sufficient to throw more energy into other styles to make up for it. Each style or each D&s activity may serve to satisfy particular needs and may not be easily replaceable with other styles.

## 28.3 Losing control is easy

Many of the pitfalls of D&s relationships are particularly relevant to the dominant and can be quite easy for the dominant to fall into. Mostly they have to do with us not taking control when we should. This is perhaps related to it often being the case that the dominant needs to take the initiative and actively claim control. Sometimes we don't notice the times or opportunities for us to do this and they slip us by.

Here are a few notes on the subject:

- Your submissive partner is not wanting or expecting your orders or directions to be a reflection of their own wants or needs. This is perhaps an easy trap to fall into. Your partner probably didn't sign up to a D&s relationship with you because you'd do what they wanted. It should be the other way around—i.e., that they'd do what you want—but in moments of difficulty or doubt it can be surprisingly easy to slip into a mode of thought where making your partner happy by doing nice things to them seems the way to go.

- D&s is not about your submissive having it easy. That's not to say that they shouldn't find their relationship with you satisfying and rewarding. But if the direction you set for them involves them often eating chocolate or cake, getting frequent orgasms, being dressed up how they like, going to parties and doing things they enjoy, having coffee with friends, socialising with other like-minded folk, and so on, then you're not really dominating them. It's more a case of you kowtowing to their desires, whether they're spoken or not.

- Your submissive partner should experience some discomfort and resistance in being your submissive. Again, this doesn't mean that they don't have a good and rewarding time. But, if what you have them do is what they'd do anyway—such as if you have them bring you a coffee when they quite enjoy doing things for you—then you're not dominating them at all. For you to dominate, you need to be in command, using your authority and control over them to get your way. They need to feel this, and so do you. This is penetration and, as we've seen, this is a vital part of BDSM. Your partner needs to deeply feel your control over them. If you push them and they easily move in the direction you have set then it probably means that neither of you will feel very penetrated, but if you move in a more challenging direction and there's resistance and you overcome it then the penetration will be much more.

- Your partner—and you—need you to not just be in charge, but to actually use the authority you have. If you use your authority merely to tell them to eat a piece of chocolate—which they'd quite happily do anyway—or to tell them to go to the dungeon and undress when they're ready to do so anyway, then you're not commanding. At most, you're simply giving them a good idea.

## 28.4 Opportunities to control

Keep your submissive on their toes so that both you and your submissive are aware of your authority. Even when out in public, or with vanilla friends or family members you can still maintain the control. Make clear to your partner beforehand that when you ask them to do something that it is to be taken as a command and prompt obedience is expected—e.g., to refill your glass, to look up something on the computer, or to serve food to you and others in a formal or semi-formal manner. You can also establish non-verbal signals (which are particularly useful at parties, whether they are BDSM or vanilla parties) so that your partner needs to keep you in sight in case you signal them. Table 28.1 on the next page has some example signals you might use.

Remember that an important aspect of this is penetration. You and your partner need to feel this control, and in the case of

| Action | Meaning |
| --- | --- |
| Rock your glass from side to side | "Get me a refill for my drink." |
| Rub your chin | "It's time to leave. Fetch our coats and bags." |
| Rub your upper arm with your other hand | If at a play party: "I want to play now. Get ready. Collect our equipment and move it into the dungeon." |
| Lightly slap your own knee | "Come and sit at my feet." |
| Brush the hair on the back of your head with your hand | "Bring me something to eat." |

Table 28.1: Party D&s signals

party signals the penetration comes both from your submissive needing to be constantly alert to what you're doing so that they're ready to respond immediately, and from you seeing them respond to your signal.

You can get similar results when you require your submissive to always walk on one particular side when you are out and about, or to only start eating a meal once you have started, or to not climb into bed until you're already in bed, etc. These all require your submissive to be attentive to what you're doing and thus feel control.

This isn't a free ride though because you have to keep in mind that what you do can't frustrate your control over your submissive or slave. You need to ensure that there are opportunities for, and no obstructions to, their obedience. For example, you can't tell a submissive to always walk on your left and then go shopping in stores with very narrow aisles and expect your submissive to be where she should.

Likewise, you also need to be attentive that they are doing what they should. You shouldn't let infractions slip by uncorrected. You can't just give orders once and then think that your job is done. The penetration side of BDSM involves you penetrating your submissive ongoing. If you just give an order once and then don't follow up, your partner only gets penetrated by you that one time.

## 28.5 Conclusion

When we compare scene-based BDSM, such as flogging or bondage, to D&s we might note that it's easy to recognise the penetration occurring in a scene because we can see the submissive writhing or flinching and the dominant feeding off that. This penetration is often quite tangible. But in D&s penetration is often more subtle or restrained and is often felt for much longer than in a scene. Because it is more subtle it can be harder to notice when it starts to fade or when it starts losing its penetrating power.

It's important to keep in mind that it is often this penetrative aspect which is the most important for a satisfying and rewarding D&s relationship rather than the simple fact or nature of any orders.

## Chapter 29

# Wrong reasons why people do BDSM

A quick first glance at BDSM suggests that it's all about pain and sex. Because of this, it has a peculiar fascination for what we might call the wrong sort of people. These include those who carry a lot of anger around with them, the socially desperate, the excessively horny, the sociopathically inclined, and the immature. These folk often don't get into BDSM to have a healthy, intimate, personally-rewarding and mutually-beneficial relationship with a partner. Instead, they get into BDSM as a way of selfishly using any potential partners they meet.

## 29.1 Unattractive and looking to get laid

Some people are unattractive. This could be because of their looks, their lack of fitness, their weight, their body odour, their ego, their allergy to soap, their personality, or their attitude towards others and life in general. Consequently, finding a partner relying on their own merits is unlikely to be successful. These socially desperate souls can get the idea that picking up a flogger or baring their back are acceptable ways to get laid. This might actually work for a while, but it's a hollow win.

Unfortunately, it can be a successful strategy because in some geographical areas there can be a surplus of tops and dominants and a lack of bottoms or submissives, or *vice versa*. When there is such a shortfall, pretending that you are available and able to fill the gap can make you attractive to people who have no better alternative.

Pretending to be into some BDSM activity when you're not is, naturally enough, a bad idea. Firstly, it reduces your own self-image or feelings of self-worth in an unhealthy way[1]. It's also dishonest. It's a strategy for deceiving a potential partner into providing sex or affection or both without providing them the actual BDSM they thought they would get.

The better solutions to finding a bed- or dungeon-mate include fitness clubs, deodorant, shaving, a good diet, and perhaps most important of all, some serious attitude readjustment. In many cases, socially desperate folk are lazy, and their choice of simply

---

[1] Note that BDSM can include healthy and constructive humiliation as a form of play, but this is very different to what we're talking about here.

making themselves available BDSM-wise is a way to avoid having to do any hard work on themselves.

Spotting these pretenders straight away can be a challenge because they've almost certainly been playing their particular deceiving game for a while and may have developed some skill at getting away with it.

Be wary of someone who claims to be into BDSM but who:

1. Tries to get the BDSM over with and get into sex as soon as possible, or
2. Shows no interest in either developing their BDSM skill, or in working with you to improve the scenes you do together.

Sad, really.

## 29.2 Sociopathic and looking to hurt someone

Sociopaths do exist. They are looking for someone to genuinely hurt or to take advantage of. They are usually quite slick and well-presented, and they seem to say and do all the right things. This is an act, and they need to be good at it because they're trying to draw you in to their own twisted reality while making it seem like the best thing since sliced bread. What they seem to be offering though, turns out to be shallow or have no value to you. They often don't care about or dismiss your feelings.

BDSM can be attractive to sociopaths because it seems—superficially—to be about hurting people and this is what sociopaths live to do. If you're after pain without any consideration of your welfare, then hooking up with a sociopath is definitely the way to go. There's more to BDSM than simply inflicting pain of course, and we've seen that pain is actually a gateway to other experiences, with the pain being a means to useful, satisfying and productive outcomes rather than being an end in itself.

Sociopaths can confuse you. They may play on your ignorance or your need to please. They may say things like, "A real submissive would be able to take what I do!" or "You want to learn to be a good submissive, don't you?". Even though you may be hurt, confused, frustrated and suffering, they can make it seem like all the problems are your own fault or that everything is due to your own shortcomings.

A common clue that you're involved with such a person is fear. If you are constantly or frequently afraid—afraid of being hurt, afraid of not being able to please, afraid of not being good enough, afraid of doing the wrong thing—then it's time to go. If you don't genuinely look forward to the experiences you have with your partner then ditto. BDSM is not a matter of just one person getting their needs met.

## 29.3 Wanting an easy way to get sex

Candles, romantic dinners, and cosy evenings on a boat on the river with champagne and canapes are just too hard sometimes. For someone who is often just plain horny (i.e., a guy), it's far easier to dress up in black, collect a few ropes, and then show up at the next BDSM social event as Master Tie-Me-Up.

Tying someone up may be enough to get sex for a while, but it's poor BDSM. If the partner of such a person is actually looking for something deeper then it's not going to be there.

There's a lot of overlap with this bad reason for doing BDSM and someone doing BDSM because they think they're unattractive. They're both manipulative and dishonest. They're also selfish and shallow. Unfortunately, some people who are enthusiastic about actual, real, genuine BDSM get sucked in by these false presentations and eventually get spat out.

Just as with the unattractive folk, the clue here is that the person you're dealing with has no interest in developing or exploring their BDSM experience or yours. They're only interested in doing as much BDSM as necessary to get into your pants.

## 29.4 Wanting a fashion accessory

A variation on this is the person who is looking to hook up with someone they think is attractive so they can then show them off as a sort of fashion accessory. This happens on both sides of BDSM—some submissives will try to connect with a desirable top or dominant who they can then present to their friends at parties, and some tops and dominants will try to find an attractive submissive or bottom who they can then have on a leash or at their feet at BDSM social events.

This becomes a problem when their focus on showing you off gets in the way of satisfying and enjoyable BDSM. If you go to BDSM social events with the expectation that there'll be socializing and play, and you find your partner is exceptionally keen on you dressing up and then doesn't play with you then it's perhaps time for a little chat.

*Wrong reasons why people do BDSM*

## 29.5 Angry and no other way to get rid of the anger

There are many pissed off people in the world. They could be angry with their bosses, with the way the world seems to be treating them, because they think they should have a life or circumstances better than they do, because they're ineffectual, or even because they have psychological problems. They may just carry anger around with them 24 hours a day.

When they're angry they want to take it out on someone. BDSM can be attractive for this because it can seem to be mainly about hitting people a lot. Using a pretence of BDSM to express their anger isn't going to help these angry people in the long term. In particular, they may come to think that all of their partners are there to be hit and this is, of course, a bad thing. Being angry isn't a good reason to be involved BDSM.

Having said that it's important to clarify something. Being angry 24 hours a day is not a good reason to search out someone to flog, whip, or cane. But when the underlying BDSM relationship is one of caring and support, then it can be a genuine service by a slave or submissive to hand their dominant a cane or flogger and bare their back or buttocks so that their partner can work out any temporary frustration on them. There are good benefits to this. Firstly, it provides a safe outlet to the top or dominant for their emotions. Secondly, it is a genuine opportunity for their submissive or slave to provide a useful service. Thirdly, they are both supporting each other in the context of their relationship with each other.

Two things are important about this latter scenario:

1. It is honest and open, and

2. It's only safely applicable when the emotions being released through the flogging or caning are temporary or occasional. Constant anger or frustration is a reason to seriously look at your life, or to find a professional to help you manage this anger.

## 29.6 Revenge

For some people there are times when they think that they have been treated badly, are angry about it, and seek revenge.

It may well be that the person who feels this way has legitimate cause, but it might also be that they themselves are the major contributor to their frustration. For example, a submissive might have gone into a BDSM relationship with their dominant partner knowing that there were some firm limits involved—such as their dominant having children and needing to work long hours to earn money to support them. When the submissive's needs grow and they need more time or attention from their dominant, they may become angry when their dominant has no more time to spare or when their dominant makes choices which don't place them, the submissive, above all else. This may seem obviously selfish, and this may well be a situation which was easy to foresee happening, but when hungers are aroused and feelings are strong, the submissive may not see it that way and may feel they are genuinely being treated poorly.

Choosing to take revenge is a choice made when there are no other choices, when the person involved doesn't have any other way of getting some compensation for a wrong they think they have experienced. It is a backdoor choice used when the front door isn't an option. Because of this, a sense of disempowerment can be involved with choosing to take revenge. The act of taking revenge can be felt as a way of taking back control.

Revenge often takes shape as some form of attack against which the person being attacked either has no defence or is unprepared. Because it's usually based on emotions, there may not be any rational or reasonable connection between the perceived wrong and the revenge taken. Anger, jealousy, and frustration are often the main motivators for revenge, and sometimes the acts of revenge can be extreme and irrevocable.

- The aggrieved person—the one seeking revenge—might target another relationship of the person who they think did them wrong so as to break up that relationship. For example, they might seduce the partner of the person who they think did them wrong simply to cause problems.

- They might target the health of the person they're pissed off with. In rare cases some have arranged for this person to get infected with something nasty, such as with Hepatitis or HIV. Sadly, university researchers have actually documented people doing this[2].

- They might go on a crusade to persecute this person and ruin their way of life. For example, they may engage in BDSM with them (with a smile, of course) and then report these BDSM activities to the police or "out" the person to their work colleagues or family.

- They also might cause damage to or steal the person's property. They could slash the tyres of their car, or spray graffiti on their house.

---

[2][MESTON2007]

Revenge often knows no logic and sometimes it can be incredibly patient. To avoid it, take the time to get to know any new partner before getting too involved with them. Try to avoid love (or BDSM) triangles. This can be difficult because many BDSM communities are quite small, and people moving from one partner to another is common.

The Internet has created additional opportunities for revenge. For example, a submissive who—rightly or wrongly—feels that she has been badly done by can join an on-line and international submissive support group and start spreading stories largely unchallenged because their target dominant isn't participating in the group. While I have no problem with someone talking about their bad experiences, there are always two sides to every story and using a forum where the other person concerned cannot reply is unfair (and is probably done for that very reason). But, revenge is very rarely fair.

It's worth noting that an imbalance of power is a requirement for BDSM, and that a submissive or slave is going to be in a position of less power than their partner. This may mean that a submissive is going to be more prone to considering revenge because fewer options are open to them.

## 29.7 Simply selfish

More generally, I suppose that doing BDSM for bad reasons is often about being selfish. Wanting something for yourself and using BDSM to get it is a bad motivation. For people who do this, it's about getting what they want and not being too concerned about the others who they trample on. Justification and rationalisation can play a part—these folk create excuses in their own mind which either justify what they're doing, or which somehow twist reality in their own mind to make it seem that their partners/victims deserve it or will thank them for it later.

This sort of relationship is one-way. They want from you but aren't prepared to give in return. They may say the right words, but it always seems that you're the one who is at fault by wanting things your way or by wanting your own needs met. At the same time, they make sure that their needs always are.

## 29.8 Misguided attempt to heal your partner

One of my other interests is hypnosis. My first book was about using hypnosis to enhance sex[3]. Because of this public interest of mine I was once approached by a dominant at a BDSM play party who came to talk to me about using hypnosis on his submissive female partner. She suffered from manic depression and was being treated by a psychiatrist for it. This well-meaning dominant wanted to use hypnosis on his partner to "cure" her. He wanted to know why he couldn't just hypnotise her and tell her to be happy all the time.

You can't use hypnosis, or BDSM, to heal your partner. If they have psychological, emotional, or psychiatric problems then leave these to people who have the qualifications and experience to treat them. Applying laymen's cures or trying to help can make things worse.

---

[3][MASTERS2008A]

With this we may be getting into an area where some dominants have a weakness. Some dominants really, really—and I mean REALLY—like, or even need to be in control. When things aren't under their control they can become uncomfortable. When some of us see our partners in difficulty we want to use our power and position in their lives to fix things even when it's not right to do so. We can feel compelled to act because we feel so uncomfortable not being in control any more. Doing something, even the wrong thing, can make us feel like we're back in the driver's seat again (albeit possibly in the driver's seat of a train on a one-way trip to a spectacular wreck!).

Some dominants get suckered into this situation deliberately by "submissives" who aren't submissive at all, but who are actually immature and don't want to accept responsibility (I also talked about this in *The knight in shining armour*, section 28.1 on page 352).

It's true that BDSM can sometimes be cathartic or provide opportunities for emotional expression and release. It can't cure though. Don't be tempted to try because you may end up with a submissive or slave who is more broken than when they met you.

## 29.9 Looking to solve a problem with BDSM when it's not BDSM-amenable

The above is a specific example of a much more general bad reason to do BDSM, and that is to try to use BDSM to solve a problem which has nothing to do with BDSM.

If by circumstance or by choice you're ugly or undesirable, then BDSM may provide a way for you to get laid. It's not a good use of BDSM if for no other reason than it doesn't make you feel good about yourself. If you have to fake or force an interest in BDSM to get laid then that's very sad and even demeaning. On top of that, it can mean misleading or taking advantage of someone who genuinely is looking for a BDSM partner.

Another bad reason someone might do BDSM is if they are emasculated in their everyday life—perhaps by a domineering supervisor at work, or because they're timid, or because they're afraid of confrontation and let people take advantage of them. They might try to make up for it by being dominant in the bedroom, or by wearing black leather and wielding the biggest flogger at every play party. This might make them temporarily feel better, but isn't a solution to the problem.

BDSM also often seems exciting to outsiders, and if someone feels their life is tedium *ad nauseum* then rather than work out what's gone wrong they instead do something exciting to fill the gap. This may be something like skydiving, insulting mafiosi, or trying BDSM. None of these solve the problem of a boring personality, and a genuinely uninteresting person can take the excitement out of anything, even out of being TASERed™.

Exploring BDSM is only a solution for BDSM-related problems. If you're genuinely hungry for someone to control you and having such a person in your life helps you grow and feel complete then chalk one up for BDSM. If an intense cutting scene is cathartic for you or helps you feel closer to your chosen partner then chalk another one up to BDSM. However, if you're a dickhead looking for excitement and you get involved in BDSM, then you end up still being a dickhead but now you have a flogger.

## 29.10　I will train you

BDSM—at least for newcomers—can be a tantalising world of strange, new, and powerful experiences. It can surprise and overwhelm, and it can be hard to know where to look or what to do. You can get lost in it.

This may be when Super Dom rides up on his black leather steed carrying a glistening array of floggers, nipple clamps, rope, candles and chain. "Follow me," he says, "and I will train you! I will show you the way to ecstasy unbounded. Your life will change immeasurably for the better and you will become my slave!"

Sadly though, sometimes what Super Dom says can be translated as, "Come with me, away from others who might know more than I, and then I will flog you and fuck you until you learn to enjoy it."

Ignorance is the problem here. The real nature of BDSM is not something which our society excels at teaching. As a result, many people enter into the world of BDSM with fantastic and unreal ideas about what to expect and about how BDSM folk really behave. A newcomer may be overwhelmed and hungry for more of what BDSM has to offer but be ignorant and ill-prepared for abusive dominants. These "dominants" might look the part and might have splashed out a couple of hundred dollars at the local leather store, but all they're doing is waiting for their chance to pick up some "fresh meat" which hasn't yet learned to recognise their true game.

Some of this—but not all of it—can be due to lack of experience and lack of imagination on the part of Super Dom combined with an overarching need on his part to get his dick wet. Super Dom may genuinely believe that all he needs is a couple of floggers and a pair of nipple clamps to bring on unlimited rapture in women because he saw another guy do it and it didn't look that hard.

Having such a "dominant" spoil your early BDSM experiences by making it about being physically abused and then being fucked repeatedly can take some of the shine off it for a new submissive.

This training game goes both ways. Super Subbie might also be lurking on BDSM websites or at parties looking for attention, and may latch on to an inexperienced top or dominant and offer to "teach" them. In reality, it could be a ploy to keep this "fresh meat" to themselves and get their own needs met—such as heavy floggings or bondage—while telling their victim that this is what all tops do for their submissives.

## The real thing

There are real teachers and trainers out there, and some of them do contribute their time and expertise to others largely out of the goodness of their hearts, so don't necessarily get turned off by what I wrote above.

Do keep in mind:

- Many people who will genuinely help you and provide training are involved with an organised and long-standing BDSM social group or club,
- Ethical teachers and trainers will have no problem with you asking around about their skill and *bona fides*, and

- Ethical teachers and trainers will sometimes say no when they see a conflict of interest in helping you, or when they recognise that they're not what you need. They may refer you to others who have skills or knowledge better suited to where your interests lie.

Things to do:

- Recognise that your genitals may get in the way of you making sensible decisions,
- Make sure to ask around,
- Your first BDSM experiences are best had somewhere you feel safe, perhaps at a play party where you know some of the people, or when you have a friend riding chaperone.

# Questions

The following questions can help you separate the wheat from the chaff:

1. If someone is offering to teach you or coach you, what do they want in return? If the dude or dudette doesn't appear to be associated with any group or club, and if their answer is that they are doing it for nothing or that they're doing it because you seem like a nice person who seems lost and they want to help you out, be very cautious.

2. Do they have verifiable experience? Do any of your friends know them? Can you get a reference? Do they have any sort of reputation to support their offer?

3. Do they straight away suggest that you go somewhere private with them?

4. Does all their equipment look conspicuously new? This may indicate that so are they.

5. Do they encourage you to get out and talk to people? If they try to hide you away or "protect" you from others who might give you the wrong idea, beware! They may be trying to keep you ignorant and thus be better able to manipulate you.

## 29.11   The gift of submission

One of the ideas which seems to have gained a footing in some sections of this very large BDSM community of which we are a part is the "gift of submission".

I can understand where the idea comes from. Many submissives have intense feelings of vulnerability in their first BDSM experiences. They feel like they have been opened up, that their protective barriers have been peeled away, and that their innermost selves have been revealed. They feel completely exposed to their dominant. This is very powerful, very personal, and very intimate. These submissives perhaps feel more naked than they ever have in the past. It's special. It can be so new and amazing that they can't imagine anyone else ever feeling the same.

And because they feel that this rarely or never-before exposed inner part of themselves is being presented to their partner they may see it as a special gift from them to their partner, that this usually-protected, delicate, and valuable part of themselves is being opened up for their partner to see and explore. In a sense, it truly is a gift.

But funnily enough, their dominant partner may be going through much the same thing, through the same intensity and the same emotional roller-coaster. Their dominant may be feeling hungers, urges, and drives which are new to them too. They can experience a need to open themselves up, to reveal, and to explore these feelings with their submissive partner. It is the same, but from the other side. The idea of a "gift of dominance" though, doesn't seem to get anywhere near the same amount of traction as the idea of a "gift of submission".

The idea that any of this is a gift from one person to the other, regardless of which direction we're talking about, is misleading and can be manipulative. In most relationships—certainly in balanced and healthy ones—what each partner gives and gets should be in equally satisfying proportions. Indeed, this is probably what you should be striving for all the time with your partner. But if you convince your partner that you are giving them this amazing "gift" then you have created a bargaining position for yourself where you can demand things from them in return: "I have given you my gift of submission and now you need to do all these things for me because my gift is so amazingly and obviously valuable that you'll have to work hard to really earn and keep it."

Sometimes this unfortunate attitude rises to a greater height when the person afflicted by this view promotes the gift to a treasure and, in fact, they themselves become the treasure. I confess that I call my partner "treasure" sometimes. I also call her "snookums" and a few other cute names. I do however hold firmly with the belief that neither of us is gold-plated. We're both

*Wrong reasons why people do BDSM*

human, and we give and take in this relationship in accordance with our abilities.

Your partner is valuable to you because they allow you to experience this gift. Rather than being a gift which you give to your partner, it is a gift which your partner allows you to give yourself. Whether you are a dominant or a submissive, top or bottom, your partner is the one who works with you to create a context or environment where your own powerful inner feelings can surface and be explored in safety.

The truth is, I think, that there are no diamond-studded gifts of submission. You're there because the feelings your partner is helping you experience are rewarding, intense, and even amazing for you. Show your gratitude for their time and for their efforts, and help them get the same sort of amazing feelings themselves.

If you're a dominant and you encounter a submissive or bottom who earnestly tries to sell you the idea of a "gift of submission", I suggest that you say you're not buying and straight away start looking for someone who will be there to share with you.

## 29.12 Let me serve you

I think service can be great. It's a sign that the person giving it is prepared to let my wants and needs influence or control their choices and actions. It's a sign that satisfying me is important to them. It doesn't need to be anything big, such as painting my house, or anything intimate, such as sex. It can be something simple, like rubbing my shoulders or bringing me a drink. Even little things, like a friend buying me some popcorn at the cinema at the same time they're buying theirs can be very pleasant.

In BDSM, service can be an excellent exercise in power. A service-oriented submissive or dominant takes their cues from their partner whose needs they want to satisfy. The service-oriented person responds to these and generally enjoys the feedback or signs of appreciation they get from their partner for a job well done.

This sometimes doesn't work quite as constructively as you might hope.

## "Let me serve you"

Over the years, one of the phrases which I have become increasingly cautious about hearing from a submissive is something which sounds like, "Let me serve you." The reason I am cautious is that it's frequently an invitation for me to do a lot of work with little in return.

The clues that this is the case are:

1. The submissive concerned has a list of things I'm allowed to ask them to do. They may not actually phrase it like that. Instead, they might be more subtle and have "limits" which prevent me doing anything except what they want,

2. The things I can ask them to do are heavy on personal reward or convenience for them and light on what I get out of it. For example, I may ask them to bring me a sandwich at a play party, and they may do this with much chatting with others and dilly-dallying along the way to the extent that I have to wait half an hour for my food. I, however, must still be grateful and tell them what a good girl they are because they brought me a sandwich,

3. I'm required to be an active participant before, during, and after these activities, and
4. None of the things they'll be doing actually require any particular skill, talent, or effort.

The submissives who do this are sometimes called "do me" submissives. They are looking for a partner to give them all the thrills they want without offering anything substantial in return. What you hear from them can sound like this:

> *"If you adopt a stern voice and let me bow my head to you, I will get you a can of soft drink from the refrigerator in the corner. You must also show your appreciation once I hand the drink to you by patting me on the head, telling me what a good girl I am, and for the rest of the evening telling everyone else what a good girl I am because I got you a can of drink from the refrigerator."*

Of course, if this is all there is to it then—as in the case of the abovementioned sandwich—I'm far better off getting the can of soft drink for myself.

You might also hear:

> *"I will let you lead me around on a leash for the evening."*

And this benefits me how?

Or:

> *"I will serve you by allowing you to tie me up any way I want."*

Again, if I can only tie her up how she wants, how does this benefit me?

And finally:

> *"I will serve you by sucking your cock as long as I feel like it."*

I don't know about you, but if you—the reader—are equipped with a cock and are like me, then having it sucked is quite nice. But I am actually looking for more than that. There seem to be many submissives who go—pardon the expression—into their own small little world while sucking cock and are actually largely uninterested in the cock owner's enjoyment.

A good way to work out what's happening when someone insists that they are truly interested only in serving you is to mention a book such as *Butlers & Household Managers: 21st Century Professionals*[4]. It is about providing excellent personal service, and it's a very good book which I strongly recommend. It is, however, quite amazing how many submissives who say they're keen to serve you have absolutely no interest in reading it. At first glance, this might be surprising because someone who swears they absolutely exist only to serve would presumably want to do a good job and any tips or clues on how to serve better would clearly be extremely valuable. Of course, their lack of enthusiasm tells you straight away that they're not interested in serving you well at all. They're actually interested in serving themselves.

The point is that they're looking to get you to make an effort to provide a context where they can get their jollies. Some

---

[4][FERRY2008]

submissives and slaves, for example, get off far more on being told what to do than on actually doing it. For others, the tasks must be simple, easy, and unchallenging, and they expect great praise, pats on the head, and compliments from you in return.

It is perhaps not dissimilar to insisting that you should be grateful that they've bared their back so you can flog it, or that you hallow their name because they've spread their legs so you can fuck them because, quite clearly, this is such amazing service to you and they, of course, get absolutely nothing out of it and it is complete self-sacrifice on their part. See also above where I talked about *The gift of submission* (p. 376).

The things to look for here are the submissives who:

- Are keen for you to know what you can do for them and the things they love to experience,
- Don't think to tell you what they can do for you, and
- Seem to care remarkably little for what you actually want or need and will change the subject if you try to tell them.

Now. I'm not trying to tar all submissives with the same brush. Far be it. But the point of this chapter is to stress that there are some submissives who consciously or unconsciously will be looking strictly at what you can do for them, rather than what they can also do for you. In some cases I am sure it is simply ignorance, that they just can't comprehend that more than a token effort from them is required for it actually to be meaningful and useful service.

## Questions and discussion

Healthy BDSM relationships are about wants and needs being met on both sides. Because the ways of BDSM can be subtle, the wants and needs involved in even a healthy relationship can be challenging to identify.

If you're feeling uneasy about your relationship with your partner, or if you don't know whether you are satisfying their needs, or if you don't think yours are being addressed, it can be worthwhile to sit down with them and ask:

- In each of the activities you do with your partner:
    - Which of your needs are you attempting to satisfy?
    - How successful is this activity at achieving that?
    - Which of your partner's needs are you attempting to satisfy?
    - How successful is the activity at achieving this?
- Are there any of your wants or needs which don't seem to be being addressed at all?
- Are there any of your partner's wants or needs which don't seem to be being addressed?
- Do you feel you are doing much more than your partner?
- Does your partner feel they are doing much more of the work than you?

## 29.13  Recognising the pretenders

A lot of what I've been writing about in this chapter has to do with pretenders. A pretender is faking some or all of their interest so you'll willingly or unwillingly help them satisfy their need. They may be looking to you simply as someone to fuck, to hurt, or to help build up their ego. It's selfish and it's all about them. Because of this, and in the worst cases:

- They don't want you to find out the truth. They'll have barriers up around themselves and won't let you in more than superficially. You'll likely feel the distance between them and you, and they won't do anything to help you get closer to them.

- They aren't really interested in your needs *per se*, and instead are only interested in what they must do to get you to comply with their needs. In particular, they won't be interested in you reciprocating their faked interest in BDSM. For example, if they discover that tying you up makes you horny and sexually receptive then they may claim to be a great bondage enthusiast. However, if you offer yourself to be tied up where sex isn't a possibility—such as a quick tie in an empty subway car between stops—they'll never be interested.

- If they're looking to hurt you then they may tend to avoid warm ups and go straight for heavy or intense play. They may justify this by coming up with an excuse that it's for your benefit, training or education.

- The shortest distance between two points is a straight line and if sex is their game then they'll only be interested in the straightest line to your cunt or to your cock. They'll demonstrate a consistent lack of enthusiasm for exploring anything else or spending more time than necessary to get between your legs.

## 29.14 Conclusion

I've talked about it before and it merits mention again. Maturity, self-awareness, and responsibility are important in making relationships work, and BDSM ones especially. When the stakes are low and only fluffy pink handcuffs are involved then perhaps not so much. But as the stakes increase—for you or for your partner—the need for personal maturity increases along with them.

A big part of maturity, self-awareness, and responsibility is being open with yourself and with your partner. The things which make many of the reasons for getting involved in BDSM mentioned in this chapter into bad reasons are the selfishness, dishonesty, and lack of openness associated with them. In BDSM terms, there's nothing wrong with wanting to flog your partner until blood runs down their back, or to tie them and fuck them until their cunt is raw. For it to be positive and rewarding for you both, it does need to be something that you're open and passionate about, not something hidden.

# Chapter 30

# Recognising pitfalls and obstacles

Like any other relationships between two people, BDSM relationships can and do fail. There are traps we can fall into which can lead to temporary or complete breakdowns of our relationships. While this is true for all relationships, BDSM has traps and pitfalls which are unique. They occur in no other types of relationships.

One of the big problems with trying to have a successful BDSM relationship is that because of the underground nature of BDSM we don't grow up surrounded by prototypes of good, healthy, well-functioning, BDSM relationships as vanilla folk do. We lack a regular exposure to examples of how things should or shouldn't be done BDSM-wise. BDSM tends to be hidden, and while vanilla folk constantly get to see vanilla-type relationships play out amongst family, friends, in the media, and in movies, we BDSM folk are often in the situation of having to make it up as we go along. This causes us to be particularly susceptible to some types of mistakes:

- Mistakes made out of ignorance,
- Placing obstacles in our own way, or in the way of our partner,
- The mistake of confusing others' outrageous fantasies—as portrayed in movies, books, or porn—with reality. These mistakes are particularly prevalent at the beginning of our journey,
- Being easily conned or mislead, and
- Falling for predators.

In this chapter I'll be looking at some of these mistaken ideas, at some predators who knowingly or unknowingly take advantage of this naïveté, and at some of the unique ways a BDSM relationship can fail.

## 30.1  Been there. Done that

Many aspects of BDSM can be interesting and exciting because:

- They can involve nude members of the opposite sex, or
- They are new and unusual.

In my neck of the woods, nude members of the opposite sex tend to be regarded as a good thing, but even full-frontal nudity can pale after a while, and nudity on its own is not BDSM anyway.

Also, the world of BDSM is quite large and it can take a lot of exploration to exhaust all of the possibilities. Initially, it can seem like there's always something new and unusual to try because there are so many different ways of practising BDSM. Unfortunately, there does come a time when you've tried all the different BDSM implements, positions, and styles. If your main motivator was the novelty and now the novelty is gone, what next?

This is an important question because some people get into BDSM precisely because it's new, risky, confronting, illicit, unusual, shocking, and perhaps even just because it seems like a kinky way to spice up sex. If the BDSM is not satisfying in itself, or if the BDSM is worth doing merely because you've never done this sort of thing before, then the time when it doesn't excite any more is already on the horizon.

It can take a fair while to get to this point. Maybe months, possibly years, particularly if the BDSM brings other benefits such as a sexy partner.

It can sometimes be obvious when the novelty is a significant factor. If you or your partner are often driven to look for new BDSM activities, new places to do your BDSM, new fetish clothes, new BDSM toys, and new people to do it with, then maybe you should reflect on exactly what you want out of BDSM with your partner. There's absolutely nothing wrong with exploration, but if the only thing you have is the exploration then your BDSM may be in trouble.

*Recognising pitfalls and obstacles*

## 30.2 When you don't know the real you

For BDSM to be satisfying and rewarding it needs to match up with your own wants and, importantly, needs. This is, I hope, obvious. Yet for reasons of guilt, fear, social pressure, or ego, many people twist what they do in the dungeon away from what they need and towards what they think they should be doing. This may not be something they do consciously; it can be due to ways of thinking they've unconsciously learned in the past. This means that instead of the right BDSM for them, they instead end up doing nearly-right BDSM or even the wrong BDSM.

Ego can be a big factor here. The voice in the back of your mind which, each time you look in the mirror, tells you that the face you see could be a movie star, is the same one which might say in the dungeon:

- "I am the most sexually desirable person in this dungeon and the guys/ladies should be falling over themselves to spend time with me!"

- "My sexual prowess has no equal and 'huge dick' is a clear understatement!"

- "I am the most dominant master in the room and I can dominate anyone or anything at any time! I can also fix anything mechanical, I fully understand abstract physics, have discovered two new planets with only a pair of binoculars, have created a cure for politics, and I construct working nuclear reactors in my spare time using only paper clips!"

- "My submission is a thing of art and beauty which none can rival!"

Fear of being seen—by yourself or by others—as being merely mortal may be a part of this. In addition, by thinking of yourself as a clearly superior specimen it means that if you don't get laid or don't get a date on Saturday night that you can blame others for their short-sightedness rather than deal with the fact that you're not such a great catch after all. My experience is that guys are particularly affected, but women aren't far behind in their own way. With guys it is often dick-related, even if just figuratively. With women, well... they also sometimes feel the need to compete for a partner. The point is that many people into BDSM have something to prove, and for this reason they are often not presenting themselves as they truly and deeply are. They consciously or unconsciously try to present themselves as shiny and flawless, and this even extends to the activities they engage in with their partner.

Regardless of where it comes from, it means that these folk aren't getting what they need out of BDSM. Instead they're getting what they'd like to think they need. A guy who actually has a strong submissive streak but who feels compelled to "act the dom" is certainly going to miss out. Likewise, a woman who has been taught that her place is at the feet of a strong man is not going to be able to comfortably pick up a flogger and attend to her partner even though it might really be the right thing for both of them.

It's worth reflecting a while on what factors contribute to how you define yourself. If you see yourself as a dominant, why is that? Is ego a part of this choice? Do you feel a need to avoid signs of weakness? How do you feel about a woman being in control? Or what about a man being in control? Do you feel guilty about what you do? How do you feel about hitting your partner? Is there some standard you're trying to achieve? Who set this standard?

If you call yourself a submissive, what is it about you that makes you think that? Is it the things you like doing? If it's just what you get out of the physical side of BDSM, what about the mental side? Does part of you shy away from taking control even though it's something you often think about? When you do kneel, how does it feel? Is there something in you which makes you think that kneeling is bad? Do you feel guilty about it?

## 30.3 Trying too fiercely to be independent

Following on from the above, one of the things we learn in our western society is to be independent and to do things for ourselves. Frequently this is not the right thing to do in BDSM, particularly for dominants. This is because many submissives like doing things for their dominant partner. They like to serve. For some, it is a need to serve. It is part of their submissive experience and it is satisfying and rewarding for them. In serving they submit to the commands, to the wants, or to the needs of their dominant.

When a dominant tries to do everything for himself he can be preventing his submissive partner from actually being submissive. He takes away from him or her the chance to submit. More than that, at the same time he also takes away his own chance to take charge, to take control, to dominate his submissive partner, and so he misses out as well.

There isn't anything wrong with being independent and doing things yourself if there are good reasons. But being a dominant means you have a duty to dominate, otherwise you should take down your shingle and go and find some other role. And dominating means directing and taking charge. It means having your submissive do what you want. It's part of the deal you have with them. Token tasks are not enough. You need them to be doing useful and meaningful things for you. This doesn't need to be all the time, but it needs to be enough of the time.

You're not sacrificing your independence by having your submissive do things for you. You are merely choosing not to assert it. Sure, you could go and get your own coffee, but if you send your submissive then you both get some pleasure—you by being dominant, and she by serving.

A dominant may inappropriately assert their independence for many reasons:

- Personal insecurity,
- His or her ego,
- Their self-image,
- Some form of denial or guilt to the extent that he feels he can't allow his partner to keep doing things for him, or
- As a symbolic way of avoiding commitment by insisting on doing things for him- or herself.

**Personal insecurity** can come from self-doubt, from not being sure that he can adopt the appropriate air of authority, or from not being sure how his submissive is actually going to take being told what to do. This latter may be valid because some submissives will only submit to rope or the lash, and trying to tell them what to do away from rope and floggers may get you the finger.

Communication is a big help with personal insecurity. If you're the dominant and you're not sure, ask. It's the dominant thing

*Recognising pitfalls and obstacles*

to do. If you're the submissive and you have a strong desire or need to serve, then say so and be openly and obviously receptive to direction and command. Encourage your dominant to take charge of you through your attitude and responses.

**Ego** can appear in thoughts such as: "I am the great MegaSupaWundaDom[1]! I am powerful! I am supreme!" When this happens any sign of dependence on another—such as a submissive doing something useful for MSWD—can't be tolerated because it damages the super-ness of his or her image. Any submissive in the picture just gets to do menial and insignificant tasks which don't impact the dominant in any way. MSWD won't allow the submissive to be particularly effective and while MSWD will happily use and take advantage of their submissive, they won't allow the submissive to dent their armour or penetrate them in any way. It is entirely one way. For some submissives this can be appealing for a while, but BDSM is about the dominant and the submissive affecting each other, about the submissive being empowered and enabled to be submissive by their partner, and by the dominant being empowered and able to exercise their dominance by their submissive. MSWD won't allow the latter and tries to be self-empowering. Ultimately, this sort of behaviour is about fear, and it is self-defeating and hollow.

While ego often relates to a more-than-perfect image of oneself, there are other forms of **self-image** which can interfere with a BDSM relationship. When the self-image is a false one, i.e., it does not accurately reflect the inner person, then it must get in the way of a satisfying BDSM relationship. The reason it must get in the way is that when we have a false self-image we work

---

[1] Also known as MSWD.

to satisfy the needs we think this false self-image has rather than our own real needs. Likewise, our partner relates to this same self-image we project rather than the real us and this reduces how much we can feel engaged by them.

Thinking that you can't be a dominant because a) striking or tying up your partner is not a right or honourable thing to do, and b) you're not like that, is possibly a throwback to your upbringing. Many dominants have this particular burdensome image which limits what they do.

In a similar way, a person with strong submissive wants or needs may be prevented from fully exploring them because of an image of themselves as an individual who kneels to no one.

**Denial or guilt** can prevent a dominant taking full advantage of his enthusiastic submissive. Feelings of inferiority can be the basis here. Rather than fully appreciating the attention and obedience of his submissive, a dominant suffering from guilt, inferiority, or one who is in some form of denial, will have feelings that he should be doing things for his submissive rather than, correctly, the other way around. In fact, by having his submissive attend him and serve him he may be doing the very best for her. This may even seem paradoxical to him.

Finally, and ominously, a dominant who was otherwise fine, may start becoming independent as an unconscious sign that he or she is getting cold feet and is starting to push their submissive away. This can be a **fear of commitment** rearing its head. He might argue that it's because of the joy or satisfaction he gets from getting his own hands dirty, or because he likes things done "his way", but you need to be cautious here. Such an argument might be an entirely valid reason for him to do some things himself, but not everything. And certainly not if his submissive could do the things equally well. On the other hand, arguing that he enjoys getting his hands dirty may be an excuse rather than a reason, an excuse which he might be making entirely unconsciously. It can be like a vanilla guy spending too much time tinkering with his car in the garage instead of being with his wife. The car and the tinkering becomes an excuse to avoid the wife.

When a submissive complains that his or her dominant won't let her do things for him, or that she's never given any serious tasks or duties, any of the reasons above can be the cause. In all of the above situations, communication with your partner, introspection, and, above all, honesty with yourself are the keys to resolving them.

## 30.4 Failing to transition from training to use

When a dominant and a submissive or a master and a slave set up shop together, one of the things which the dominant or master may do is begin to train the submissive or slave. This can be a mutually satisfying and exciting time in the relationship.

For some BDSM partnerships, the training can take the form of the dominant or master teaching his new partner about the various activities he does. This can be the way he conducts an impact play scene, how he runs a pain play scene, the positions, postures and implements he prefers to use, and so on. For a dominant with a service-oriented submissive or slave the training might also consist of assigning duties, monitoring how well they are performed, applying correction, etc. In either case, the dominant has a lot to communicate to his partner, and this can be a very "hands on" and rewarding process.

## BDSM Relationships - Pitfalls and Obstacles

What happens when the training phase is over? When the submissive or slave is educated in the ways of the master, or when the submissive has learned all the tasks and duties her partner desires her to do, what then?

The risk—and, indeed, the consequence—for many is summed up in the typical Internet post shown in figure 30.1 on the next page.

Training can't go on forever. At some point, the person who is being trained has learned all their trainer or partner has to offer. After training, what comes next?

The ideal answer is use. Once a submissive or slave has been sufficiently trained, the dominant should be able to use the submissive according to how she has been trained. If she's a service-oriented submissive, then she should be serving him drinks, cooking his food, performing oral sex on him, etc. If she's been trained instead to absorb all the punishment he can hand out in the dungeon, then that's where she should shine and he be happiest. We've seen though that one of the key parts of BDSM is penetration. During training of a slave or submissive, there is a lot of penetration between the master and the submissive. The master is constantly monitoring or correcting. Once the training is over, the level of penetration often drops dramatically. Certainly, the slave or submissive will be useful in their own way, but the dominant doesn't really get to be dominant to the same extent as during training, and the slave may well feel left alone or even abandoned because while their partner is still there physically, the actual D&s penetration has gone.

We can see this happening in the example in the Internet post. The initial phase of this slave's relationship with her master was based on training. This required her master to compel or

> Dear mailing list,
>
> When my master and I first began our relationship he knew exactly what he wanted and expected from me. I put in a *lot* of time, effort and struggle to adjust so that I could be the slave he wanted me to be.
>
> I remember how hard it was. Many of my most personal beliefs and values were challenged by all this—not just because he was asking for a lot, but also because I had to confront myself and really closely examine what it was that I wanted and needed. The exchange of power which I felt with each way of thinking I confronted, and with each behaviour I learned or unlearned was palpable.
>
> Now most of the challenges from the early days are behind me. I have adapted so that all his requirements and expectations are second nature to me now.
>
> But now I have a question: because all the change in me has been done, does this mean that there is no more power exchange between us?
>
> Slave Sue

Figure 30.1: Failed training-to-use transition post

require her to achieve standards which he set. The intensity of the penetration she felt came from his determination. As she says, "he knew exactly what he wanted and expected".

But once she has learned how to behave or not behave, and has learned the standards and values which her master requires, the penetration stops happening. There is no need for any effort from him to reshape her. Indeed, there is no need for her to reshape herself in light of his needs or desires because she has already done so.

This is a common scenario when any form of training is involved. At some point, the trainer has done all of the training possible. What then? In the case of someone who is purely a trainer, the trainee (the slave in this case) goes back to their owner to be used.

However, in the example we have a trainer who is also nominally the master or owner of this slave, but the transition from trainer to owner hasn't occurred. What appears to have happened is that there has been an awkward fading from trainer-who-trains to trainer-who-doesn't-have-anything-to-train, and this is, of course, unsatisfactory (probably for both concerned).

There's a big difference between how a trainer engages their trainee and how an owner or master engages their slave. The risk with failing to make this transition properly is that you end up with something like the above example—namely someone who is in service but who is not being engaged or penetrated.

The main problem is that new BDSM couples faced with this often started out in their relationship recognising that training would be very exciting and powerful for them both. In fact, it can be intensely exciting, and it is one of the main, easy ways of getting a lot of engagement and interaction with lots of expressions of power. Wonderful!

## BDSM Relationships - Pitfalls and Obstacles

However, phase two is often neglected. What do you do with a trained slave or submissive that will engage both you and them? If your slave is trained to serve coffee with immaculate perfection, then while the training phase might have been intense and painful, once trained the slave doesn't need correction and, in fact, possibly won't need any correction or masterly expressions from their partner ever again. And, of course, serving then becomes a chore or unsatisfying because it's no longer about a productive BDSM engagement and exploring and experiencing power, it's merely about coffee.

There are a couple of ways around this problem.

Pessimistically, you could simply accept that there won't be any joy once training is complete. You simply move on to a new partner. In fact, this happens rather a lot.

Alternatively, you could plan for the use phase well before the training ends (preferably even before you set yourself up with your trainee). Having concrete goals for your trained submissive which include opportunities for you to command and direct them, to engage them, and to create situations where they can feel used and even objectified, may keep the relationship ticking along quite nicely.

- You could use your submissive as a tool in activities you usually perform just by yourself. For example, if you do your own car maintenance, or run your own business, or do your own computer repairs, then while you are busy with this use your submissive to fetch things, to watch a screen, to hold something, etc. If you enjoy cooking, put them to work cutting onions or celery, or stirring the pots while you do more critical things like adding spices or cooking the meat.

- Try to avoid "invisible service". This is where your submissive or slave does things so that you aren't involved at all. While this may be OK for a servant you employ, it can be a disaster in D&s. Instead, make sure you are involved authoritatively in most or all of the service they perform, such as your approval being required for the breakfast, lunch, and dinner menus each and every day before they are prepared; your submissive not being allowed to dress in the morning until you have chosen or approved their clothes; them not being allowed to arrange outside activities—such as shopping, hairdresser appointments, social visits, pleasure outings, etc.—without your prior approval in each case.

Unfortunately, some people can't make this transition from training to use. A lot of the time, in fact, it's probably and actually inappropriate because it is the training itself which is what is exciting for the master and for the slave.

We live in a society where we are encouraged to do for ourselves and this makes using someone (as opposed to training someone) a difficult step for many. I have come across a number of masters who are quite comfortable with the training, or the tying up, or the flogging of their partners, but who are very uncomfortable with being served. Instead of preparing the daily chores, or assigning tasks or errands to their slave partners, they do the things themselves.

Tasks, duties and errands also provide opportunities for penetration and engagement. A master need not make this up just to keep their partner busy, but can take their own ordinary, everyday activities and farm them out to their slave. For example, sending one's slave out to do the banking, chase up quotes for a job, organise invitations to party, or get master's car repaired, can all provide exciting and satisfying duties for a service-oriented slave.

Once training is done—and if he successfully makes the transition from trainer to master—the master then gets to direct her in the execution of the tasks and duties he assigns her. In return he, ideally, gets to see his projects being developed and pushed forward by more than just him. Done well, he will feel that his slave is an extension of his will and desire which is focussed on his personal priorities. His slave will feel herself being moved and directed by his determination.

A final note here: once training is completed, the master must also have goals which he expects and wants to use his slave to achieve, such as to have her perform as *maître d'* at his formal dinner parties, or to help him run his business. Her uniqueness then determines how these goals are achieved. This is important because rather than the goals being achieved as he would do them himself, she achieves the goals with her own unique stamp. When the service slave is combined with a master, the end result is not merely the same work as the master would do multiplied by two, but is instead the master's goals and projects achieved by two unique individuals working towards them.

## 30.5 Power decay

Failing to transition from training to use is an example of what we could call power decay. One of the pillars of BDSM and of BDSM relationships is a disparity of power, and one of the main sources of power in BDSM is motivation or drive. When a dominant has a strong drive to tie up, hurt, flog, or control their partner then this is a power that they have. This is an intensity which they can express with their partner.

While a top or dominant may have a significantly higher skill level at some BDSM activities than their submissive, or they may be physically stronger than their submissive, often it is the need or desire to use this skill or strength which is the actual source of power which the dominant feels and which their submissive is subject to.

When hunger, drive, or passion diminishes, power tends to diminish with them. Failing to transition from training to use may simply mean that the dominant or master concerned has a strong drive or need to train his submissive, but that he then doesn't have a strong need to use her once she is trained. When this is the case, his passion or drive is obviously going to diminish as her training with him reaches its end. The disparity of power component of their BDSM fades, and with it goes any penetration both he or she may feel.

This decay in power can occur for other reasons. For example:

- When BDSM is used to satisfy a need, a change in circumstances may mean that the need disappears. Someone with a stressful job who used BDSM for catharsis may not need it any more if they change to a less stressful job.

- A submissive who enters into BDSM looking simply for pain or hotter-sex-through-bondage may find that as their tastes become more refined and as they gain experience that simple rope play or a quick flogging no longer does it for them. Their current partner may not be able to go where they need to go and so the submissive effectively disempowers their dominant as they outgrow them.

- BDSM may initially seem exciting or titillating, and this novelty may be enough to maintain the passion, but with experience the novelty will necessarily fade and if it was the novelty which was keeping the fires alive then the power fades with it.

## 30.6 Imagination, images and engagement

One of the issues I see which causes a breakdown in BDSM relationships is actually more of a failure to start them properly. This is related to something I explored in *This Curious Human Phenomenon*[2], namely how is it possible for two people to meet at a BDSM play party, chat for a while, and then go off into a convenient dungeon and have a most intense BDSM scene? How can a dominant engage and penetrate so intensely someone he or she has only just met? How can a submissive have such an intimate experience with someone she doesn't really know?

I wrote in *Curious* that they weren't actually having such an intense experience with the actual person, but instead were largely projecting their own internal ideas and needs onto this person they had just met. In their own minds, they imagine that this person they have just met is more than they actually are. They project an image of their ideal partner onto this new person, even if they aren't an ideal fit.

This is OK strictly in this play party context because it serves to get things started and let off some steam. But it's only

---

[2][MASTERS2008, pp. 77 - 87]

useful in this play party context. Beyond the play party the whole experience can be misleading because it might suggest that there's some actual chemistry involved.

Let's look at this a little more.

Suppose a guy goes to a party and meets an amazing vision of female goddess-ness. If she deigns to speak to him or, amazingly, rests her feet on him or gets him to fetch her a drink, then he might have a most powerful reaction. But who or what is he really reacting to? If he has just met her then it can't be her. She might have just walked in the door and he feels compelled to drop to his knees. But it can't be her who he is reacting to because he doesn't know her at all. He may later discover that she, in fact, is not dominant in any way but that doesn't stop him getting turned on in this first instant.

If he can't be reacting to her, then he must be reacting to an image in his own mind of how a female dominant should look or act. This process frequently happens when one person sees or meets another, and it may work to kick start a relationship—i.e., "I'll spend time with you because you look like the sort of person I'd like to spend time with".

However, for a relationship starting this way to go the distance, a transformation needs to occur. Instead of being excited by the image in our mind of our partner, we need to become excited by this partner themselves. For the abovementioned guy and the female dominant, he needs to be excited by her herself rather than by the image in his mind which excited him initially.

Trying to continue a relationship just with an image is like masturbation. It's having a relationship with yourself. While this may be nice—and certainly precludes disappointment—there is little engagement with your actual partner and hence it's not going to lead to a satisfying BDSM relationship.

## BDSM Relationships - Pitfalls and Obstacles

Some BDSM activities are more likely candidates in which such image relationships can occur or persist than others. Flogging is a good example. The most common targets for flogging are the back or buttocks. Due to the way we humans are built, most floggings are not done face-to-face. This means that during flogging neither the dominant nor the submissive gets to see their partner's facial expressions, winces, grunts, or exertions. This is ideal territory for relating to an image rather than our real partner because if we can't see our partner's face, how can we really engage or connect with them?

Indeed, most of the time we might not be connecting with them at all during a flogging scene but instead be connecting to an image of them. Because we can't see their face, we might be imagining or guessing how they feel or how they are responding. We might base this on what we know about them in particular, or on our previous experience with other partners.

When we can't directly communicate with our partner, such as when we can't see their face, or when they are covered up during mummification or are wearing a hood, we rely on other signals and messages. These other messages and signals which we get from our partner and which help us to engage them, especially when we can't see their faces, include hand-waving, grunts, moans, wiggles, writhes, muscle movements, laughs, and even occasional words or phrases. But even with these we might interpret a particular wriggle as meaning one thing when our partner is really feeling something else.

This is where engagement with our real partner comes in. As we learn about our partner and become familiar with their actions and reactions, we have less of a need to fill in the gaps with our imagination or from how previous partners reacted because we <u>know</u> our partner and don't need to guess or imagine. Getting back to flogging as an example, this means that when they wriggle a certain way or make a particular sound we don't have to guess what this means or try to think back to how other submissives or dominants behaved. We know exactly what it means, and thus we are engaging our real partner rather than an image in our mind or some generic or average partner from our past experience.

This leads us to one of the problems with some BDSM scenes: it can be hard to feel engagement with your partner when they are playing at being a dead fish (i.e., not moving or responding in an obvious way but hopefully not really dead). This feedback is vitally important both to preventing the image problem, and to allowing our partners to feel engaged and penetrated by us.

Being able to engage our real and actual partners means knowing what they feel, how they react, and what they mean when they communicate with us. After a scene we tune into this more by sitting down with them and talking about how they feel, what they were thinking during the scene, what certain actions or sounds meant and so on. At the same time, we share our thoughts and reactions with them so they can be better tuned in to us.

## 30.7 Testing and challenges

A submissive or slave who needs to feel a firm hand—metaphorically speaking—is going to tug on their metaphoric leash from time to time to check that their partner is still paying attention. They do this when they feel that perhaps they have too much freedom, or that their partner isn't supervising or correcting them sufficiently.

Remember that BDSM is about penetration and if a slave or submissive isn't feeling sufficiently penetrated by their partner then they may consciously or unconsciously do things to get a reaction from their partner. They may become disrespectful, inattentive, or downright disobedient.

There are, of course, SAMs (Smart-Assed Masochists) who may deliberately be disrespectful, frisky, or mischievous to provoke a reaction from their partner, often as a power play (i.e., to try to demonstrate that they're in charge). But others may be doing it because they are genuinely feeling a lack of something from their partner.

If you notice that your submissive or slave partner has periods of restlessness, lack of attention, or disobedience, then look to see if it is their way of getting you to tighten things up. They may be feeling a lack of direction from you, and just a little more attention from you in regards to their discipline may be all that they require.

## Sabotage

A SAM may also behave the way they do defensively. When they are consciously or unconsciously afraid they can behave in a smart-assed way to change the course of what's going on to protect themselves. For example, if they are unconsciously afraid of the intensity of their feelings once these feelings are released, or are afraid of surrendering to their own reactions with someone they don't know well or who they don't trust, they may do something to irritate or annoy that person or to deflect what they're doing so as to reduce the threat of exposing themselves or of becoming too vulnerable. It can be the case that they don't consciously know why they do this. As they say, "I don't know why I did that."

What they're doing is sabotage to prevent themselves getting into a situation which scares them. For example, a submissive who knows that they easily slip into a state of surrender or sub-space in which they are quite vulnerable might still enjoy the attentions of a dominant, but when the action or context starts to get close to where she might get triggered, she'll do something to deflect this, to change the context to one where she feels safe again. Being a smart ass is one way of doing this.

In section 30.15 on page 426 we'll see some other strategies which are specifically aimed at avoiding surrender.

## 30.8 Boredom

If BDSM stops inspiring you or your partner for some reason it can manifest itself in a few obvious ways:

- Boredom with what you and your partner are doing together,

- Feeling that what used to be satisfying is now merely ho-hum,

- The difficulty and challenge is gone. What used to be demanding and hard work is now such familiar territory that you can do it with your eyes closed and one hand tied behind your back (which may actually be the case anyway!), or

- Not feeling a connection with your partner any more. You're both going through the motions, and the BDSM activities themselves still work mechanically, but it's like there's no one on the other end of the flogger.

It might be that the original reasons you and your partner got into BDSM are no longer there. Some people outgrow BDSM. For others, their life circumstances change and BDSM loses the importance it once had. If you feel that your BDSM has lost its edge, talk with your partner. Maybe exploring some other areas of BDSM will bring the zing back.

## 30.9 Failure to communicate

Many relationship problems come down to poor communication. Talk deeply and talk often. Don't let things get bad before saying something. Don't feel embarrassed. Be open. Don't judge.

The important thing about all this is that some BDSM misconceptions can get in the way of communication. I've mentioned a few already in this series of books, but communication is always a topic worth revisiting.

Although a dominant is supposed to be in charge, they aren't necessarily supposed to have all the answers. That doesn't mean that your submissive will either, but they are another source of information. When you don't know what to do or are puzzled then ask. Admitting that you don't know is more a sign of strength than weakness, and it can often indicate that you want to include your partner rather than exclude them. This is a good thing. Muddling on when there is better information available, or when your partner can help, is not a sign of strength and can seriously damage your image in the eyes of your partner and of those people around you, e.g., other BDSM folk.

If you're a submissive then the story is similar. Just because you wear a label that says "submissive" or "slave" doesn't mean that you know what to do, what to think, or how to achieve everything. If you don't know how to do something, say so. E.g., if you don't know how to do a slick 3-step kneel and how to smoothly rise to your feet, find someone to show you or who will teach you. Don't just cobble something together and hope it's right.

There's an odd idea about that you should be able to do everything yourself. Learning the physical and mental skills to be an effective submissive is not always easy, and you might not be able to learn them just on your own or just with your usual partner. Ditto for dominants. If you are married and you and your partner have only just discovered BDSM, it can be difficult to consider going outside the marriage to learn more. But learning about BDSM, getting training on how to tie knots or how to flog, getting tips and advice from other dominants and submissives, or even inviting someone along to your own private dungeon to show you both how some BDSM activities work, is not going to violate your marriage oaths.

Communicate with your partner. Communicate with other BDSM folk. Don't let ego or insecurity get in the way.

## 30.10 Not showing reactions

In most scenes or engagements with your dominant partner, they need you to react. They are not there just to hit you, they want and need to see you react to being hit. They need to see the effect of the pain. Likewise, your service-oriented partner doesn't bring you drinks and massage your feet because it turns them on to do so. They need to see and feel your reaction to it.

Don't be a black hole into which your partner pours their attention and energy and from which nothing escapes. Show your feelings. Respond. Wriggle. Squirm. Moan. Often it is the case that your reaction—whether you're a dominant or a submissive, master or slave—is going to be what makes things work best for you both.

Displaying your reactions creates a connection with your partner. They get to *feel* you rather than being in the poorer position of having to guess what you're feeling. In other words, displaying your reaction increases engagement.

One way of thinking of this is that rather than being two separate individuals doing BDSM together, you and your partner are a team, even a tightly-bound single unit. What you do together is not two individual experiences which just happen to be occurring in the same location at the same time. The most intense times for you both as partners in this relationship is when what happens between you is actually one intense experience which you share. The less you communicate—either verbally or non-verbally—the more it becomes two separate experiences. The more you communicate, the more it becomes one single experience.

It's not always the case that the times with your partner are one shared experience though. As we've seen, some folk have different needs than their partner and it can easily be that sometimes one partner is getting more out of it than the other, or that each is using what they're doing together to take them to two separate places.

## 30.11  Not knowing your partner's needs

If you or your partner don't say what you want or need, or you don't show how you're feeling, or you don't display any reactions to what they do, then they have to guess what you want or need. And they may get it wrong.

If you don't know what your partner needs at any particular time, clarify. This applies regardless of which side of the power fence you're on—dominant, submissive, master or slave. Avoid guessing or assuming. It can be tempting to try to guess or to assume because if you're trying to impress someone then you don't want to appear ignorant.

In the middle of an intense scene you may not want to disturb the mood by suddenly pulling off your partner's gag and quizzing them on the finer points of clitoral stimulation as regards them, or you may not want to disturb the mood by stopping the scene and asking what they're trying to achieve by hitting you *there*; but do file the question away to ask later because the more you and your partner know about what works, what doesn't work, and when, the better you will be able to relate to each other and make things work really, really well.

## 30.12  Failing to adapt to growth

Imagine, if you will, an architect straight out of university. His first few projects out in the real world may be small—a public toilet block, a fountain, an extension to someone's garage, a scenic footpath in a park, etc. He is, however, likely to grow out of doing these as his skill and experience increase. His

*Recognising pitfalls and obstacles*

career may lead him to happily designing suburban apartment blocks for the rest of his career, or to designing civil engineering projects such as highway interchanges or bridges. Or maybe he will end up working for years at a time on individual projects, such as office towers or tunnel links between islands. At some point though, he will find where he is most comfortable. Not every architect aspires to design the world's tallest building. Maybe he will find his place and settle there doing medium-sized urban design projects.

In any case, the point here is that while he may start out with small projects, he will invariably rise above them. Exactly where he will rise to is difficult to say. And even if two different architects rise to the same level of technical expertise and challenge, they may be working on entirely different types of projects—such as office buildings versus bridges.

Something similar happens in the world of BDSM. Someone might enter the world of BDSM via fluffy handcuffs or through fantasies of leather-clad ladies holding whips, but where they end up is often next to impossible to guess. What we can be fairly sure about is that they will grow. Their BDSM tastes and preferences will develop and mature. Perhaps even their tolerance for pain will increase.

How does this effect their partner? If it was a mutual decision by two BDSM "virgins" to enter into the world of BDSM in a serious way together, they may find that they grow closer together if their interests remain shared and they mature in parallel. But if they discover that their maturing interests are taking them in separate directions, or if one is content with less intense or less severe BDSM than the other, then they may find their relationship breaking down.

## BDSM Relationships - Pitfalls and Obstacles

Sometimes breakdown is unavoidable. I've seen numerous cases where a couple spends many happy years together, perhaps bringing up a family, and then one urges them both into an exploration of BDSM. After a short time one of them discovers that BDSM strikes a deep chord in them and they throw themselves into it with a passion, leaving their long-term partner trailing along behind.

When BDSM appears to be leading you in separate directions there are things you can do which may prolong your relationship. There are possibly even things you can do which may keep you together. The most important thing is—as it always is—communication.

If you feel that BDSM may be moving you and your partner apart, discuss it with them. Be open and honest. Be clear about what's important for you. In particular, be receptive and understanding of their wants and needs and look for options where you can both find what you need. Be prepared to step back and reconsider your own position.

- If your partner is interested in doing or trying things which don't motivate you at all, or which actually turn you off, look for alternatives. Look for what's behind their interests or needs. Find out if there are other things which work for you both. BDSM is a big wide world involving many, many different activities and types of relationships. Maybe something you haven't yet thought of will provide the level of satisfaction which you and your partner are seeking. In book two of this series I have a chapter called *The lists* where I categorise over two hundred different BDSM activities. Maybe you will find something there.

- Consider alternate ways of getting wants or needs met. If your partner, for example, discovers a powerful

*Recognising pitfalls and obstacles*

and overwhelming need for very heavy flogging and it's something you simply can't do but otherwise your relationship is sound, then maybe your partner could offer themselves up as a practice dummy for flogging training courses, or maybe you could both frequent BDSM clubs or social events where he could get his flogging needs met by someone else. You both could even consider engaging a professional BDSM mistress or master from time to time.

- Seriously look at yourself and your views on things. If your partner discovers an intense desire to be submissive and your conservative upbringing shies away from being part of this, then step back. Maybe having someone to grovel at your feet, worship the ground you walk on, give you great massages while dressed in a G-string, and bring you food and drink, are things you could learn to love and even lust after yourself.

While not always possible, if there is a solution to growing apart due to BDSM, it definitely involves communication, openness, honesty, being receptive, and being prepared to reconsider or change your position.

## 30.13 Accelerated growth

While changes in people which might affect their relationships often take a long period of time to occur, sometimes growth in BDSM is very quick. Take someone who is into flogging, for example. They may have started out their BDSM journey receiving light floggings and avoiding anything to do with blood, bruising or marking. Fast-forward a few months and you might find them involved in the heaviest caning or flogging scenes and being left with bruises and weals which last for days. What has changed in that short time?

Have they become enlightened? Have they changed in some profound way? Has their physiology morphed in those few short months so that now they are extra-human?

What's happened is that they have learned about themselves. They haven't fundamentally changed, but what they thought they were, what limits they thought they had, has been replaced by a better understanding of themselves.

One could say that what they thought they were, and what limits they thought they had at the start of their BDSM journey were not real or were possibly incomplete. If the poundings that they take now are profoundly satisfying, what were the quick stings and tickles those few months ago? Perhaps they were licentious hints of what was to come.

We could argue that if what they are doing now is right for them, then what they were doing a few months ago wasn't. Those few months ago they were experiencing what they thought they needed or wanted, but it was all aimed at a false or incomplete image of themselves. And because it was aimed at a false image it was probably not fully satisfying.

It may have been new, exciting and thrilling, and this can sometimes pass for something profound. But being merely new, exciting and thrilling rarely satisfies for long. To be profoundly satisfying and fulfilling it needs to be aimed at the real person and at their real needs, not at an illusion, false image, or idealised presentation.

## 30.14 Unconscious limits

When we talk about limits in BDSM, most people think of the sorts of limits which get negotiated before a scene. For example, a bottom may tell her top that she doesn't want rope marks or rope burns, doesn't want any bruising except on her butt, and that she doesn't agree to unprotected sex. These are her limits for the scene.

Limits provide protection. For example, no bruises or marks except on the butt might be necessary for a woman who works as a model, or for a guy who plans on going to the beach the next day with vanilla friends who aren't aware of his BDSM inclinations. This sort of limit protects them from embarrassment, awkward explanations, or even social rejection.

Someone might have other limits because they find an activity terrifying, against their beliefs, just plain unpleasant, or because they have legitimate medical concerns, such as an allergy or a fear of infection.

As someone gets more experienced or skilled in BDSM activities, or as they become more comfortable with their own reactions or with their partner, they may refine their limits. They may look for more intensity and risk the marks, or they may schedule some of their activities so that any marks will have faded by the time they need to show the affected parts of their bodies to others.

A certain respectful awareness of your own weaknesses, strengths, and background can help you to create useful and effective limits. While bruises and abrasions are obvious limits for some people, less obvious limits—such as avoiding play rape scenes for someone who was abused as a child—are important to others.

Up to this point I've been talking about conscious limits, about the rational choices we make to protect something we're fully aware might be at risk.

Many people, on the other hand, will automatically and unconsciously avoid some activities—both in their vanilla and BDSM lives—-which present some sort of risk or threat, and they'll automatically and unconsciously embrace other activities which are safe and reassuring. They do this without consciously thinking about it. Their unconscious mind guides their choices in such a way as to keep them safe. For example, someone who was raped or abused as a child may unconsciously and automatically avoid situations which have the potential to remind them of what they went through such as being tied up in particular circumstances, the use of knives on them, verbal threats, and so on.

In an ideal world we'd be able to discuss all of our limits with our partners, and we'd negotiate with them and agree on what's in and what's out. But what about unconscious limits? What about the choices our unconscious mind makes which we're not aware of?

One of the ways the unconscious can get involved with and interfere with our BDSM is in our choice of partners. It can push us towards choosing a partner who simply can't cause our limits to be breached because they are either physically or psychologically incapable in some way.

## Someone who is physically incapable

Let us suppose we're talking about a submissive who is afraid of surrendering, or who has had an unfortunate experience with a top in the past who physically harmed her through an unsafe flogging. Her unconscious mind may push her towards choosing someone who has some physical or medical handicap as her next top or dominant. This is a very effective way of ensuring that her limits will never be exceeded.

For example, she may choose a dominant or top who is extremely unfit or overweight. They are unlikely to ever place any physical demands on her. They're not going to be able to engage in heavy or intense flogging scenes because they don't have the stamina or energy for it. Likewise, unless she is very tiny, they're not going to be able to haul her around and do physically challenging scenes such as suspension bondage or intense military interrogations with her.

She can still do whatever her dominant or top wants while being safe in the unconscious knowledge that he won't be able to get anywhere near her limits. For her unconscious this is a win-win situation because she gets to be as submissive and compliant as possible while never getting near anything that her unconscious considers unsafe.

You might think that this sort of situation is not 100% guaranteed to protect her. For example, what happens if her top enlists the aid of another, fitter top to help out in a more demanding scene? With this extra horsepower shouldn't she be facing the same sort of risk her unconscious was trying to avoid?

At first glance, this might seem true, but this is the unconscious mind we're talking about here, and it has an answer. This situation is easily defeated by her unconscious insisting that she's shy or embarrassed in front of others, or that she is just a "one-man woman" and will only play with her top. Her kind and considerate dominant will never force her to do something she doesn't like and so she's safe.

Medical problems—such as blindness, diabetes, heart conditions, asthma, and even allergies—can also create physical limitations for some tops and dominants which a submissive can unconsciously exploit. While the submissive can say they are up for anything, by choosing such a limited partner they have created a situation where their dominant's own physical limits protect the submissive from getting anywhere which the submissive unconsciously thinks is unsafe.

This behaviour of unconsciously choosing a partner with physical limitations has D&s ramifications because the submissive's unconscious mind has already taken control of much of the shape of the couple's BDSM relationship and there isn't really anything the top or dominant can do about it, even if he is aware of it... which is probably unlikely.

It isn't just submissives who make such unconscious choices like this. Dominants can also unconsciously choose partners with physical limitations so that they don't have to go into certain areas or perform certain activities which they feel uncomfortable with or which they find challenging. For example, a dominant who lacks confidence in his flogging ability, who lacks strength in his arm, or who doesn't have a lot of stamina, might be attracted to a submissive who has back problems. His unconscious might tell him that her charm, wit, intelligence, or ability to go into sub-space are highly attractive and this gives him an excuse to avoid flogging almost completely. It may be that she's not really that attractive after all, but if his unconscious mind pushes hard enough he'll come to think she is and this protects him from having to confront his shortcomings.

## Someone who is intellectually or emotionally incapable

When we stray into the areas of BDSM which are less physical and more intellectual or psychological such as D&s or M/s, then a very effective way for a submissive to unconsciously ensure that she isn't dominated more than she's comfortable with is simply to pick a partner who isn't as experienced or as smart as she is.

This works for a submissive or bottom who is, for example, keen on the physical side of BDSM—the floggings, canings, piercings and bondage—but who unconsciously doesn't want anyone who can psychologically dominate her. Thus, a muscle man with limited brains who can barely string two grunts together may seem very attractive to her. He can certainly push her physical buttons, and at the same time she can manipulate him fairly easily so that he thinks he is getting the whole D&s package when he is actually only getting the wrapping.

The unconscious mind can be quite subtle, and a dominant may not even realise that he or she is in a situation where they are being manipulated by the clever and devious unconscious of their submissive partner. In the present example, this unconscious is aiming to allow the submissive any number of physical experiences, and at the same time is protecting her from being dominated or controlled psychologically. Surrender is probably an element in this. Psychological surrender is sometimes more threatening than physical surrender and is potentially easier to avoid—and stay safe from—if the submissive is smarter, quicker, or more experienced than the dominant.

The dominant may even think how lucky he is to have such a smart submissive at his beck and call!

Like all the unconscious limits I am talking about here, a dominant can create or impose them just as much as a submissive. For example, a dominant who is unconsciously insecure may pick a submissive who is intellectually his inferior and thus be certain both of his ability to dominate and of her inability to resist.

In contrast, for someone who is looking for the experience of actually controlling his partner, having control provided on a platter in the form of a submissive who simply cannot provide any resistance can take much of the excitement away because there is little challenge and, importantly, little penetration with them.

## Someone who is geographically incapable

There are all sorts of BDSM connections and activities which truly flower when there is long-term, ongoing, and continuous contact between two people. Profound explorations of control are a good example, and these can be found in some forms of D&s and M/s. For these to be successful, it generally needs the people involved to be together frequently such as when they live together or work together in the same small office or local area. This extended contact creates the opportunity for deep control to be imposed, developed and enjoyed.

This isn't going to happen for people who don't live or work together or who live in different cities. A submissive who only sees her dominant every second weekend will still need to retain extensive authority over her life. She'll have to earn money without her dominant being involved. She'll have to do shopping, prepare food for herself, clean her apartment, make important life choices, plan her financial future and retirement, and deal with all sorts of day-to-day issues without him. This isn't because he can't give her direction, but with him having such a tiny involvement in her life he can't actually make effective decisions because he simply doesn't have the awareness of her life to do so.

So, for a submissive or slave who wants only to experience superficial control and surrender, or who is unconsciously afraid of experiencing anything more, picking a partner who can only have a long-distance relationship can be ideal. Someone who lives in a different city, or who is perhaps in the military and is away frequently, is perfect.

It's worth considering that on-line BDSM relationships can fit into this sort of geographical incapability. Internet-based, real-time chat offers a chance for people to engage in limited forms of D&s or M/s, but the same sorts of limitations apply here as they do with geographically distant partners. Time spent facing each other from behind the glass screens is limited. It may be that the two people involved really only have an understanding of what they can see through the camera. Life must go on when each person is away from their screen. Food must be prepared and eaten, clothes bought, bills paid, and so on. The control in such situations may only be transient and shallow without the possibility of anything more.

## Someone who is time incapable

If a submissive enjoys D&s but unconsciously either doesn't want it full time or wants frequent time-outs, a good choice can be to pick a dominant partner who runs their own business—and who, therefore, often works late—or a dominant who has children who either live with them or who they see frequently.

Business and family frequently create times when BDSM simply can't be done. While Sir Diddums might still be the master or dominant when the kids are around, he's not going to be in a position to have his submissive crawl around on all fours in front of them. This can be her respite from anything too intense.

A dominant might also unconsciously choose a submissive who has time constraints because it can limit how much responsibility he needs to shoulder. If the submissive works in an area of emergency services and might get called out to work at any time, it means the dominant escapes having to do intense scenes because their submissive must be ready to go to work and deal with other people's traumas at any time. They can't be in a state that needs too many bandages or too much aftercare.

## Problems with this strategy

The big problem with consciously or unconsciously picking a partner who is actually incapable of pushing your limits today is that he or she will be just as incapable of pushing them tomorrow, next month, or next year. When you reach a point where you want to increase your limits and look for more variety, intensity or challenge, your limited partner can't go with you. The only real choice you have is either to abandon your BDSM and personal growth and stay with them—which may be necessary if you have set up a family or had kids with them, or give up your partner and move on to someone else who has fewer inherent limits.

Avoiding having to make this choice sounds deceptively easy: pick a partner who can grow with you. However, if you find yourself attracted to someone who is clearly inferior, who is somehow or sometimes unavailable, or who is lacking in some important areas—such as health, fitness, wit, cleverness, or IQ—then you really should be asking yourself what you see in them and what sort of future you can have with them. Your unconscious mind reacts to the here-and-now. It may be pushing you towards someone who is "safe" today, but who may not be able to keep you company on your BDSM journey in the long term.

## 30.15 Avoiding surrender

An important part of BDSM is being engaged by your partner and being engaged by them, but for this to happen you need to open yourself up to what they do, and they need to open themselves up to what you do.

I need to digress for a moment here because I have a little linguistic problem. I want to talk about surrender and "limited surrender", but some dictionary definitions and some writers on the subject of surrender consider surrender to be absolute and that you can't surrender in a limited way. When you hold something back, they instead call this "submission". This is a very important distinction, and it's one I need to make and use in the following paragraphs. Unfortunately, the term "submission" has a different connotation for many people into BDSM and I don't want my use of it here to cause confusion or offence by implying that what they do and how they label themselves is in any way inferior.

## BDSM Relationships - Pitfalls and Obstacles

So for the moment, when you open yourself up completely to the experience I'll call it surrender. When you only open yourself up in a limited way, trying to keep control of the experience, I'll call it submitting or submission. You'll see why I want this distinction imminently.

Submitting is sometimes a preferred option to surrender. Suppose you know that after a few taps of a flogger your inhibitions go out the door and you're anyone's. Clearly, being anyone's is not a safe thing all the time, especially with a new partner who you don't know and can't fully trust. However, you may like being tapped with a flogger even without getting to the point of being anyone's. This means that with someone you've just met at a BDSM play party you need to stop the flogging action before you reach the critical point. Part of you needs to hold back and keep a supervisory eye on what's happening so that you can say your safe word, wave a red flag, or whatever, at the necessary time. This means you can't completely surrender to the experience. You need to hold something back for the duration of the scene.

There are many other times and reasons when submitting, rather than surrendering, is the best option. For example:

- When you only have a limited amount of time and you need to keep an eye on the clock,
- When there are kids, family, or others nearby and you've got to limit how much noise you make,
- When you or your partner are trying something new and don't know quite how it's going to work out, and
- When you're with someone new and you don't want them to see how truly weird you are until you know they can handle it.

*Recognising pitfalls and obstacles*

It might seem that this discussion of surrender versus submission applies primarily to the folk on the receiving end of the cane or flogger, or to the ones being tied or humiliated, or to those who provide personal or sexual service to their partners. This isn't true. A master, top, or dominant can equally be in the position of needing to choose between submitting to the experience they are having with their partner or surrendering to it. For example, a top who is flogging a relatively new partner needs to pay close attention to the reactions of this bottom in case they become overwhelmed, distressed, or simply reach a physical limit such as starting to bleed. The top can't completely surrender to this shared experience because he needs to be ready to stop or change what he's doing at any time. On the other hand, if this top is flogging a partner with "leather skin"[3] he doesn't need to be on guard to such an extent and can really let himself go in terms of how hard he hits and for how long. He can surrender fully to the experience.

So all of this discussion about surrender applies equally well to masters, slaves, dominants, submissives, tops, and bottoms. By holding back for any reason, you can't fully immerse yourself into what's going on between you and your partner. You can't surrender to it.

All of the situations I've mentioned so far are good reasons to hold back. You know what's going on, you understand the situation, and you make the choice to proceed with engaging

---

[3] The term "leather skin" is sometimes used to refer to someone who has been flogged so often that their skin has adapted and become toughened. They can endure and embrace long, intense floggings with minimal bruising, redness, or abrasion.

your partner BDSM-wise knowing that you have to hold back. This is a conscious choice.

However, some people will hold back unconsciously. It's often fear of one sort or another. They may have problems with being intimate and therefore won't open the door all the way to you and what you're doing with them, or they'll stand at the door ready to push you out and slam it shut at a moment's notice. Others may have been hurt in the past and the fear they learned back then stops them being open now. They can't immerse themselves in the BDSM experience completely because part of them is afraid and is unconsciously holding themselves back.

## Strategies

People who unconsciously avoid surrender often have some interesting strategies to achieve this. For example:

- They may only play at parties. This is quite effective because play at a BDSM party is unlikely to be too intimate. Scenes at play parties are usually limited to about half an hour or so due to others wanting to use the play equipment or dungeon. Also, play at most parties tends to be conservative and this avoids anything too challenging, too intense, or too risky.

- They only agree to particular types of activity which don't risk surrender being triggered. Some types of scene compel surrender; it's unavoidable. For example, while you might gird your loins, endure a flogging, and not surrender, with some scenes involving intense stimulation or pain—such as cutting—no amount of girding is going to help you resist the pain forever. You must surrender to it eventually. By not getting involved with such scenes in the first place you can avoid surrender.

I hasten to add here that just because someone doesn't like intense pain or cutting it doesn't mean they're avoiding surrender. It might simply be something which doesn't have a positive outcome for them. For others for whom it is a doorway to intense and positive surrender, it can be something which they only do with someone they trust.

- They physically close their eyes so that they can be in their own little world and not have to see or face their partner. They may surrender to the physical feelings and sensations, but by closing their eyes they can exclude their partner from this experience. This means that they can avoid the risk of the bonding which can occur through the shared intensity or power of their BDSM experiences.

Following on from an earlier discussion, two other effective strategies someone might use to avoid surrender in a D&s context, as opposed to a physical play context, are:

- To unconsciously choose a partner who simply cannot physically or mentally dominate them, or
- To choose a situation where they can't be completely dominated such as only playing at D&s at a party where time is limited.

## Questions

1. Are there any activities you avoid—either as a dominant, top, submissive, bottom, etc.—because you feel nervous

about them even though they are, in themselves, technically quite safe?

2. Are there activities which make you uncomfortable for no obvious reason?

3. Are there activities or times when you feel yourself completely open to your partner, to what they're doing, and to where it's taking you?

4. Are there people who you can be more open with than others? What's the difference?

## 30.16 Being worshipped

I don't mind being worshipped. It can be a very nice thing. One of the key parts of a BDSM relationship is power disparity and the power disparity must be used or manifested to have any effect. Worship is a way in which each partner gets to represent or enact that power differential. The submissive or slave gets to lower themselves, debase themselves, or grovel below their master, mistress or dominant, while their master, mistress or dominant gets to stand over or take a place above their partner. Worship can and does allow the status or rank of each partner to be concretely played out. The way each person behaves clearly identifies one partner as being dominant or higher ranked, while the other is submissive or lower ranked.

This can be a good thing. For example, when worship is used to reinforce rank or role, or when it's used as a way to express the power the dominant or master has over their partner—such as by compelling the submissive to their knees, or to require them to kiss or lick their dominant's boots—this can be very effective and empowering.

However, worship can also be twisted into a bad thing such as when the dominant or master is *required* by their submissive to behave, or dress, or speak in particular ways to remain "worship-able"; then it becomes one-way and manipulative of the dominant or master. This can happen without the dominant being aware, and it means that the submissive is the one doing the controlling. This is not uncommon.

At first glance, being idolised might seem like a very nice thing for a dominant. It can seem quite complimentary and a boost for your ego to be put on a pedestal and treated as if the very ground you walk upon is sacred.

It is however, hard being an idol. For a start, you have to be available whenever your worshippers want to worship you. You don't get to set the schedule. They do. And like other idols you might not actually get anything from your worshippers. Many worshipful submissives are looking for a dominant who doesn't actually do anything except basically stand there, "look like a dom," and maybe occasionally wave a flogger or tie a knot. Being an idol means you have to maintain certain standards. Your submissive or slave may even demand it. If your halo drops, if you have a late night out on the turps and look a bit worse for wear in the morning, or if you don't dress to their standards, your worshipper will not be happy because you're not living up to the standard they require. They'll even get pissed off with you because you've damaged the image they need you to maintain and because you have, they feel, taken away their object of worship. In effect, you've descended from the pedestal they put you on without their permission.

This, I think, explains why the original gods and buddhas long ago moved on and left behind carved or sculpted statues in their place. Statues never let worshippers down. In fact, the worshippers construct them that way. The statues always have their hair in place, never have bad days, and can be constantly happy, jolly fellows—religion permitting.

A submissive or slave who approaches you AND who is all bubbling and effusive in their praise of you and your wonderfulness AND who insists on grovelling at your feet or worshipping you is someone to be wary of. There's nothing wrong with someone thinking that you're wonderful and amazing because you actually might be that as far as they are concerned. It is the worshipping and grovelling bit where things can go astray because these can easily become one-way. For someone to grovel at your feet, for example, you need either to be standing still or posing majestically instead of doing something you'd rather be doing. You stand still, you let your submissive grovel at your feet, and you're doing them a favour. It might even cost you because as well as the time lost, later on you'll have to clean the saliva trails off your shoes.

On the other hand, someone who thinks you're amazing and would like to spend time with you, maybe attend you or serve you, fetch you drinks and such like, could genuinely be trying to learn from you, or enjoy your skills and abilities, and give you something in return.

This idea of being compelled to maintain an image is, in itself, not a bad thing if it's open and honest. A worship-based relationship needs to be two-way, just like any other relationship in BDSM. Worshipping must be done as an adult. Worshipping your partner should mean that they have your respect as a person, as a dominant, and as your partner in the relationship. The key idea here is "partner" because your relationship is supposed to be mutual with both of you benefitting more-or-less equally.

Needing to present a certain image all the time is a chore, just ask a professional dominatrix. They always have to maintain a certain image, wear particular types of clothes (often uncomfortable if worn for long periods) and act in certain ways, otherwise their customers will stop coming back. They get paid to look and act this way and that is one reward they get out of it. For a dominant in a non-commercial relationship to feel compelled to do the same without compensation is manipulative and one-way.

Putting a dominant or master on a pedestal and worshipping them can also be a defensive move on the part of a submissive or slave. It can be done consciously or unconsciously as a way of creating distance between them and their master/dominant in a similar way to the strategies I discussed in section 30.14, *Unconscious limits*. As long as the dominant feels compelled to remain on the pedestal, they can't actually get down, become mortal, and fully engage their submissive or slave. This ensures that there always will be distance between the two of them. And if the submissive isn't feeling consciously or unconsciously safe enough, they just worship and grovel a bit more and thereby move their dominant to a taller pedestal.

This can all happen the other way around as well. If a dominant or master insists that his slave or submissive worships him all the time, or that they treat him like a minor god, it could be that he is trying to place distance between himself and his submissive or that he is trying to create a barrier to prevent getting too involved.

Although I'm focussing on the abuse of worship here, I would like to stress that worship can be a useful part of a BDSM relationship. It does reinforce rank, which can be very effective, and it can be helpful in maintaining distance when distance is needed. There's a saying that "familiarity breeds contempt" and it means that by getting to close or knowing too much about someone that they are lowered in your eyes. This may not be a good thing in some BDSM relationships and encouraging or even requiring worship can help prevent this... assuming that the dominant behaves in a way which merits worship, of course.

Worship is also a good tool where distance must be maintained for other reasons, such as in a part-time BDSM relationship where the people involved have other interests or obligations and can't do 24/7 BDSM. In this case, using a worship as a behavioural way of not getting too close can be excellent.

Worship can be a situation which leads to lack of engagement. If your partner metaphorically thinks that the Sun shines out of your rear end... well, it's obvious that it doesn't and if they're labouring under the illusion that it does then they're not engaging you. To have a strong and healthy relationship they need to be dealing with the real you. This is something I discussed right at the beginning of book one of this series. If they're interacting with someone who has solar radiation coming out of their butt hole then clearly they're not interacting with you. They're interacting with someone who they're imagining and even though this imaginary person might look like you, wear the same clothes as you, and be standing in the same spot you are, it's not you.

## Questions and discussion

For submissives and slaves:

- When you worship your dominant, or when you kneel or grovel at their feet, what do they get out of it?

*Recognising pitfalls and obstacles*

- You might find it very powerful, but what benefit, reward, satisfaction, or pleasure, do they get then and there?
  - How does your worship actually help them meet their own needs?

- Is there something your dominant or master could do, or stop doing, which would make it difficult or impossible for you to continue worshipping them? How would this effect your relationship?

- Do you serve your master or dominant? What relationship does your service have to worship?

For dominants and masters:

- Do you find that you need to maintain a certain image or certain standards for your submissive? Is this a burden?

- If you enjoy being worshipped, what is it that you find satisfying or rewarding?

    - Is it the implicit flattery?
    - Is the way they worship you physically or sexually exciting or pleasing?
    - Is it what happens after the worship?

- Does your submissive or slave serve you? How do they serve you, and is there any relationship between their service and their worship? If they no longer worshipped you, would the service continue? Would it change?

## 30.17 Avoiding responsibility

There are some folk who enter into the world of BDSM—particularly in areas such as D&s or M/s—who are there because they don't want to be answerable either for themselves, for their lives, or for much of what goes on around them.

They style themselves as submissives or slaves and see D&s as a way of handing off as much responsibility as possible to any poor sucker dominant who will take them on. They argue that their dominant takes control and, therefore, takes responsibility so that they—the submissive—can do whatever they want and they're never at fault.

Their dominant, on the other hand, is the one who gets blamed, who cops the flak, or who gets seen as a "bad dominant" who can't keep his submissive out of trouble. Should anyone try to talk to the submissive about any perceived attitude or behaviour problem, the submissive simply refers everything to their dominant: "I belong to Sir Dude and you have to take up any issues about me with him."

Inexperienced dominants can easily be taken in by such submissives. The submissive proclaims that they want or even need to be under the dominant's control and that they'll do whatever they're told. Indeed, at some superficial level they do seem attentive and responsive. The dominant is wooed by the submissive who insists that they are their partner's property, how much they love them, and how much they long to obey and be treasured. This can be very attractive to some dominants.

In reality, the submissive is manipulative and will have a ready supply of legitimate-sounding reasons and excuses for behaving badly or inappropriately. Their dominant will find that they're actually powerless to change their submissive's behaviour. The submissive may act profoundly apologetic if taken to task by their partner, but nothing will change.

These sorts of people exist throughout society. They look for other people to take responsibility for their actions, or they look for ways of denying responsibility for what they do. They aren't confined to BDSM. BDSM though, provides an environment where, on the face of it, someone else actually does take control and responsibility.

Neither responsibility nor answerability are diminished or destroyed in a healthy D&s relationship. What can and does happen is that a submissive makes themselves answerable to their dominant partner. Their dominant acquires the right and duty to set standards, and can insist on obedience and conformity to these standards. Failure leads to discipline or punishment. There is no decrease in responsibility here. On the contrary, responsibility and answerability increase in D&s.

It is not, and never is, the responsibility of a dominant to ensure that their submissive behaves politely, respectfully, and with consideration of others. This is a responsibility which we all have, regardless of whether we are in a BDSM context or not. Trying to invoke the magic phrases, "I'm XYZ's property," or, "I am a submissive," to avoid that responsibility is a good warning sign of someone who doesn't want to be a productive member of society.

## Recognising that this is happening

When these so-called submissives show up they can be difficult to spot. In all likelihood, they've been playing this game—and it is a game—a long time and are very good at getting away with it. More than this, they are very good at getting other people to play their game with them.

Here are some questions to consider:

- Do you feel disempowered in relation to your submissive?
- Do you feel like things are out of your control?
- Do you feel emasculated?
- Do you feel like there's nothing you can do to keep your submissive on the path of good behaviour?
- Do you feel actual fear of what they'll do next?

## Getting out

If you are a dominant involved with such a submissive, here are some important notes:

- Get out. You can't change them. They are experts at what they do. They would have changed a long time ago if they'd wanted to. They will not change for you. This can be a difficult thing for you, as a dominant, to accept, namely that you're powerless to make this person change or do what you want.
- By staying you are enabling them to continue playing this game which is harmful to you and to them.
- While you keep playing their game they are winning, and this is a bad lesson to give them.

## Dominants who avoid responsibility

Nominally it is the tops, dominants and masters who are in control. They are the ones who are supposed to make the decisions, direct the action, and set the priorities. There can be a lot of responsibility tied up in these things.

In purely physical scenes, such as cutting or bondage, there are a number of potential risks including infection, nerve damage, permanent scarring, broken bones or worse. When we start getting into long-term relationships, D&s relationships, M/s relationships and psychological play—such as humiliation, interrogation, and mind fucks—there's scope for emotional damage, trauma, fear, abuse and more.

A dominant, master, or top needs to step up to the plate and be ready to deal with these very possibilities. Sadly, some don't.

Some will say:

- After breath play gone wrong: "I didn't know she had a cold!" or "I didn't know she was asthmatic!"
- After their partner collapses during bondage: "I didn't know he had a blood pressure problem!" or "I didn't know I might need to get him out of the bondage in a hurry!" or "How was I to know the ropes were too tight?"
- After a flogging or whipping scene goes bad: "But she didn't say her safeword!"
- After a surprise play rape scene has a less than happy outcome: "How was I to know she was raped as a child?"
- The day after an intense scene: "How was I to know he might react badly?" or "How could I know that he'd need to talk to me the next day?"

## BDSM Relationships - Pitfalls and Obstacles

- In general: "It's not my fault! I did everything right!"

The point is that BDSM has risks. While we might talk about SSC[4] or RACK[5], neither these nor any other magic words take away the need for both people involved in any BDSM relationship to take responsibility for what they get into.

For dominant, tops and masters, they need to inform themselves, ask questions, read books, and talk to others before engaging in any activity which might put their partner at risk. In particular, they need to know the physical, emotional, psychological, and skill limits of both themselves and their partner. They need to know what might go wrong and have planned for it.

When you're the top, dominant or master you're often in the best position to prevent things going bad. Not taking advantage of that position to do so is irresponsible.

And if your partner is the top, dominant or master in your relationship and they avoid taking responsibility, find the nearest door and use it.

---

[4] A common BDSM motto: Safe, Sane and Consensual.
[5] Another common BDSM motto: Risk-Aware Consensual Kink.

*Recognising pitfalls and obstacles*

## Chapter 31

# Pushing the kinky sex line

In book one of this series, *Understanding BDSM Relationships*, I have a chapter called *Uncomfortable thoughts*, and one of the things I talk about in it is how some people dress their BDSM as kinky sex to make it more acceptable, often to themselves.

Even someone who is not very conservative can have trouble with the ideas that they like being hit or hurt by their partner, or that their partner likes hitting them or hurting them. The general idea in our society, in many families, and in many religions, is that you don't go around hitting people, especially someone you care about deeply. There are even laws which say hitting and hurting people can land you in prison. These attitudes generally encourage us to think of being hit or hurt as something which we shouldn't accept.

On the other hand, and particularly over the last few decades, sex—and even casual sex—has become more acceptable, more widely discussed, and even anticipated between two people who have only barely just met.

On top of this, it's easy to link our BDSM play and sex play. There are forms of BDSM which don't involve pain or ropes—such as sensation play or wax play—which can be quite sensual. It's one thing to talk about dripping hot wax on to someone, which can sound like a medieval torture, and quite another to describe dripping cooling wax onto our naked partner's nipples and then sensually peeling it off with our fingernails once it has set. The latter clearly sounds sexy while the former perhaps sounds pathological!

Sex shops invite bondage play between innocents when they sell the now-famous, fluffy pink handcuffs. The fact that we can buy them in sex shops means they must have something to do with sex, and the fact that using them is "about sex" makes the BDSM part more acceptable.

Heavier forms of BDSM, such as flogging or rope bondage, also become more acceptable if they don't involve blood, do involve nudity, and end with sex.

But as we have seen through the course of this series of books, hitting someone, tying them up, humiliating them, ordering them around, injuring them, bruising them, and so on, even when there's no sex in sight, can be positive, constructive and life-affirming for two people in many, many ways.

This all means that for many people exploring BDSM there is a line to cross, and that line separates seeing BDSM as kinky sex, and seeing some or all of BDSM as being quite distinct from sex. While you try to see BDSM as merely kinky sex then you can't see what might be positive aspects of BDSM without sex. If your BDSM play always needs to involve nudity, sex, or orgasms, then it can be hard to find some of the forms of surrender or catharsis which many other people look for and achieve in their BDSM.

Dominant and submissive relationships, and master/slave relationships, can especially become restricted and highly limited if you can or will only see BDSM in terms of sex. Topping and bottoming are typically scene-based, and these are quite amenable to being done in a one-on-one or sexual context such as in a bedroom or *sans* clothes in a dungeon. But D&s and M/s often extend outside of the dungeon or bedroom and for much or all of the time may be non-sexual. Embracing the idea that BDSM need not be about sex can liberate D&s and M/s relationships.

Going even further, when you can completely separate yourself from the idea that BDSM is about sex, it means that you can freely see which wants and needs you and your partner have which can or should be done without sex, and those which are compatible with sex. Sometimes sex can get in the way of meeting needs when it, and not the need, is the focus. But at other times, such as when BDSM is used for recreation, sex can be part of the play without interfering.

However, going back to acceptability for a moment, because we aren't encouraged by society to think of hurt, pain and restraint as acceptable, it can be that we simply don't think about them and whether they are important to us or to our partner. And because they may never come to mind we might not consciously realise that there is more than kinky sex going on in our BDSM, even when what we do is already heading in that direction.

*Pushing the kinky sex line*

## BDSM Relationships - Pitfalls and Obstacles

It's worthwhile then, especially for people who have been actively exploring BDSM for more than a short while, to periodically reflect on what they enjoy doing, the role of sex, and especially the role of things other than sex. Because there can be so much going on in BDSM, with so many different motivations, wants and needs involved, teasing out the individual aspects which are important and making sure they are addressed can make what we do much more satisfying and rewarding for us and our partners.

## Chapter 32

# Incomplete needs meeting

As we've seen throughout this series of books, BDSM is often about exploring and satisfying wants and needs which aren't always obvious. Certainly, some of the reasons why people do BDSM can be quite private and intimate, and for this reason they won't always communicate what they're pursuing to their partner unless they trust their partner completely... and sometimes not even then.

When two BDSM folk get together for a casual encounter it's implicit that what they do together must be satisfying, rewarding, or exciting for both of them. If one has to put in a lot of effort to satisfy their casual partner and doesn't get enough back then it's not worth their while to get involved in the first place. But in a longer-term relationship it doesn't need to be this way. Because there are going to be regular BDSM encounters between the two people involved it means that there doesn't need to be this per-scene balance that casual play tends to require. One partner can afford to devote themselves in one scene to the needs of their partner knowing that this will be balanced in the future.

This is particularly relevant because some of the needs which BDSM can satisfy are explicitly one-sided anyway. For example, and as I've already noted earlier, there can be a physiological release associated with tight rope bondage. This typically involves a comfortably-positioned submissive or bottom in a tight, full-body rope tie. Once tied they need to be quietly monitored for 15 minutes or so. This can be profoundly relaxing, a deep release and very calming for the submissive. Obviously, for the top who tied them up it's not very engaging. They need to just sit around, keep an eye on their tied partner, and then release them once the time is up.

There's a not-so-obvious aspect to this, which is that if you tie your partner up for such a session and then untie them too early you may end up with them feeling very irritable or less satisfied than when you started. Many BDSM activities can be like this. Too little or too much can be worse than nothing at all. Pain play, such as cutting, generally needs a certain amount of pain for a certain amount of time in a certain environment (e.g., quiet, alone with partner, warm, no music) to be effective. The wrong sort of pain, or too much pain, or too little pain, or pain which goes on for too long, or pain which doesn't go on for long enough, or the wrong environment may not lead to the necessary emotional or psychological release.

The rhythmic thudding of heavy flogging can take a submissive or bottom into what's called sub-space, which is quite relaxing and can be cathartic, but it can take time to get there and if

*Incomplete needs meeting*

you stop flogging too early they may end up, again, irritable or unsatisfied. If you flog too long or too hard then they may also end up only half-way there.

Part of the irritation can come from the let down. If someone has been looking forward to a satisfying scene with their partner and the scene is cut short before their needs are fully met, or if the scene doesn't go the way it usually does—such as when their partner surprises them by trying something new—then needs also might not get met. It can mean waiting for another day or another week to try again.

More than this though is that an incomplete needs-meeting session or scene can create an additional problem rather than solve one. What do you do with half a catharsis, for example? Or if someone is looking for that physiological release associated with a tight bondage tie and they're untied too early, what do they do with half a physiological release? Someone who uses the stimulation, the pain, the impacts, the restraint, and the interaction with their partner to get to a certain mental state is going to follow a particular path to get there. If the stimulation stops too soon, then they end up stuck part way along the path, neither at the beginning nor the end. It can leave them in a sensitive or vulnerable state for hours, days, or longer.

Dominants and tops, too, need their release and where a dominant uses a BDSM activity for this, their submissive partner also needs to be able to go the distance. This can be apparent when a dominant uses a heavy activity, such as a long and strenuous flogging, to get built-up nervous energy out of his system. If his submissive partner is unable to endure the flogging and needs to stop early, then the dominant can be left feeling unsatisfied and with energy left that he doesn't want and can't get rid of.

*Incomplete needs meeting*

## BDSM Relationships - Pitfalls and Obstacles

A top or dominant who uses BDSM as an opportunity for self expression—such as through artistic rope work, or creative needle play—can also be left hanging and unsatisfied if he doesn't get to finish what he started because of an interruption or if his partner calls it off early.

Regardless of whether you are a top, bottom, dominant or submissive, it may not be obvious to you when your partner is using the activities you share to achieve such an internal catharsis, some sort emotional release, or some other profound outcome. You should talk to them to make sure that their needs are being met. You need to know—and this, of course, has to do with engagement—when they have wants or needs which they satisfy with you through BDSM, what they need to do or what you need to do for this to happen, and when it's enough.

When you are a bottom or submissive it can be useful to devise a system of signals, possibly hand signals, which tell your partner of your changing needs throughout such a scene. For example, you might have a signal for "Harder!", or for "Slower!", or for "Stop! Now I need to be quiet for while." These can help your partner help you navigate through your own internal feelings using what they do with you while distracting you as little as possible.

What we're talking about here is meeting needs, and in the context of a longer-term relationship needs meeting can take on a whole different shape to what's possible in casual encounters. When profound needs or profound forms of release are being sought, a longer-term relationship can provide times when only the needs of one partner are addressed and this focus means that the needs can be met much more deeply than in a casual encounter. Also, a longer-term relationship allows each person

*Incomplete needs meeting*

to learn their partner's particular needs intimately, to learn what triggers them, and how to help meet those needs.

This point about engagement and knowing your partner's needs can be quite important because if someone does have a strong need and they try to get it satisfied with someone who doesn't know them well, or who doesn't know about this need, and the two of them do some sort of scene together, then there's a risk that the person without the strong need will be focusing on having a good time or on getting what they want out of it, while the person with the strong need may end up being left high and dry when their partner reaches their own desired level of satisfaction and stops.

A benefit of a longer-term relationship is that you can focus on one need, meet it fully, and then at some later time visit other wants, needs and lusts. Particularly where one partner has stronger BDSM needs than the other, or where they both have strong needs but which are satisfied in entirely different ways, recognising that there must be some times put aside for focused needs meeting and then other times which can be used for fun, bonding, sex, recreation, or whatever, can avoid one or other partner being left unsated.

*Incomplete needs meeting*

# Chapter 33

# False righteousness

One of the problems which afflicts BDSM generally, and which affects BDSM relationships in a particularly negative way, is false righteousness. The Oxford English Dictionary[1] defines righteousness as:

> righteousness, *n. The state or quality of being righteous or just; conformity to the precepts of divine law or accepted standards of morality; uprightness, rectitude; virtue, integrity.*

False righteousness is having the absolute conviction that what you are doing is right when it isn't. More than this, it also extends to conveying this conviction to others.

---

[1] [OED]

## BDSM Relationships - Pitfalls and Obstacles

In the BDSM world, false righteousness typically develops in individuals and groups as a result of isolation. I've already noted one form of isolation a number of times through this series of books, and that is the isolation which society-in-general imposes on us through lack of acceptance of BDSM and its practices. This social isolation means that some people develop their BDSM interests and understanding in hidden geographical pockets with little or no contact with other BDSM enthusiasts.

With no yardsticks against which to measure their understanding, skills or abilities, these people can come to believe that what they're doing is good, safe, healthy or productive simply because in their limited experience or in their own small social group it all seems to be going smashingly. Indeed, it might be going smashingly simply because through luck they haven't encountered any problems and what they do is, in fact, quite risky.

I'm reminded of such a situation where a gathering of BDSM practitioners from all across the state was organised for the first time in a number of years. This gathering lasted a whole weekend and was an opportunity for people to demonstrate, share, and discuss their interests. One demonstration was from a top who lived in a small town which had just a handful of enthusiasts. He wanted to demonstrate fire play. This involves wiping a cloth or swab soaked in a volatile liquid—such as an alcohol/water mix—across a small patch of a bottom's skin, setting fire to the vapour, and then quickly extinguishing it to prevent their skin from getting too hot. This can have a powerful psychological effect on a bottom because it looks and feels like they are on fire when it is not actually their skin which burns, but the vapour above their skin instead.

Anyway, this top got his bottom, a well-endowed and very "forward" young female, to sit topless in a chair and then he wet the top of one of her breasts with the volatile liquid and set it alight. A small plume of flame rose from her boob as expected, and he quickly put it out. A number of other tops in the audience then immediately stopped his demonstration for safety reasons.

There were two problems. Firstly, done the way he did it there's a serious risk that flames rising up towards the bottom's face can get inhaled and damage nasal passages, throat or lungs. Secondly, hair can easily catch fire and while this particular bottom's hair was quite short, long hair can hang down towards the breasts and it invites future disaster to demonstrate such a risky way of doing fire play to an audience which contained inexperienced BDSM folk who then might go home and try it on someone with long hair.

This top had learned his fire play skills in isolation, and because he had successfully set fire to a number of people without problems, he had come to believe that what he was doing was right. It only needed for him to try this "seated fire play" with a bit too much alcohol, or with too much delay in putting out the flame, or with someone with long hair, or with someone who breathed in at the wrong time, and he might have had a major medical problem on his hands.

This same sort of skills problem can develop in a number of areas of BDSM such as flogging, caning, suspension bondage, and so on. While light-and-fluffy play is often fairly safe, when overconfidence develops in isolation, people can be taking risks which they don't appreciate and can be getting themselves into serious trouble.

Isolation and lack of shared experience also leads to a false righteousness in attitudes and beliefs. This is something which

*False righteousness*

we can sometimes see in *The gift of submission* which I discussed in detail back in section 29.11 on page 376. A submissive who experiences intense submissive feelings or intense feelings of surrender for the first time may not have the experience or understanding to be able to correctly and realistically deal with these feelings. Because they may never have heard of these feelings before, they may think of them as special or magical and might come up with romantic or impractical theories to understand and handle them. With no one around to tell them otherwise, these ideas may become entrenched and even graduate to being "obvious". Similarly, a submissive who has been raised on the BDSM equivalent of Mills & Boon novels[2] may have completely unrealistic ideas of how BDSM relationships actually play out and may bring these hard-to-change ideas with them when they set up shop with a dominant. Dominants, of course, aren't immune to this. Literature such as *The Story Of O*[3] can easily give them the wrong impression about what to do with a submissive or bottom and lead them to extremes which the average bottom or submissive might never survive, let alone endure.

I'm reminded of some strong-minded young female virgins here because many of them inflict this same sort of righteousness on their first boyfriends. A female friend with whom I was discussing this commented that sex changes a woman. When she becomes sexually active, she behaves differently and has different values than a virgin. Similarly, BDSM experience changes both a dominant and a submissive. It might be that they

---

[2] A famous line of hundreds (thousands?) of escapist, romance-heavy novels from Britain - see http://en.wikipedia.org/wiki/Mills_%26_Boon

[3] [REAGE1954]

don't get the full idea until they have had a couple of partners, but the same can probably be said about virgins, too.

Righteousness can develop entirely out of ignorance, but often ego has a place in holding on to it. Someone who has devoted a lot of time to practicing what they think is right may react badly if they start to get the idea that they may not be so right after all. They may go to extreme lengths both to avoid being educated and to avoid contact with those who might be better informed. They might avoid going to workshops or reading books about BDSM, and may attempt to encourage others around them to similarly isolate themselves. All this to ensure that their own standing, and any power or influence they wield in their local group is not diminished. This applies to submissives just as much as it does to dominants because in a small pond it's easy to be a big fish, and being a big fish means you have social standing. If the pond suddenly becomes bigger through an influx of knowledge or through an influx of people with better skills, the previously big fish might end up looking fairly small and lose their social position.

When it exists, false righteousness creates an artificial foundation for a relationship. In book one of this series I described three characteristics of BDSM relationships—disparity of power, penetration, and engagement—and referred to them as pillars. These pillars support a BDSM relationship and implicitly they must rest on a solid foundation. If they don't, if the foundation on which they rest is soft and mushy, then it doesn't matter how solid the pillars themselves are. When the foundation is weak then the relationship itself will be precarious and prone to collapse. In the case of false righteousness, this collapse occurs when the foundations begin to shake, typically because of growing knowledge or awareness in or around the people in the relationship.

## 33.1 Entitlement

Along with righteousness can come a sense of entitlement. Entitlement can have to do with anything, but someone who has come to believe that they are a superior dominant or submissive because of their experience can come to expect the social standing I mentioned above, or that their utterances will be treated most seriously, or that they get first pick of any new "meat" which walks in the door of the local monthly BDSM play party, or that their way is clearly the right way.

When they're challenged about any of this they have little to fall back on. Being challenged means that they have to justify or prove themselves, and if they have nothing except their own beliefs or limited experience on which to draw then they may see their little world start to crumble. When there is such a sense of entitlement, they may become loud when challenged or criticised, or may clam up and simply insist they are right and refuse to discuss whatever it is.

# Chapter 34

# Conclusion

When we're looking at pitfalls and obstacles to a BDSM relationship then it always will be that we're looking for something going wrong with one or more of the three pillars of BDSM relationships:

- Disparity of power,
- Penetration, or
- Engagement.

A breakdown in any of these three things, or failure of the foundations on which they rest, can change the nature of a relationship, change it from BDSM into plain vanilla, or even bring the relationship to an end. As we've seen in this book, there are many ways in which this can happen.

## BDSM Relationships - Pitfalls and Obstacles

Communication and trust are always going to be important elements of any relationship and BDSM relationships are no different. However, while vanilla relationships can be less susceptible to problems in these areas and can keep chuffing along even when there are serious communication or trust issues between two people, BDSM is often a lot more sensitive. In particular, engagement is likely to be the first thing to suffer when there is either a communication or a trust problem. As well as creating feelings of distance when engagement diminishes, the depth of our BDSM explorations and their ability to satisfy us and our partners also suffer, often badly.

Another interesting problem which afflicts many BDSM relationships, particularly those involving people new to BDSM, is unrealistic expectations. I mean, *The Story Of O*[1] is a very good read and can be quite a turn-on, but you wouldn't want to try what's in it with a brand new submissive. Many of the things which BDSM and erotic literature tell us are fanciful and often physically dangerous. They make for a good read, but they should stay in books and not venture off the page. Unfortunately, people who are new to BDSM have no way of telling the possible from the unrealistic and may think that what they read can actually be done, or may believe that knights in shining armour (or shiny black leather) are waiting around the corner to carry them off into a world of ecstatic flogging and endless orgasmic delights to which they merely have to surrender. They are in for an unfortunate surprise.

I'm a keen believer both in reality in BDSM and in clearing out any junk which prevents us seeing reality. When there's distance between us and reality, or when we replace reality with fantasy,

---

[1][REAGE1954]

engagement with our partner suffers. Instead of focussing our energy on what our partner needs, on what we ourselves need, and on what our shared relationship needs, part of our energy goes towards the fantasy and is lost.

First reactions to the realization that a relationship is in crisis, or nearly so, can be denial or to go for a quick fix, such as having more scenes, flogging harder, or going to more workshops. Often however, dealing with a BDSM relationship in crisis can be just a matter of stepping back a bit, then working out what motivations or needs have to be met on both sides, how they have been met in the past, what might be interfering, and how these needs can be met now. It's my hope that this series of books can help you do just that.

# Bibliography

[ANTONIOU1995] Antoniou, Laura. *Laura, Leather, and Life*. Lecture at Crossroads Learning Center, Seattle, Washington, November 1995

[FERRY2008] Ferry, Steven M. *Butlers & Household Managers: 21st Century Professionals*. BookSurge Publishing, 2008. ISBN 1-4392-0967-7

[GRANDIN1992] Grandin, Temple. *Calming Effects of Deep Touch Pressure in Patients with Autistic Disorder, College Students, and Animals*. Journal of Child and Adolescent Psychopharmacology, volume 2, no. 1, pages 63 – 72, 1992. ISSN 1044-5463

[HILL1996] Hill, Craig A. and Preston, Leslie K. *Individual Differences in the Experience of Sexual Motivation: Theory and Measurements of Dispositional Sexual Motives*. The Journal of Sex Research, volume 33, no. 1, pages 27 – 45, 1996. ISSN 0022-4499

[KRAUSS1987] Krauss, Kirsten E. *The Effects of Deep Pressure Touch on Anxiety*. The American Journal of Occupational Therapy, volume 41, no. 6, pages 366 – 373, 1987. ISSN 0272-9490

[MASTERS2008A] Masters, Peter. *Look Into My Eyes: How To Use Hypnosis To Bring Out The Best In Your Sex Life*. CreateSpace, 2008. ISBN 1-4404-4986-4

[MASTERS2008] Masters, Peter. *This Curious Human Phenomenon: An exploration of some uncommonly explored aspects of BDSM*. The Nazca Plains Corporation, 2008. ISBN 1-9346-2568-X

[MASTERS2009] Masters, Peter. *The Control Book*. CreateSpace, 2009. ISBN 1-4421-7386-6

[MESTON2007] Meston, Cindy M. and Buss, David M. *Why Humans Have Sex*. Archives of Sexual Behaviour, volume 36, no. 4, pages 477 – 507, 2007. ISSN 0004-0002

[OED] OED. *Oxford English Dictionary (Online Edition)*. Oxford University Press, 1989

[REAGE1954] Reage, Pauline. *The Story Of O*. 1954

# Glossary

24/7      short for 24 hours a day, seven days a week. This refers to a type of D&s or M/s relationship where the two people involved always interact and engage each other in D&s or M/s terms.

BDSM      an acronym for Bondage and Discipline, Dominance and Submission, and Sadism and Masochism.

Bondage      a BDSM activity where a top, dominant, or master uses rope, chain, cuffs or any other method to physically restrain their bottom, submissive, or slave.

Bottom      a BDSM role. A bottom is the one on the receiving end during a BDSM scene such as the one being tied up, the one being struck with a flogger, etc.

Cutting      a BDSM activity using very sharp knives or scalpels to cut designs into the skin. These can be shallow cuts, usually through only a layer or two of skin and which are more for psychological effect than to be actually painful, through to deep cuts which bleed and leave scars.

D&s a short-hand way to refer to dominant/submissive relationships.

Discipline any BDSM activity involving an aspect of punishment. Typically things like bare-bottom spanking and caning fall into this category.

Dominant a BDSM role. A dominant takes charge of some aspect of their partner's activities. This can be solely for the length of a scene, or longer term when they live together.

Dungeon a special area reserved for BDSM scenes. Usually equipped with specialised and BDSM-adapted furniture such as spanking benches (padded, comfortable benches used during spanking scenes), wooden frames with anchor points used during rope bondage, etc.

Fire play an activity involving fire, typically where a top applies a thin smear of a volatile liquid—such as an alcohol/water mix—to the skin of a bottom, lights the vapour above the bottom's skin, and then quickly extinguishes the flame to prevent burning.

Flogger a type of short, multi-tail whip. Usually designed more to thud than sting, the tails are often shorter than one metre and are typically fairly wide and soft. The tails can be made of leather, rope, cord, hair, rubber, etc.

Impact play   any BDSM activities where striking one's partner is the goal. Includes slapping, spanking, paddling, whipping, flogging, and so on.

M/s   a short-hand way to refer to Master/slave relationships.

Master   a BDSM role. A master claims ownership or rights over a slave.

Mistress   a BDSM role. Can be the female counterpart of a master, but often this role is merely a female top.

Mummification   a type of bondage in which the whole body is encased in a form of wrapping in a manner reminiscent of an egyptian mummy (with holes for breathing, of course). Most commonly the material used for wrapping is something like kitchen cling wrap because it's quick and easy to apply.

Needle play   using hypodermic needle tips to thread through the skin, genitals or nipples. Usually done for psychological effect because the needles are actually designed not to hurt (much) unless larger diameters are used. Can also be done for artistic reasons where large numbers of needles are used at one time to create patterns.

Pain play   any BDSM activities where causing sharp or dull pain is the goal. Includes caning, whipping, flogging, cutting, etc.

Paddle   a paddle similar in shape and size to a ping-pong paddle made out of wood or thick leather. Used for paddling, which is similar to spanking but is done with a paddle instead of a hand.

*Glossary*

BDSM RELATIONSHIPS - PITFALLS AND OBSTACLES

Play party   a type of BDSM event where people get together to engage in BDSM activities and BDSM play with each other. Usually held in a private location, such as someone's home, warehouse, loft, or other dedicated space. Rooms or areas are usually put aside for such play, while other areas are put aside for talking, socialising or eating.

Rope bondage   using rope or cord to physically restrain someone partially or fully. Includes full-body bondage, hog-tying, wrist or ankle cuffs made out of rope, etc.

Scene   a collected series of activities with a BDSM focus having a clearly defined start and end; hence *bondage scene* or *discipline scene*, etc. Often performed in a dungeon.

*Scene* is also sometimes used as a verb meaning to engage in a scene or to perform a scene. For example, *the dominant intends to scene with his submissive*.

Slave   a BDSM role. A slave assigns ownership or rights over themselves to their partner.

Squick   to cause to feel repulsion, to disgust.

Submissive   a BDSM role. A submissive hands over control over some of their activities to their partner for the length of a scene or longer term if they live together.

Switch   a person who can adopt the role of top or bottom to suit their own and their partner's needs.

Suspension  a type of rope bondage where the person being tied is first tied and is then suspended in the air from a frame or from a bolt in the ceiling.

Top  a BDSM role. A top is the one who does things to their partner, the bottom, during a scene. This could be bondage, spanking, caning, flogging, and so on.

Toys  Equipment used for BDSM play such as floggers, canes, chains, cuffs, etc.; hence *toy bag*, i.e., a bag used for carrying around BDSM equipment.

# About the author

Peter Masters is a BDSM dominant and author who lives in Sydney, Australia. He has enjoyed taking control of fine women since his early twenties (which was thirty years ago) and is the author of a number of BDSM and kinky-sex-related books.

He has a website, which is more a wiki than anything else, where you can find hundreds of articles on BDSM and related topics:

```
http://www.peter-masters.com/
```

Printed in Great Britain
by Amazon